Lot 12

EVERY ARTIST HIS OWN SCANDAL

The Metaphor in the Jungle (verse)
Yesterday's Children (verse)—with Pavel Tchelitchew
The Granite Butterfly (verse)
The Hollywood Hallucination
Magic and Myth of the Movies
Chaplin: Last of the Clowns
The Three Faces of the Film
The Young and Evil—with Charles Henri Ford
Conrad Marca-Relli
Classics of the Foreign Film
Florine Stettheimer: A Life in Art

EVERY ARTIST HIS OWN SCANDAL:
A study of real and fictive heroes
PARKER TYLER

HORIZON PRESS | NEW YORK | 1964 ♭

Foreword: EVERY ARTIST HIS OWN SCANDAL

No one could title his book as I have done without laying himself open to the suspicion of having taken a shot at sensationalism. I suppose I have, mildly, taken that shot, yet not without due reflection on all I have said of the artist and the flaming, or black, dead ends (actually very various) of his careers. Let us avoid the glances of those who deny one can speak of "the" artist, much less "every" artist; not to mention also the plain implication that a scandal would seem, according to my title, something that happens to all of them. My plea is that I don't at all designate here *all* artists or *all* their scandals. Scandal itself must be properly distinguished in histories and in situations where often it is never mentioned.

The "scandals" featured automatically in newspapers (one might say so poorly defined in them) are quite beyond my range of interest; that is, the range of my natural interest, which I can identify as the perfectly drastic way in which an artist conducts himself when it comes to having a deep, deep scandal of his own. He doesn't (by which I mean he didn't up to fifty years ago) care if he should raise the Devil himself. Yet all he wishes to do, no matter which his medium, is to have his own way with it, regardless of advice, threats, tradition, fashion, comforts and common, even normal, rewards. The Prometheus image has crept into my deliberations here and not without a much weighted meaning.

The artist, when necessary, is one who, having "stolen fire from Heaven," is used to making from it the most lunatic conflagrations in sober, calculated sense, and then, before whatever gods there be, grimly offering his unprotected liver to be annihilated. And what gods, or god, could there be but those, or the one, of his choice?—the hero's choice? What the custom of the ages has described as the offender's "punishment" comes to the artist, whose special kinds I have been at pains to discuss, as a mere part of his own creative logic, within a closed pattern of frightening freedom: some stark necessity of cause and effect. This is why Nijinsky, a real hero, and Stavrogin, a fictive one, are brothers having the same militantly pure flesh, though under different skins, in different times and places, in different "arts." All the created and creators in my pages have the high, mighty heroism that looks lightning in the eye—and then, perhaps, proceeds to parley with it.

Hamlet, his own creator's most penetrating eye among human flesh (human flesh which Prospero is not!) is the kind of artist-seer who sees and acts from behind a tantalizing veil but all-knowingly, superbly, as does the professional artist himself. An artist does not concern himself, strictly speaking, with an "original creator": he starts dealing, rather, with a given, if somewhat unpredictable, situation whose primary element (whose "ground" so to speak) is precisely himself; if he doesn't like the way the situation is going, he tries to change it (he may even defy the onward, implacable flow called history); if paradoxically he somehow fails, or, like Hamlet, realizes he has lost once and for all the great opportunity, he throws up the whole outward scheme of things in the twinkling of an eye—literally, as did Huysmans, he may vomit it—and goes his own singular, arbitrary, unsobbing way; that is, *he continues to the end in his own style* . . . to the lunatic asylum, in step with death or with the vogue, out of step with death or with the vogue . . . anyway, a particular artist's living or dead profile remains clearly marked against what Mallarmé called *le Néant*. He has, *wishes* to have, no other raison d'être; maybe, I should say, he is allergic to a raison d'être—unless it is very ironic like that of Socrates' terminal capitulation. He carries off any incidental failures, or possible reproaches or honors from posterity and the world of connoisseurs, as so many medals for "distinguished service." That is all.

Yet I must not speak, in what may seem to present itself as a preliminary, clarifying argument, too much in parables. A scandal, semantically speaking, must be a *scandal,* however elusive, however deceptively or vulgarly so named. Far be it from my purpose in the following pages to have implied that the inherent scandal is the misunderstanding between an artist and his public, resulting in a tragedy of real, seeming, or alleged neglect or wrong of him. Count their heads! Among these real and fictive heroes you will find no alibi-boys (unless wearing sinister fun-masks), no malingerers or apologists. Rather, each one (obliquely blank; surly and macabre; sweet tempered and generous) has a face empty of envy, grievance or *self*-accusation —least of all the last, unless made with elegant and demonic sarcasm. Such an artist (he is heroic for the same reason) is, if empirically a kind of scapegoat, not *docile,* for he has no acknowledged community to save; he concentrates only on his own conscience and, whatever the consequences, in the utmost privacy. It is a pattern followed by Henry James and Franz Kafka as well as by others treated here.

Are all these fine fellows, allowably, too proudly insulated—just too big for their britches? Are they—baleful words!—neurotics and psychopaths at the worst, or self-indulged Narcissuses, in the traditional sense of which artists, I believe, are still spoken? The reader will find here no consciously adduced evidence to that effect. My conclusion is keyed to the note of exultation, not exculpation. It might be obvious from my first chapter, in fact, that no one could be more discouraging to the fiats and the pious assumptions of the laws of pathology (however much braced by the modern clinic) than I. It might be noticed, moreover, that I sympathetically let the artist as hero speak for his fatal innocence of any self-nurtured idea that his behavior is really "scandalous." Scandal, in reality rather than in the newspapers, is exactly like Oedipus: one leg is shorter than the other through a maiming not of his own daring and not of his own doing. Yet he walks straight ahead, gaze never flickering, toward an ultimate image of rectitude. And his heroes, "scandalously," mirror him.

In placing this unique eye in the artist's forehead, I may have put him in danger of being deemed monstrous, as some observers before me have concluded anyway. There are, it may well be, anti- (or non-) social artists, and technically these are to be rated, perhaps, as monstrous. Although I think that that would be a lamentable error, one to be skirted, its risk is one in which I gladly join my protagonists. The blacks of melancholy, the reds of outrage, the greens of disgust, the yellows of nausea (pre-Sartre), the off-whites of sublimest madness, are a palette of emotions which I think natural to men who obstinately regard art, or any other action, as no mere dream of success-come-true. I hope, in the stretch of my book, not to have omitted any humor and its appropriate color in the artist's emotional palettes as I have composed them. Such humors are not subject to the inspiration of outer fashion but of inner necessity.

So far as I can make the matter out, to date, the only thing to equal the longevity of our civilization's future will be the artist's demonic self-confidence and his ability to meet his fate without tears of joy or grief. All in all, do I exaggerate? Does he, my self-indulgent artist, demand too much of *our* indulgence, so "unreasonable" as his last gesture may seem? I should dislike the reader to think that I unwisely celebrate these abdications or put a false, bright face on these self-approving denials and truncations, these flights into hiding or finest ambiguity. They are terrible enough! But they are alight with the only grace that really saves: free choice.

On the level of the great creator, free choice *is* the only grace, in the midst of which (to our horror) we see him isolate or immobilize himself, or else adopt, through insight or compulsion, the rôle of a criminal: acts which are, indistinguishably, beautiful and scandalous. They are beautiful because impregnated with poetry; they are scandalous because that poetry, supreme in aloneness, has been determined by a secret terror. Is it always "terror"? Well, perhaps only pride, disdainful of comprehension —but above all of sympathetic *in*comprehension. I know I touch on sore social dissidences of today, kept hidden by an unofficial pact between artist and public that demeans all aesthetic values: a pact that directs the artist, as clown, to ape the average weaknesses, the social humiliation of too many failures in human self-government, national or individual, too many botches of human dignity. . . . For the style of the scapegoat inevitably derives from the style of the "saved society," and the style of the "saved society" ("ours") is not so good, my friends, not so good!

CONTENTS

INTRODUCTION TO THE CELL

Shakespeare was the first artist in the world to place the artist type tragically on the dramatic stage. The case was, of course, Hamlet. The well-known opposition detected between thought and action in Hamlet's character is rightly felt to be crude. Certainly, I do not propose to contrast art with action. However, I realize that I join the persistent urge of criticism to supply a more relevant formula to justify the magnitude of the pure enigma flashing from Hamlet's legend. In the attempt to provide a psychology (and thus, in modern terms, a motivation) for Hamlet more coherent than the one seemingly offered by the play, critics have tended, unfortunately, to overlook the real dramatic tension of Hamlet as governor of the play's development.

Hamlet is an artist who is aware of being a seer rather than a craftsman; in other words, he anticipated the nineteenth century's desire to fuse these capacities. When the Ghost reveals the secret of the murder, his response is: "Oh, my prophetic soul!" This is not in the least a conventional exclamation. Murder is the missing half of the "incest crime" he has already divined and whose essence he has read in his heart. Sending love notes in verse, he goes on to mock the custom of a lyric poet, and with the most heroic and compressed language of which Shakespeare was capable, he speaks throughout the play as a critic setting himself above the poetry of the simple affective life. When Ophelia laments that she "suck'd the honey of his music vows," the line invokes all the sweet verse of Shakespeare spoken by love-mastered beings. But when casting off Ophelia, Hamlet does so on the basis that he can foresee for himself a future like his father's, and a son on whom the duty of vengeance would be laid as unwelcome as that on Hamlet himself, one of the "breed of sinners." Hamlet can satisfy himself in predicting the future for he has had a special illumination into the past, which came to him as an inspiration and which the Ghost's words have verified.

Hamlet is a seer intoxicated with a vision which he dare not put into words any more than he can readily act upon it. When he says to Ophelia, "I am very proud, revengeful, ambitious, with more offenses at my beck than I have thoughts to put them in, imagination to give them shape, or time to act them in," the words have a second edge forged in the most lucent irony. The maddened prince, whether voluntarily or involuntarily, invokes a classic metaphor for the boundlessness of supernatural wisdom as well as for the multiple characters which both god and artist have needed to define themselves. Nor is he faking in the least. When he writes dramatic verse, as in the player's speech, it is not only satirically flavored and facilely rhymed, but also has a disdainfully bestowed function: it travesties the situation of his father, mother, and stepfather. It cannot remotely compare with the true poem of his intuition, which was cryptic and "prophetic."

Hamlet's projection of the past as a play is an ironical reflection of his own inward illumination. As his father *might* have seen the truth of his Queen's future infidelity, and perhaps (according to the Player King's speech) did see it, Hamlet the son, in any event, is in possession of the complete design, including his own role as filial avenger. But after the imagination, the flesh —and especially now—is redundant. This is the point where Hamlet the son, as the plot's chief motivator, wants nature itself (in the dramatic sense) to end. At one stroke, and as though not by aim or desire, he stands at the summit which is ever the artist's anxious goal.

This is the curious miracle of premature victory that has gained such an eminent fame in three and a half centuries. Shakespeare makes Hamlet relatively innocent at the beginning because of necessarily conforming to a plot which could not have existed if Hamlet's genius was to blossom in one stroke, achieve itself in a single moment of insight. That Hamlet should fail in action: this is Shakespeare's *sine qua non*. It is the obvious plot for public consumption. But also, as James Joyce has intuited in *Ulysses,* Hamlet is his author's whipping boy no less than a case of supreme insight and poetic articulacy. Behind his outward and formal innocence rests the immeasurable quantity of all Shakespeare's wizardry of human divination. That Hamlet's apparently boyish ignorance and manly dutifulness are a dispensable cloak is nowhere better revealed than when the machinery of playacting is deliberately underlined by Shakespeare, when the Ghost, now only a voice, adjures Horatio and Marcellus to swear secrecy on Hamlet's sword; Hamlet proceeds to mock the adjuration because, at the Globe Theatre, it presumably was to be uttered by someone standing beneath the stage: "Ah, ha, boy, say'st thou so?" This mockery of his father's spirit, toward which he has seemed so awed, serves as a divining rod for the play's, and especially Hamlet's, ambiguity.

The Ghost has exhorted him: "Remember me!", and with unequivocal emotion Hamlet has assured the spirit, ". . . thy commandment all alone shall live / Within the book and volume of my brain." But Hamlet knows better than the audience that the metaphor of "book and volume" illustrates precisely the fictitious and mutable nature of the moral life, a fact which is given conscious point when the Player King says, "Our words are ours, their ends none of our own." Briefly, Hamlet's soul consents and does not consent to carry out the commandment of revenge. The soliloquies remove only the one, the fourth, wall of his secrecy, and are particularly the window-dressing of his wavering; what is positive in their sinews is an intellectual and emotional illumination so blinding that no one but the subject can bear it in its simplicity.

When the oath takes place, Hamlet must move the group twice—and with ironic indulgence—to accommodate the Ghost's subterranean fluidity. This direction and pace of unseen movement suggests the unconscious life itself and that the Ghost (a "boy") is Hamlet's other self; a "mole" and "worthy pioner," indeed, for in this sense the Ghost "in the cellarage" anticipates the Freudian structure of the past and the unconscious. Despite his youth, Hamlet remains the play's only truly knowledging person. Everyone else, intellectually speaking, is conventional, obeying the rules of discourse, mood, and sentiment which *he,* with Jovian arrogance, perpetually ignores or travesties; where *his* madness is a desperate form of play, Ophelia's is a desperate form of reality. The very oath of secrecy given the Ghost would seem to contain, in Hamlet's baroque, punnish fashion, an *exorcism.* We have a cue for this not only in the bitter famous last couplet of the scene, but also in the later claim that the apparition may have been a fraud of the Devil's.

Hamlet knows that which "passeth show" and yet which he insists, with violent certainty, on showing; thus, he is a supreme exhibitionist. In *The Murder of Gonzago* he finds a symbolist-poet's way of communicating his crucial information to the very parties most involved. The symbolic substructure of reality has

already been formed by his strategic position as the potential
Oedipus, whose actual role has been stolen by his uncle. Hamlet
uses the players' performance merely to prove to his mother and
stepfather that he has "guessed" all; that, in short, he is a seer,
a master of the imagination. The overwhelming success of the
device (for it sets the King's guilt beyond possible doubt) might
be enough for this proud, precocious poet with his guilty secret.
If fate were satisfied with this academic, or legal, proof of the
King's guilt, Hamlet the appointed punisher would be relieved
of the role he does not want.

About Hamlet there clings something passionately chaste, an
odor of omnipotence, as of an initiate just imbued with a high
mystery and gazing at the gross world as at a stranger. But the
world is *too* gross; Hamlet is *too* fresh. This is the flesh of the
tragedy under the pied silk of the parody. "O God," he says, "I
could be bounded in a nutshell and count myself a king of infinite
space, were it not that I have bad dreams." In his case, reality is
the bad dream, the profanation of the truth. Hamlet wants to
handle one of the recorders and mocks Guildenstern's efforts to
"play" upon him, to "pluck out the heart of my mystery." The
pun on "recorder" is obvious; such "music" would reveal the
truth of the past. But this has already been done, beyond further
ornament, through the abortive performance of *The Murder of
Gonzago*. And the very truncation of the plot is appropriate.
Hamlet too would like nature to end with this statement. For
nature to continue the plot means his necessary participation, but
this would be more "a play" than the mummery he has just
helped to devise.

Reality has become a play for Hamlet because of a law whose
validity is adequate for the artist type alone. When the imagination has completely absorbed into itself the essence of a possible
deed, that deed (i.e., outward, physical reality) becomes superflu-
ous. Such a situation may be very rare in an artist's life because
his life, like that of others, is dynamic and dialectic, but if it

appears, it pronounces, as it did for Hamlet, the irrevocable word of inner withdrawal. This word is all the more valid (though here impracticable) in that future possibilities dwindle in an artist's eye as that eye tends to absorb the future into the past through the very ritual of work. Analyze the plot of Shakespeare's tragedy and you will see that Hamlet assumes all the problems of authorship and is constantly "reading in," revising, and stopping work.

What does it matter? He is his own play's *saboteur*. Hamlet's insight into his incest feelings (the center of his clairvoyance) has put the essence of reality into his keeping, and he has no incentive to gain anything at all by acting. Nature itself has muffed his moral role; Claudius has fulfilled all possible action: horrible but ultimate. The situation touches a rule of all human existence. Action can have no appeal in prospect unless it promises a reality hitherto incomplete in feeling and understanding. The skull appeals to Hamlet because it is the true fruit of his psychic tree; he is a stillborn Oedipus.

A subtle fact palpitates throughout the lines of Shakespeare's play, perpetually modulating the rhythm of the action as it unfolds scene by scene. It is the image of Hamlet as a hero who, already complete in character, acts only as the mechanism to bring about the catastrophe. This is, too, the irony. Hamlet belongs to Ophelia, only, as he writes her, "whilst this machine is to him, Hamlet." How easy it would be for him to *write* this tragedy rather than *live* it. If he does the latter—if all his frowardness cannot stem the tide of the Ghost's explosive word—it is because he is indelibly the Ghost's son, and obedient. Yet this is not what makes him "Hamlet," uniquely an individual in relation to other individuals. The essential truth we can see in the weave of Shakespeare's rhetoric as though it were a clear plastic substance. It is that "platform" from which Hamlet always speaks: the knowledge that through personal insight (of which the Ghost, objectively, is but an outward, literary device) he alone comprehends life from a viewpoint making past, present, and future into a timeless absolute. His destiny extends in a pure line, with unfaltering feet, from his heart to the stars. What can the gestures of earth contribute?

I
CONSPICUOUS SELF-SACRIFICE

1
NIJINSKY'S ANTI-SANITY

"When I was a boy and my father wanted to teach me to swim, he threw me into the water. I fell and sank to the bottom. I could not swim, and felt that I could not breathe. I kept the little air I had, shutting my mouth, thinking that if God wishes, I shall be saved. I do not know how I walked under the water, and suddenly saw the light. Understanding that I was walking towards shallow water, I hastened my steps and came to a straight wall. I saw no sky above me, only water. Suddenly I felt a physical strength in me and jumped, saw a cord, grasped it, and was saved."—The Diary of Vaslav Nijinsky (Simon & Schuster: 1936).

Vaslav Nijinsky's diary, written in 1919 and published seventeen years later (after being discovered by his wife in 1934), is preceded in the published volume with thanks to distinguished persons helpful in the accrual of funds for the Nijinsky Foundation, and with a Preface by the dancer's wife explaining the circumstances of the diary's composition, and is followed by a Note on the Nijinsky Foundation, its purpose, and an appeal for more funds. So not only cardboard covers keep the record closed; it is bound within the conventional world whose laws and modes Nijinsky sought always to escape but which finally, as he realized the endlessness of its trap, became intolerable to him. At this juncture, he abdicated from collaboration with it, but he could not escape (as he learned for a quarter of a century) the continued persecution of its "well-meant" offices.

Nijinsky's tremendously moving document and his tremendously simple sentences (each as dynamic as a match flame) proclaim that their author constantly sought a freedom to be termed unprofessional, unorthodox, and irrational. However, the desires of people attracted to him and the structure of society consistently opposed the dancer's negative efforts; freedom (which, as he asserts on the Diary's first page, was entirely a matter of "feeling") escaped him even when he abandoned his positive and special means of seeking it: the dance; it escaped because he was hopelessly trapped within the limitations of the ordinary, real world in which he was never happy. The fundamental environment of the world did not alter for Nijinsky when he was committed to an institution; it only narrowed down, trapped him a little more thoroughly.

His wife, Romola Nijinsky, begins her Preface by saying: "This Diary is Nijinsky's message to mankind. . . . I am giving it . . . in the hope that it will be helpful to many." It will be, indeed, if one knows how to read it. We must be grateful for Mme. Nijinsky's generosity, even if unavoidably she is to be included in that unceasing and "innocent" conspiracy of the world to appropriate, utilize, and control the human sources of its spiritual wealth and power in the manner it does its grain and chemicals, without regard for the innate desires of the wonderful, individual exceptions: its geniuses. Above all other examples of maladjusted genius, Nijinsky's is the classic one to be studied, because it is an artistic tragedy: a "case history" so astonishing in its crystalline purity and the starkness of its outlines that it is like some limitless area of reality revealed by a single flash of lightning.

Nijinsky wrote: "I do not like Shakespeare's Hamlet because he reasons. I am a philosopher who does not reason—a philosopher who feels." Constantly, in the Diary, he identifies himself with life (as directly opposed to death), with God, and with love.

He also said: "I am not Christ; I am Nijinsky, a simple man."
But Christ, on occasion, said much the same thing of himself.
And it is possible to say it in the same sense only by denying, as
Nijinsky did, that one is Christ. Nijinsky was right. When he
went insane, he merely became a philosopher of pure feeling.
Physicians call his state pathological, and it is possible that some
traumatic condition (even, theoretically, inherited, "in the
blood"), was the direct cause of his mental breakdown. But the
Diary establishes this quite clearly: before Nijinsky lost his
capacity to think coherently in words, he wrote down the
apologia that conceals in its pleas and prayers a curse. Endlessly
he proclaims his love for everybody, including among particular
persons his wife and child, and reiterates his repulsion from and
fear of Diaghilev, the impresario who had such great influence
on his life, although he denies his hatred for him. Endlessly he
cries out how deeply he loves to dance, how much he wanted
everyone to understand his dancing, and that he always wished
he could dance without recompense in money. Repeatedly he
insists as well that his wife does not understand him and that
Diaghilev tortured and persecuted him, forcing him to create a
ballet, "Jeux," he did not want to do because it represented
Diaghilev's perverted sort of love. This ballet was the worst
thing Diaghilev could have done to him, since joined to its intrinsic theme was the fact that it was hackwork.

In the Diary, it is not a mere question of facts in the journal-
istic sense, or even of logical relationships among events, people,
and ideas. It is the certainty and lucidity of Nijinsky's feeling that
matter, the observer's knowledge that he was dominated by extremely simple emotional reflexes, and that these reflexes controlled his inner workings without letup or compromise; that his
concessions to normal social and professional life were always
superficial. In this trait, Nijinsky was much like the child who
arbitrarily refuses to obey a parental order. What can make this
issue clearer than that moment in the Diary when Nijinsky (according to a note) is called to bed by his wife, and writes: "I do

not want to be told to go to bed, and I will go only when God orders me to. I told my wife that I would come soon, but I will go on writing for a long time." Here is the universal experience of childhood: placating the mother with a false promise to gain precious time for his own disposal. Moreover, this incident furnishes us with a clue to Nijinsky's complex, which is undoubtedly that of Oedipus. The image of his father, who had thrown him into water to make him swim, was displaced by that of Diaghilev, and the image of his mother by Mme. Nijinsky, his wife, who looked after him as a man. "God," who constantly appears in the Diary as a Being in complete harmony with Nijinsky, became the ideal parent, the one who really "understood" him. And God, in terms of displacement, was obviously the apotheosis of Nijinsky's own ego, his inner desires.

The Diary is divided into four parts: *Life, Death, Feelings,* and *Epilogue.* In the part called "Death," Nijinsky tells about his money difficulties with Diaghilev. "I knew well," he writes, "that if I left Diaghilev I would die of hunger because I was not ready for life. I was afraid of life. Now I am not afraid any more. I wait for God's wishes." Why was Nijinsky afraid of life, and why, at the time of writing, waiting for "God's wishes" (i.e., his own impulses), was he so no longer? It is hard to make the public believe that so personal and pyrotechnic an art as the dancer's has any object but that of technical virtuosity and brilliant style. But if it was hard for Diaghilev, a talented and sophisticated man, to realize that Nijinsky was deeply wounded by having to compose ballets he did not like and to dance when he was exhausted, how much harder would it be for those who adored the "thousands of red rose petals" in "The Spectre of the Rose" and the dancer's sensational leaps to believe that Nijinsky "meant" anything by the entire form of ballet, that dancing was for him a subtle, precise, and mature expression of his inmost feelings, of his spirit—and, more than this, that it was a fetich against fear, a ritual to exorcise fear? Yet the fact is that again and again in the Diary we learn that dancing was the refined summit of

Nijinsky's personal expression and that nothing upset him so much or made him so desolate as things that interfered with the ideal nature of his performances. "I am not mad," he wrote, "and Dostoievsky's 'idiot' is not an 'idiot.' I felt nervous and therefore made mistakes." This nervousness was fear—fear of making a mistake as Myshkin was afraid of knocking over the vase. His madness was a raising to the "infinite" power of his fear that, because of personal quarrels with Diaghilev, fatigue or general unhappiness, he would not dance well, and so would fail to receive the great and final spiritual release that dancing gave him.

Increasing pressure from forces alien to the pure performance of his art brought Nijinsky to the point where he could not be sure of the spiritual coefficient of his gymnastic prowess. This was the fatal turning point of his "madness." Just as he had feared, during the legendary period of his intense and hazardous rivalry with a fellow pupil in the Ballet School, that he "would not leap high enough," he began to feel he would not scale the *spiritual* heights, would not be able to climb the Faun's little symbolic stairway. In the section called "Feelings," Nijinsky explains the essential spirituality of his love for his wife, that he does not love her "as a woman," and that God wishes her to leave him. Earlier he has expressed his reluctance to eat meat and his resentment of Mme. Nijinsky's fondness for it. He connected (as he says) the eating of meat with sex, and in his case, with self-abuse, which weakened his physique and therefore his dancing. Evidently a libidinal struggle took place in Nijinsky as in all of us. The manner in which he relates that he scorned Diaghilev's sexual advances and ran after girls, frequently whores, indicates that he wished to dispose of his sexual feelings spontaneously and without moral obligation to the object. When we learn that he submitted himself to treatments of autosuggestion in order to identify himself more entirely with the Faun while on the stage, it is not hard to guess that Nijinsky rationalized his sexual expression into the spiritual form of Mallarmé's conception of onanistic trance. Nijinsky feared the ravages of onanism and, in symbolizing them in dance motion and gestures, he probably took away some of the power of the actual impulse. Eventually he seems to have been disillusioned with whoring, not for his own sake but for the sake of the girls, who felt little or nothing, their spirits having been ruined. Nijinsky's spirit could not be ruined, but it was fearful. Out of fear he was married, for a wife proposed a tentative answer to his animal need that likewise promised spiritual sustenance.

To finally comprehend the pattern of Nijinsky's fear of life and profound need to dance, as well as what he refers to as his "nervousness," it is necessary to invoke the incident described at the head of this chapter: his father's act of throwing him into the water. Although Nijinsky's recollection (as is natural enough) emphasizes his own self-rescue and its manner, the "boy of six or seven" must have felt that his father might have succeeded in killing him, but at least that the desires of his father entailed the risk of the boy's life. "I am life," he wrote Diaghilev. "You are death." Clearly the man who wanted him to swim by violent edict and the man who wanted him to dance by parallel violent edict are one and the same in the deepest realm of Nijinsky's feeling. Nijinsky was mortally afraid of not pleasing Diaghilev because he identified him with public success; not with art, that is to say, for of that he was inwardly confident, but with the worldly reward of art: a livelihood. But more than to live as an animal (even a luxurious animal), Nijinsky wished to live as spirit. He was constantly "nervous" because Diaghilev had convinced him that it would be fatal to make a "mistake," and if he did not take his (Diaghilev's) advice, he *would* make a mistake. Nijinsky sought in the woman he had married an escape from Diaghilev's tyranny as he must have turned to the tenderness of his mother from the severity of his father. But Romola Nijinsky could only extend the tyranny of the ordinary "power-world" of success by providing its semi-private nature: the success of marriage and the home. To Nijinsky, every success but one, the act of dancing well, was alien and a nuisance.

During the space of ten years, articles and photographs continually appeared in the press, announcing that Nijinsky's "recovery" might be near at hand, that he was coming to America, or that he had "danced" before the Russian soldiers. These articles presumably aroused the hopes of dubiously sensitive beings who would find pleasure in contemplating Nijinsky's "return to sanity." Although enfeebled somewhat in body, the man was far too clever to do anything so stupid as voluntarily to return to "sanity"; however, it was possible he might be conscripted. In terms of space and visual variety, his world then was much narrower and humbler than in the days of his glory, but the world he gained had a relative freedom: a choreography of the mind that was unshackled by any professional and social exactions. I do not mean that madness was a conscious device of Nijinsky's to escape from the world, although the feigning of madness has often been proven close to "the real thing," but that the positive greatness of Nijinsky, his genius as a dancer, may have had its innately *spiritual* impulse in the trauma of fear probably incurred when his father plunged him into the swimming pool, and—lips shut tight—he sank helplessly to the bottom. . . .

The genius of life is that it offers to very exceptional beings the unique challenge of death that, shaking them to their deepest depths, causes them *by reaction* to reach the heights for which they are destined. Nijinsky has described without flaw the sublimity of his self-resourcefulness in the terrible moment when he might have died. His words and tone leave no room for doubt that he was certain of the transcendent strength of his legs to make the life-saving leap that he completed over the window-sill into the chamber where the young girl dreamed of the rose. But if Nijinsky always leaped *into* life (even if it was life as a dream, half illusion and half reality) he leaped *from* death. ". . . children do not forget what happens to them," wrote Nijinsky. "I saw my father diving into the water," he says, "but I was afraid. I disliked somersaults." The leap is always upward, and the body is not inverted, merely being momentarily in air and stretched in all directions to its uttermost. Air and life replaced water and death for Nijinsky. Only the shut mouth of subaqueous terror could reply to Diaghilev's quick tongue and implacable will. Only the birdlike surge of the leap could provide escape from the remorseless paternal critic that was magically revived in Diaghilev, who was immeasurably terrible because he criticized the very form of Nijinsky's life-saving "device," which had revived as *the dance*. In the eyes of the child, the father's dive was a descent, a descent into death, and that is why Vaslav feared seeing it. When forced into the same situation, therefore, he had to use his utmost strength to convert the descent into the rise, to complete his father's downward arc by leaping over the wall-of-death that was the side of the swimming pool.

2

RICHARD II'S REBELLIOUS ABDICATION

NORTHUMBERLAND: *My lord, in the base court he doth attend*
To speak with you; may 't please you to come down?
KING RICHARD: *Down, down I come; like glist'ring Phaëthon,*
Wanting the manage of unruly jades.

—The Tragedy of King Richard II,
Act III, Scene III

So Richard, having taken refuge from Bolingbroke at Flint
Castle, obeys the behest of the usurper to parley with him below.
The metaphor he chooses for himself expresses the downward
motion of what is, in myth, Icarus' and Prometheus' fate as well
as Phaëthon's. It represents man's pretension to divine or quasi-
divine powers which the gods, when intimately touched, were so
prompt to punish. Apollo, who delegated official powers of musical instruction to Orpheus, was the god who punished Marsyas
for presuming to rival divine musical talents with earthly. He
was, moreover, the god whose management of the Sun's chariot
Phaëthon sought to emulate. Noble heirs to the throne of England in the fifteenth and sixteenth centuries secreted the Prome-

thean intention of stealing "Heaven's fire" by setting at naught the established sanctity of the ruling office.

Shakespeare's contribution as poet, in his histories of kings, lies chiefly in his evocation of the paradox inherent in the idea of divine right, inheritable, after all, by human blood and placed in the unreliable keeping of human temperament. In these plays, Shakespeare did not decide whether the king suffering the ordeal of power, and sometimes its questionably brought-about destruction, was right or wrong in his adherence to the idea of divine right. What Shakespeare did was to show us the kingly ordeal and accentuate its human pathos no less than its actual modes. We might conclude, from the play in which this ordeal is most singularly concentrated, *The Tragedy of King Richard II,* that Richard is a "usurper" in the Promethean sense simply through identifying his personal fortunes with absolute powers, an identification as fatally naïve as Phaëthon's own.

In just what dramatic sense "naïve," was the inevitable point to be demonstrated inasmuch as Richard is convinced, in moral temperament, of the metaphysical or ultimate nature of his kingship and yields only to what he presumes consistently to be illegal force. Nowhere else has Shakespeare shown so purely the vulnerable earthly condition of the king's "divine right." True, near the close of the tragedy, the Bishop of Carlisle intervenes between the throne itself and Bolingbroke, the usurper about to mount it, and predicts all the woes that are to come as the result of this trespass on God's will: Richard's deposition. But Shakespeare was so powerful a dramatist exactly because he could recognize as the way of the world the capacity of mere force to defy God's will as invested in king and priest. In a sense, this predicates what actually befell the divine-right doctrine: it was repudiated both in worldly political form and the Protestant schisms from the orthodox church as well as in the official break of the English Church from Rome.

What, indeed, could divine will signify as soon as earthly rule should become a game of military force and mundane suasion:

the *problem* of generalship rather than the *right* of the blood royal? Hence, in the eloquent person of Richard II, we witness the death throes of a concept of inevitability: the metaphysical concept by which the sacredness of the king's person protects him from evil, including the supreme evil of deposition. The image of this absolute identification of earthly powers with divine will is explicit in Shakespeare's language of metaphor in Richard's history. The king, as shown at once on his return to his rebellious country, feels so metaphysically identical with English ground that he considers himself of its substance as *creator* ("mother") rather than *created* ("child"):

> As a long-parted mother with her child
> Plays fondly with her tears and smiles in meeting,
> So, weeping, smiling, greet I thee, my earth,
> And do thee favour with my royal hands . . .

All too clearly does Richard cultivate the illusion of divine parenthood; all too clearly in that, as the poetic seer of his kingly fate, he is saturated with irony for his own supposed omnipotence, and as bad news comes after bad news, his words play steadily on the uncertain tension of the One in quality, which is metaphysical, to the Many in quantity, which is earthly and which —despite his myth and his personal desire—he feels will decide the issue of temporal power. Asked by Aumerle, in the same scene, why he looks so pale, Richard replies:

> But now, the blood of twenty thousand men
> Did triumph in my face, and they are fled
> And till so much blood thither come again
> Have I not reason to look pale and dead?

Richard is so sensitive a gauge of the flux of kingly fortune as to seem lacking in the essence of the very virtue in which he believes, and admonished for this remissness by the optimistic

Aumerle, he pretends to come back to himself only to assert the same numerical equation as before:

> Awake, thou sluggard majesty! Thou sleepest.
> Is not the king's name twenty thousand names?

The scales of fortune have on one side the king, identical with his followers constituting his earthly power, and on the other side all his enemies. Richard needs only the further news of the deaths of Bushy, Green, and the Earl of Wiltshire to fashion in speech, without ado, his own epitaph.

Richard's temperament seems ideally designed for the *elegiac* aspect of kingly destiny. And so the actual case falls out for him. As the poetic and pessimistic register of royal metaphysics, Richard is very much part of Shakespeare's metaphoric language. In Act III, Scene IV, in the Duke of York's garden, when the Queen learns of Richard's ill fortune, the Gardener who informs her observes:

> In your lord's scale is nothing but himself,
> And some few vanities that make him light;
> But in the balance of great Bolingbroke,
> Besides himself, are all the English peers,
> And with that odds he weighs King Richard down.

Thus the explicit metaphor of the scales appears when a common man, an "objective" observer, speaks: one who does not explore a subtle poetry of feeling but rather produces a single crude metaphor. Not that Shakespeare would have written the scene for this crude metaphor alone. The Gardener and the First Servant have already compared the garden to England as a place having to be kept in order by pruning and plucking, and have envisaged the kingdom's present situation in terms of horticultural strategies. But just when Richard has been condemned by their practical minds as the negligent horticulturist of his native land, the Queen, having eavesdropped on their colloquy, appears to reproach the Gardener:

> Thou, old Adam's likeness, set to dress this garden,
> How dares thy harsh rude tongue sound this unpleasing news?
> What Eve, what serpent, hath suggested thee
> To make a second fall of cursed man?

This—by no means Shakespeare's most inspired metaphor—is very serviceable to the pattern I am describing—and not merely because of the literal analogy with Phaëthon's adventure: another "fall." In the Queen's speech, the earthly garden of political rule is forced to yield place to the garden of myth, where the divine unfortunately becomes human or, in closer terms, where kings are subject to common misfortunes. The Queen speaks, like her husband, the mythical language of royalty, in which evil is the modification of an absolute quality: what amounts to a maladroit or "illegal" conversion of *quality* into *quantity*.

But if the Queen's Edenic metaphor is naïve—which I would not gainsay—it has the identical weight of poetic irony that issues in the quality of Richard's naïveté when later he compares himself with Phaëthon. Kingly failure is accountable only in terms of direct abrogation of God's law; nothing less suits its verbal explication. However, in the two parts of *King Henry IV*, Shakespeare was to show the mundane education of a prince and the demise of his predecessor (his father) in a way hinging royal responsibility on the growth of worldly reason, opposing to the practical notion of political power only the distracting indulgence of the senses; it is the latter as typified by Falstaff, Prince Henry's nurse and teacher, that the newly crowned king unfalteringly repudiates. In this royal history, the conflict devolves on two aspects of the mundane. And the mundanity is maintained not only in the transition from roisterer to ruler but also in the quality of exuberance with which Henry takes over from his father, who suspects the worst of his son's motives when the Prince, thinking the King dead, has placed the abandoned crown on his own head. After his initial accusation, the dying Henry IV is reconciled with the Prince, and father and son are shown conferring on the nature of kingly responsibilities, joined as one in what amounts to the more valiant part of royal bad conscience. The elder Henry concludes:

> How came I by the crown, O God, forgive!
> And grant it may with thee in true peace live.

To which Prince Henry modestly retorts:

> My gracious liege,
> You won it, wore it, kept it, gave it me:
> Then plain and right must my possession be,
> Which I with more than with a common pain
> 'Gainst all the world will rightfully maintain.

Though Henry V is but one remove from Richard II, we have taken the extensive royal step from the attitude of metaphysical poetry to that of tough worldly realism. Henry's attitude is the power dogma, to which the crown is more a physical property than a symbol; Richard's is the fountain of bleeding kingship, in which poetic form reveals the substance of royal being and is not merely its conventional mouthpiece. That this requires of the latter the objectivity of a poet, we observe when Richard, on being asked to read the charges against him, replies:

> Mine eyes are full of tears, I cannot see:
> And yet salt water blinds them not so much
> But they can see a sort of traitors here.
> Nay, if I turn my eyes upon myself,
> I find myself a traitor with the rest;
> For I have given here my soul's consent
> To undeck the pompous body of a king;
> Made glory base and sovereignty a slave,
> Proud majesty a subject, state a peasant.

This king is a poet who continues to view life from the plane of absolute values, where glory is always glory, state always state. In the very motion of being separated—with the accord of an ego instinctively passive to force—from his royal condition, Richard judges the event from above but not outside; as king, he cannot have utter (poetic) detachment. When he calls for the mirror, the split in the narcissean image is perfectly calculated by the dramatist, and if it is "the very book indeed where all [his] sins are writ," it is so because, though metaphorically still King Richard, he is also the Richard who has consented to bend the knee to Bolingbroke. When he declares that the broken mirror signifies "How soon my sorrow hath destroy'd my face," Bolingbroke bluntly amends the figure with

> The shadow of your sorrow hath destroy'd
> The shadow of your face.

On this, Richard is quick to thank him for what is actually the opportunity to reassert the inwardness of his grief, and thus his persistent metaphysicalism: while kings, like mirrors, may remain whole or be destroyed, the royal "substance" lies in the sensibility of beings destined to fail or succeed in a divine mission on earth. Consigned to the dungeon at Pomfret, Richard attains greater metaphysical detachment:

> I have been studying how I could compare
> This prison where I live unto the world:
> And for because the world is populous,
> And here is not a creature but myself,
> I cannot do it; yet I'll hammer it out.
> My brain I'll prove the female to my soul;
> My soul the father: and these two beget
> A generation of still-breeding thoughts,
> And these same thoughts people this little world
> In humours like the people of this world,
> For no thought is contented. The better sort,

As thoughts of things divine, are intermix'd
With scruples, and do set the word itself
Against the word. . . .

Here is the self-consciousness of the sacred king who has come to
understand the theological paradox of the divine invested by the
earthly, a paradox of which the rightful king, appointed by God,
is at once the keeper and the quintessence. As a result, the king's
own person becomes the metaphysical scene of the reversals of
earthly fortune, whose final condition, naturally, is death. Later in
the same soliloquy, Richard says:

    . . . Sometimes I am a king;
Then treason makes me wish myself a beggar,
And so I am: then crushing penury
Persuades me I was better when a king;
Then I am king'd again; and by and by
Think that I am unking'd by Bolingbroke,
And straight am nothing: but whate'er I be,
Nor I nor any man that but man is
With nothing shall be pleas'd, till he be eas'd
With being nothing.

The something/nothing paradox needs only the religious affirmation to reproduce the metaphysical experience of the seventeenth
century. Indeed, the play on the clock metaphor that immediately follows here and especially the climactic brooch metaphor
are close to the manner of Herbert and Donne. The metaphysical
gesture is to recreate the world in terms of thought; thus, to
imitate the act of divine creation. Hamlet, too, with his "O what
a rogue and peasant slave am I," is well within the metaphysical
sensibility that placed man's intellect philosophically correspond-
ent to God's initial creative act in which all existence is implicit.
In Act IV, Scene IV, echoing Richard's numerical figure given
above, Hamlet visualizes "The imminent death of twenty thousand men" as Fortinbras' army passes, and climaxes this solilo-

quy with "My thoughts be bloody, or be nothing worth!" Both his and Richard's individual reverses of kingly fortune hold, as temporal experience, what must take place ideally in the poetry of the metaphysical, whose law—because of the basic matter/spirit paradox—rests on the ultimate identity of opposites.

As Phaëthon, Richard finally conceives himself as the ridden rather than the rider. He is crushed by the groom's information that his own horse, Barbary, carrying Bolingbroke, went "So proudly as if he disdained the ground," rails on the horse and then asks his forgiveness, concluding with a figure that characterizes the depth of his reversal:

> I was not made a horse;
> And yet I bear a burden like an ass,
> Spur-gall'd and tir'd by jauncing Bolingbroke.

The dynamic antithesis is epitomized in his dying words:

> Mount, mount, my soul! thy seat is up on high,
> Whilst my gross flesh sinks downward, here to die.

The elements in previous centuries which led to the typical seventeenth-century concept of man as a microcosm are as well known as the verse containing the imagery of this concept. It remained for the poets to express the inwardness of the spiritual revolution, especially with regard to religion, which had traditionally interpreted the universe to man. Christ as king, for the devotional poets, redeemed man's something from his phenomenal end and beginning in nothing, and provided intrinsic justification of the formal paradox as well as a mythical model for his earthly conduct. But the principal change, determining the pivot of metaphysical verse, was the Protestant reform that concerned precisely the individual's immediate confrontation of divine being. Technically and historically a presumption, this had to be redeemed by the poet's profound humility.

What is striking about Shakespeare's kings is their egotism, which is either narcissean as in Richard II or practical as in Henry V; in brief, their "protestant" spirit which relied on their personal responsibility for a settlement with God when they went to chapel and to the Hereafter. In the Shakespearian histories, it is a cliché that the king's foot repeatedly rests on a spot slippery with blood. The Bastard's lines closing *The Life and Death of King John* show that the basis of the foothold—or rather, its animating spirit—is temporal power inspired by patriotism:

> This England never did, nor never shall,
> Lie at the proud foot of a conqueror,
> But when it first did help to wound itself.
> Now these her princes are come home again,
> Come the three corners of the world in arms,
> And we shall shock them. Nought shall make us rue,
> If England to itself do rest but true.

There were two main sources of interference with English independence: Rome and France. In King John's history, the temporal invader is expelled before the Pope's legate, Pandulph, has failed to induce him to lay down the arms whose assumption the legate himself had previously advised. The legate's politics are purely religious: King John, having been reconciled with Rome, has regained Pandulph's allegiance. With Richard, however, the problem of government is quite internal, and that this king is against the ancient superstition that virtue will triumph in arms, is proven by his abrupt dissolution of the planned combat of honor between the mutual accusers, Mowbray and Bolingbroke, on both of whom he at once imposes exile. Richard represents the ideal, static, and Narcissean element of chivalry, Bolingbroke the practical and dynamic; the former is pacific and effeminate, the latter belligerent and masculine. Bolingbroke's victorious heroism is animated by the intolerability of separation from native ground. Thus, his is the concrete politics, not the abstract metaphysics, of kingship. He is the Henry who fathered Henry V.

The moral relation of the tragedies to the histories is here significant: Macbeth and Hamlet are respectively alignable with
Henry IV and Richard II in regard to kingly office. Richard and
Hamlet discover in language (that is to say, in poetic metaphysics) ripe extenuation of the postponement of, or abdication
from, official duties. Macbeth and Henry contrarily measure language only by deeds, kingliness only by the possession of the
crown. If Richard, as has been demonstrated here, strikes the
metaphysical note more accurately than does Hamlet in any of
his soliloquies, still the latter are animated by that absolute confrontation of the universe by the ego that is the essential condition of metaphysical verse.

One prime rule of this condition is closeness to nature, the
actual confrontation of the elements, found alike in "The Garden" and "To His Coy Mistress," of Marvell, and in Hamlet's
"sea of troubles" and its "currents." The *inward* directly reflects
the *outward,* and the quality of infinity saturates the tension between them. The famous couplet,

Annihilating all that's made
To a green thought in a green shade,

as an efficient emblem of the metaphysical quality, may be fruit-
fully contrasted with the isolated use of "green" as natural metaphor in *The Life and Death of King John* when Pandulph ad-
monishes the youthful Dauphin: "How green you are and fresh
in this old world." The legate means that Lewis is immature in
political strategy, which situates the metaphor within the actual
process of nature as a *relative* quality. The place of "green" in
Marvell's line indicates the opposite: it is outside nature; that is
to say, in mind, and thus represents an absolute, not relative,
quality of maturation.

We may then note, in Richard's tragedy, the metaphysical
movement contained in the Queen's reprimand of the Gardener,
who has just compared Richard's England to the garden in which

they stand (an actual portion of English ground). The Queen's language makes the ground of all action *mythical* and thus, in relation to Richard's conduct and fortunes, purely metaphysical. Marvell's garden is a benign climax of thought, Richard's prison a malign climax of thought. The words of the King's soliloquy (above quoted), "yet I'll hammer it out," indicate truthfully that *his* poetic metaphysics has matured in duress rather than in free choice; though Richard's instinct is poetic, he *remains a king* rather than *becomes a poet*.

In the legend of evil invoked by Richard's Queen lies that mythical schism in consciousness which it became the destiny of the metaphysical poet to assume and mend. Adam the individual, states the legend, was divided; and so in the domain of sex, logically, would lie the process of self-reclamation that was to be so large and important an experience of the poet as human lover. For the metaphysical, indeed, the erotic partner became a landscape, a ground of action, by which the awareness of the universe, an absolute unity of nature, was attainable. Already the seeds of metaphysical love had entered literature in The Song of Solomon, and whether the Biblical text be construed as purely sensual in origin or as a parable of the love of God, its metaphysical mode is unimpeachable: the beloved individual offers an infinite nature, a symbolic body, in which the lover gains (or following the logic of the Eden myth "regains") his sense of wholeness in the visible and invisible universe.

Typical evidence of this from the metaphysical school may be cited in Donne's "The Extasie": the image of the violet resting on the "Pregnant banke" and representing the union of the lovers:

> A single violet transplant,
>   The strength, the colour, and the size,
> (All which before was poore, and scant,)
>   Redoubles still, and multiplies.
> When love, with one another so
>   Interinanimates two soules,

> That abler soule, which thence doth flow,
>   Defects of lonelinesse controules.

Although Donne well knows that the sexual union, as complete and "controlled," is on the transcendent level of soul, both the "single violet" that is love's original seed and the universal ground of the "Pregnant banke" are necessary to the metaphysical unity, the attainment of the One. The poem's coda asserts:

> So must pure lovers soules descend
>   T'affections and to faculties,
> Which sense may reach and apprehend,
>   Else a great Prince in prison lies.

The beauty of this metaphor is no less surprising in the poem's context than the relation suggested now for it may appear: that to Richard II in the dungeon of Flint Castle. Love as well as kingship requires experience of the physical domain—that is, human love (aside from the Socratic tradition) does. Nevertheless, it is the further implication of superhuman love, love for God and other divine persons, by which the metaphysical tension undergoes its most vital test. For, as Donne well knew, the body of the beloved passes from integrity into dissolution as does the body of the lover.

If, from the strictly religious standpoint, the danger of metaphysicalism in the lover is the possibility of error through ultrafetichism, so, from the strictly political standpoint, the danger of metaphysicalism in a king would be the possibility of error through the same; in effect, an error of radical disproportion. Richard's naïveté therefore resides in a confusion about the laws of kingly conduct comparable to Phaëthon's confusion about the laws of human conduct when he essayed to drive the Sun's horses. I think both may be considered parables in the same light. The success of the illusion of omnipotence—an absolute

equation between ego and universe, human individual and God
—depends exclusively on action *as language,* God's or the poet's;
or, as it is put in Richard's prison soliloquy, a cohabitation between "brain" and "soul" producing "thoughts." And if, in the
case of this king, "no thought is contented," "the word itself" set
"against the word," it is actually because the speaker remains in
a cell of imposed physical inaction, of which Hamlet's symbolic
"cell" is the psychological paradigm in drama. The discontent
and opposition among Richard's thoughts arise from their bastard situation, where they are but the reflection of forces still
warring within the world; thus, forces held in dynamic suspense
without final resolution.

The difference between the quasi-metaphysical poets who are
Richard and Hamlet and the true metaphysicals becomes clear:
in the quasi-metaphysicals of drama, the reflective impulse is but
the psychic mirror of real action; that is, the psychological *reaction* to willed or unwilled physical *inaction.* In the true metaphysicals of seventeenth-century poetry, the means of language is
sufficient to reflective thought as a willed end. Through language,
thought becomes the final resolution of all conflicts involved with
a single tension. This *is* the metaphysical tradition. Therefore the
tensions of its poets arise and subside with the constant reappli-
cation to language for an adjustment between ego and universe,
the devout individual and God. All the same, love must ever
watch against the mundane danger of property-feeling, which
assumes that individual, society, or God, as illusively subject to
the human will, may be coerced into providing ground for the
transcendent union. The poet who has triumphed morally over
this danger (and it is intrinsically contemporary as well as historic) is the assured metaphysical. The means of his triumph is
the understanding that mutual consent, or love in reciprocity, is
the law of the ideal union.

George Herbert and the early and late Donne have direct relations with the world and with God through love of God; in
Donne's case, primarily through the love of woman that was

superseded by the love of God. The personal element, the projection of the ego, is important here because of the Phaëthon image I have chosen as this chapter's emblem. Before Richard II compares himself to Phaëthon (who represents the pseudo-function of the Sun God), Bolingbroke, catching sight of Richard as he enters on the wall above, exclaims:

> See, see, King Richard doth himself appear,
> As doth the blushing discontented sun
> From out the fiery portal of the East,
> When he perceives the envious clouds are bent
> To dim his glory. . . .

The king as sun god is a remote mythic tradition. But, despite the strict conventionality of Bolingbroke's salute, it is profoundly situated within the play's esthetic structure and enters the present theme. Comparable to the interpersonal relation of the king and his intimate supporters—the nobles conscious of shining in his aura—was another interpersonal relation of the time: that of the noble patron and the poet-commoner.

The male patron was the generalized image of a specific cultural value denoted by the entire noble caste, and as such could assume (as suspected in the case of Shakespeare's "Mr. W. H.") the ideal characteristics of both intimate muse and erotic image: could be the king-queen of the poet's private worship. Thus, it is quite in conformity with custom that we find Donne addressing six of the seven sonnets of his *Divine Poems* to the Earl of Doncaster and beginning the dedicatory sonnet:

> See, sir, as the sun's hot masculine flame
>   Begets strange creatures on Nile's dirty slime
>   In me your fatherly yet lusty rhyme
> —For these songs are their fruits—have wrought the same.

Sexuality as such is not, of course, a component of the erotic metaphor here any more than it is in Richard's above-quoted soliloquy where he contemplates proving his brain "female" to his soul. At the same time, Donne *is* in a passive relation, metaphysically and dynamically speaking, to the patron he addresses: a passive relation made vivid by evoking the physical generative process. This dedication has a special appropriateness, moreover, as indicating Donne's own evolution from "lusty rhyme" to sacred verse, an evolution which had taken place because of the pivotal shift of his attention from the real feminine image to that transcendent virgin-image of the anniversaries and thence to the images of God and Jesus.

It is instructive to recall the author's note prefacing Crashaw's "A Hymn to the Name and Honour of the Admirable Saint Teresa":

> Foundress of the Reformation of the discalced Carmelites, both men and women; a woman for angelical height of speculation, for masculine courage of performance, more than a woman; who yet a child outran maturity, and durst plot a martyrdom.

No matter of which sex, the poet's muse tends to place him in the "feminine" attitude of one who submits, who primarily is acted upon. We are reminded of the lady-lords of feudal times to whom lovers paid suit in the masculine form of address. Here is a reflection, also, on the "masculine" ascendancy of the virgin queen, Elizabeth, whom a recently developed theory has identified as the covert subject of Donne's poems in honor of Elizabeth Drury.* The humility of the metaphysical before his god, muse, or patron is the emotional basis for his use of language as passional action. In order to achieve the transcendent union that is his aim, his love—whether for woman or divine being—must be humble and suppliant, open and passive; never dominant or aggressive unless in the fervor of a Teresan avidness.

---

* The theory has been independently announced by Marjorie Nicolson and Marius Bewley. See the latter's essay in *Kenyon Review,* Summer, 1952.

Richard II proved his love for the divine right of kings by stepping down in favor of the masculine, practically aggressive Bolingbroke; yet, not being a true poet, Richard was destined to rue his loss of the temporal crown. This monarch, seeking martyrdom in a manner parallel to Christ's, still could not purely allow his person to be metaphysically the scene of the divine king's earthly destruction; nor could his experience have entitled him, even in prison, to speak lines such as those of Donne's that begin "La Corona":

> *Deign at my hands this crown of prayer and praise*
> Weaved in my lone devout melancholy. . . .

The great traditional function of soldiers has been to make a throne secure, as it was also their collective function, in Richard's poetic sense, to keep the blood in a king's cheek. But Richard confesses his own pseudo-functionalism by being constantly thrown back in mind on the importance of externality, seeing only too well the sentiment of divine right as distinct from the objectivity of mundane right, which is concentrated in force rather than in sacredness. In his own way, Richard is as naïve a metaphysical as Thomas Traherne. In "The Apostacy," Traherne virtually states a valuation of the world commensurate with a child's valuation of toys in a shop-window. To all kinds of property, he has as naïve and pseudo-functional a relation as does Richard to the throne of England and its crown.

"Toys" and "hobby-horses," mentioned in "The Apostacy," stand generally in Traherne's verse for objects in their pseudo-functional aspect. When a child plays with paper dolls and thinks he is dealing with living adults, he imagines himself in control of the real world: it is his first practice in the hypothetical problems of metaphysical control. Myth is that medium in which men exist on the same plane as the gods but are to the gods as children to adults. It is the physical opacity of myth and the physical transparency of metaphysical poetry that appear in crucial contrast.

Psychologically, Phaëthon's aspiration is that of a presumptuous child who dreams of guiding a splendid team of real horses attached to a real chariot. Apollo's horses, as the myth reveals, demonstrate when tried that they are not the "hobby-horses" of Phaëthon's dream-world whose models are the true horses of the actual world. The naïve poet, hesitating before the catharsis of real experience, falls back upon the wish-fulfillment phase of experience, and with this condition (primitive and radiant and full of love though it is in Traherne) submits himself to God by grace of *in*experience.

The most primitive desire of the child is for things, objects, regardless of their use, of which at first, naturally, he is ignorant. The survival of this primitive property-sense into adulthood is reactionary, and accounts for the accumulation of material wealth as luxury. Only the maturity of the spirit as intellectual understanding can transcend the property-sense: this is the essential condition of metaphysical poetry. For the static modes governing the tension between child and adult, man and God, ego and universe, the sophisticated metaphysical, such as Donne and Herbert, substitutes dynamic modes derived from worldly experience, in which physical objects are desired, experienced, and then rejected. This is Donne's specific evolution as revealed quantitatively in his verse.

If the typical failure of the child is the failure of the adult, the typical failure of man is the failure to be God. In the recognition of this ultimate failure by the naïve or sophisticated metaphysical lies that peculiar tension of the ego confronting the universe whose physical existence, whose deepest exploration as *matter,* has had to be abandoned in favor of the consciousness of God or Infinity. Jesus was a "king" among men because, ultimately passive before the world's physical aggression, he could reject the world in favor of the prospect of eternal life and reunion with His Father, and so was triumphant in humility. Shakespeare bestowed on his Richard II an intuition of this same humility, for only the hypothesis of this intuition can adequately explain

Richard's readiness to see his eventual eclipse in every aggressive step of Bolingbroke's.

With what irony, afterwards, was Bolingbroke's breed, representing the cult of the acquisitor, to issue in Henry VI, his grandson and Richard II's parody. This Henry's kingly bad conscience utterly neutralizes his will, so that in the last part of his history he becomes no more than a pawn in the fluctuating War of the Roses. The pendulum-like movement Shakespeare has traced from Richard II and Bolingbroke to Henry VI and Richard of Gloucester (Richard III) is of a dynamic profundity with eloquent moral implications. The movement suggests not so much the classic nemesis as a eugenic antithesis: an irony of biology. Henry VI of aggressive Lancaster is more inert, less inwardly passionate, than Richard II of passive York! The latter at least does not selfishly bargain for the crown on his head as does Bolingbroke's own grandson. In the third part of Henry VI's history we find him bereft of the throne and wandering: ". . . disguised, with a prayer book." His meditations do not accomplish the metaphysical movement of Richard's meditations previously cited, but he muses upon the antithetical nature of men's fortunes. Apprehended by two gamekeepers who recognize him, he rebukes them as men who once took oaths of fealty to him:

> Look, as I blow this feather from my face,
> And as the wind blows it to me again;
> Obeying with my wind as I do blow,
> And yielding to another when it blows,
> Commanded always by the greater gust;
> Such is the lightness of you common men.

This is a pointed irony of the material world; that is, the world dominated by materialistic values. Christ was the "king" who had already understood the "commonness" of belonging to a world which, on the metaphysical level, unites a king even with his humblest subject. So Shakespeare's figure just quoted is not finally so true as the one he invented for Richard II: the mirror. From the metaphysical standpoint, the dynamic irony of this figure applies to all humanity, where kings are as immaterial as those who obey them, men being as feathers among the inscrutable urges of the universe—or, as one might say, the "driven" rather than the "driver." Phaëthon wrecked the Sun's chariot as Richard broke the mirror. Only one factor—and it is the pivot of metaphysical control—reëstablishes the equilibrium of this destroyed tension: the *love* of the driver for the driven.

Whether or not the universe the poet faces is concentrated in the anthropomorphic image of God does not matter to the issue. What the poet's ego confronts is an Infinity and a Totality which do not appear in the aggregate of natural experience and can only resolve themselves in the intuition of Eternity. This is the absolute norm of the metaphysical tension: the only possible means of translating Phaëthon's desire into Apollo's capacity. The myth can apply to universal experience, including the metaphysical poet's along with the ruler's, through the linguistic and other arts. It is thus a metaphor for all kinds of human government. The "political" ideal of the metaphysical poet—now, previously, and always—is the perfection of a paradoxical technique: to be the ridden and the rider.

3

DOSTOIEVSKY'S PERSONAL DEVIL

Stavrogin, hero of *The Possessed*—in one of those oblique, laconic insights somehow wrung from him—defines the quality of Verhovensky, the terroristic Nihilist, as "enthusiasm." The term "enthusiasm" has suffered a degradation of usage, for Webster's Dictionary gives "elevation of fancy; ardor of mind; fervent zeal; fanaticism." Today its Dostoievskian perspective, for a variety of reasons, is altogether lacking; it is now a quality exposing its truest expression at picnics, the theatre, conventions of political parties, and in the euphoria of beatniks; that is to say, it is no longer serious excepting as defining the appreciation of an esthetic spectacle. In *The Possessed,* Yulia Mihailovna's "literary fete" makes it clear what status and order Dostoievsky accorded "enthusiasm for art." The meaning of Stavrogin's attribution to Verhovensky is to be filled out "enthusiasm . . . for life." If there is one quality of human character untypical of our age it is precisely enthusiasm for life . . . enthusiasm, not care.

If it be said, on the contrary, that Europe still breeds its Verhovenskys in radical political movements, and that the Communist successes in Spain many years ago and the historic rise of Marshal Tito's party comprise evidence that enthusiasm for life still issues springlike from the human breast, the reply must be that, as reflected in culture, this enthusiasm does not survive (and has not for the last three decades) the criticism of reason, common sense, and the ethical conscience. The work of a few painters may be excepted, perhaps, and for a while the Surrealists seemed to have struck a universal key, but it turned out that the heart of the movement was esoteric—it was avant-garde esthetics pure and simple. The dada and surrealist "madness" at one point had a Dostoievskian aspect of electrifying energy, but it could do very little for society in general, of which *The Waste Land* was a much more adequate, truthful, and (one might say) consoling expression.

The fact that the man described by Stavrogin as an enthusiast, Verhovensky, was a Nihilist of the most extreme terroristic kind, may indeed be an index to the culture of political types in modern Europe—as different in spirit as prominent modern examples of political leaders are, and as much as Dostoievsky strove to discredit Verhovensky's politics. Yet without Dostoievsky we would not have a profoundly vivid portrait of this sort of Nihilist, the progenitor of the more rational Bolshevik. The connection between the abiding liveliness of timbre given off by Verhovensky —like that of a perpetually tuned musical instrument—and its motivation, cannot be ignored. Verhovensky's enthusiasm arises specifically from his devotion to what in the novel is termed "The Cause."

The political cause in *The Possessed* means, roughly, something with large vague aims for which the individual committed to it is constantly expected to commit outrages and risk his life on orders from a mysterious "center." Verhovensky's "cause" is expressly revealed in the novel as entailing a plan to confuse and terrify communities throughout Russia to a point where the malcontent elements will spontaneously rally to a sudden raising of the standard of revolt and find those in power so disorganized as to be incapable of resistance. The outline plot of *The Possessed* covers an interrelated series of events which are nothing but engines for creating such a state in one unnamed Russian province. Yet, involved in the implacable human passions and wayward wills of the persons in this novel, the reader cannot help reflecting that Verhovensky's motivation, as a fundamental cause for the sequence of catastrophes, is but a superficial principle for the general organization of Dostoievsky's plot—a purely formal principle which the author, whatever his political opinions, has used to hold together an interaction of human lives much too explosive (in the generic sense of "enthusiasm for life") to be defined as mere symptoms of enthusiasm for a Cause.

This observation is in order because all the male characters in the novel, without one exception, are or have been, actually or in imagination, involved with the machinery of "The Cause"; that is to say, Dostoievsky is artistically sound in relating the nihilistic sentiments of the period of which he writes to the self-destroying, plangent, unreckoning motives of the chief persons in *The Possessed,* including most of the women; Marya Timofeyevna, whom Stavrogin marries out of mockery, is mad; Lizaveta Nicolaevna a hopeless enthusiast for romantic love; Yulia Mihailovna a fanatical narcissist; Varvara Petrovna, Stavrogin's mother, an obdurate feudal tyrant; Marya, Shatov's wife, a hysterical "freethinker" and one of Stavrogin's victims. The truth is that where Dostoievsky virtually denounces his professional Nihilists as doomed madmen or fools, so seeming to negate any moral virtue in the idea of social revolution, his instinct as an artist has seized upon the Nihilistic movement in Russia as a symbolist device, recognizing it as another symptom of the Russian temperament and thus, basically, of the human temperament of his time and place. So the Nihilistic "Cause" is actually a symbol of a deeper, humanly wider cause in the scheme of individual emotions in *The Possessed*. In this sense, *cause* may be understood as motivation of act in the individual's relation with his own soul no less than his relation to his organized social action. Surely the ex-Nihilists, the morose and taciturn Shatov and the quasi-religious Kirillov, demonstrate that the political idea as such is but one of the "chemical" properties serving to drive the individual toward self-revelation, the creation of his soul. Not that here Dostoievsky is concerned, any more than elsewhere, in a specific definition of the individual's relation to his soul—but this is only because this novelist was never concerned primarily with *definitions* (as are, for example, novelists of the modern existentialist schools) but with *actions*. And yet in the mystery surrounding the "center" of the Nihilistic movement—the physical and spiritual kernel of the Cause—is there not a parallel with that mysterious "center," with its invisibly communicated power, the human soul?

The term used by Dostoievsky for his title has an esthetic ambiguity, whether or not this ambiguity was reckoned by the artist. The element of *possession,* directly related to the classic definition of enthusiasm as "fanaticism" or "ardor of mind," is not only a standard quality of Dostoievsky's character creations in the single gallery of all his fiction, but in this novel it is particularly related to a "madness" with an ideological, or conscious and deliberate, content: revolutionary terrorism and its socialistic objective. How significant it is that when Kirillov, the near-Nihilist who has decided to take his life on strictly moral grounds, describes to Shatov a state of ecstasy he has just achieved, Shatov warns him that he has exactly the symptoms of epilepsy. It is of special interest today, when moral negation and the absurdity of life deeply occupy contemporary novelists, that Dostoievsky should, with some instinctive design, have related decadent revolutionary fervor to epilepsy, which in turn he relates (as also in Myshkin's character) to Christian humility and goodness. Kirillov has reached his decision to commit suicide through his belief that Christ is the divine absurdist, having expected on the Cross his early advent to Paradise. Kirillov cannot believe in God; he can only believe in the man Jesus who "absurdly" thought God was his father and would elevate him to eternal happiness without making him suffer as a human being. As Shatov believed in Stavrogin, who failed him, Kirillov believed in Christ, who apparently was proven "wrong." Of the two men, the Christian Kirillov is the more truly "possessed" by the symbol of a person, because he wishes to leave a world rendered absurd by Christ's alleged failure; whereas on the contrary, the Stavroginist Shatov, however morose and inactive he becomes, still values his own life as though clinging to an obscure hope.

A characteristic of "possessed" persons is that they are precipitated into action, more or less violent, or that they constantly plan such action. "Possession" is therefore a state of being prepared for immediate action, the "cause" of such action being the thing which possesses, however it be identified. It is easy to see how revolutionary temperaments (and especially the Nihilists of the 19th century) fit into this pattern. But I have observed that in this novel Dostoievsky formulates a human condition wherein emotions are galvanized by a social-revolutionary objective—in short, by *an idea*. A most witty and important observation is made of Verhovensky by a minor character in *The Possessed*: He can "make up a man and live with him." One of the most astounding scenes in the novel is the one where we learn just what it is that makes the enigmatic, slippery, scheming Verhovensky "tick": it is nothing less than the vision of Stavrogin as a revolutionary "tsarevitch," a sort of political messiah, whom he —Verhovensky—will manage to place in power. This is the explanation of the malicious *mot* on his curious propensity to "make up a man." As Verhovensky himself asserts while frantically begging Stavrogin to consent to the future role he has assigned him, his faith in Stavrogin is precisely due to his knowledge that Stavrogin is "indifferent to everything." This means that his purely imaginary man, "Stavrogin-Tsarevitch," seems possible, capable of being real, by the fact that Stavrogin is essentially empty, in that, committed to "nothing," he is capable of "anything"; that is to say, apparently he is not "possessed." But, as the long suppressed chapter "At Tihon's" tells us, Verhovensky is wrong. Stavrogin's ostensible, neo-nihilistic indifference is a mask for pathological guilt. Truly, Stavrogin cannot be "possessed" (it becomes evident) by a definite person; he cannot even fall in love with Liza, whom he finds so attractive, and with whom he has a one-night affair, during which she tragically guesses his inability to love her.

The deepest spiritual revelation in the book occurs from the mouth of the monk, Tihon, to whom Stavrogin shows his written confession of having seduced a little girl who thereupon committed suicide. Tihon suggests that Stavrogin's confirmed desire to publish the confession may be his ruin, for he will discover that his crime is not "great" enough, that, after the initial public shock, people will ridicule him and he will not survive their contempt. Stavrogin is profoundly dismayed by this idea, which apparently is a valid insight into his nature. Thus, incapable of a truly great sin, he is incapable of any state rightly to be termed "possession." Stavrogin, I suggest, is possessed by one idea—or, so to speak, a non-idea—that of being *not possessed*. However, previously he has indeed been a quasi-nihilistic idealist, a believer in the Russian God whose "body is the Russian people." So Shatov, diehard disciple of Stavrogin, insists to his "master" two years after their last previous meeting. In having renounced his beliefs meanwhile, Stavrogin has "committed suicide" in Shatov's consciousness, thus destroying Shatov's belief in God and gaining Shatov's mortal reproaches. For both Verhovensky and Shatov, Stavrogin exists as a made-up man! But why can Verhovensky continue living with his "made-up man" and Shatov have found him destroyed, dead, a useless phantom? Because Shatov's enthusiasm for life depends upon fitting ideas to idols, and so it is *the idol* that is essential and primary; with Verhovensky only *the idea* is essential and primary. To regain any enthusiasm, Shatov has to wait until the re-entrance in his life of Marya, his wife, who has been got with child after being originally seduced by Stavrogin. Here is an extraordinary if blasphemous parallel to the story of Mary and Joseph, a sort of immaculate conception. Shatov accepts Marya's child as a "savior" of his soul and acquires new enthusiasm for life with the appearance in his wife's womb of fruit which, if not Stavrogin's own, was "permitted" by Stavrogin's wanton, "godlike" authority. The spirit— "the word"—has been made flesh. But before it was a word *made* flesh, it *was* flesh: Stavrogin.

The fundamental question asserts itself: just what is enthusiasm for life? In relation to the characters in all Dostoievsky's other novels, as well as those in *The Possessed,* this enthusiasm appears as an entirely irrational faculty in that actually so little about any of his great characters can be called "sensible" or "practical." Modern psychology and philosophy have tended to assign to this faculty, so typical of Dostoievsky's characters, an inscrutability—a realm of blind ultimate cause, as in Freud's *libido instinct,* Bergson's *élan-vital,* or in a more commonplace term, *joie-de-vivre.* Roundly, it is the "life force." But such terms are of no help to us, in regard to individual moral attitudes, unless we accept the logic of some science or philosophy as a reading of human motives conceived without conscious recognition of such logic by the persons motivated. Freud has analyzed Dostoievsky, as he did also Leonardo da Vinci.

Right here, since Stavrogin's own "case history" is actually presented in documentary form by his "confession," the question of the relevance of psychoanalysis to Dostoievsky's novels might well be disposed of. The value of Stavrogin as an index to human character in general is not adequately assessed by a Freudian or any other psychiatric method, for the simple reason that the data of his "psychosis" do not define him as an individual. If a man be no richer than his psychosis or neurosis, he is of no schematic worth to anyone but a professional analyst. Stavrogin, being "unpossessed," is capable of "gratuitous action"—as evidenced by the two incidents in the early part of the book, his actual leading of one man by the nose and biting another's ear, and by his will-less incident with Liza, whom he offers to marry in the same arbitrary, motiveless spirit in which he bit the Governor's ear. People such as Liza, with genuine enthusiasm for life, guess the absence of it in others, and she guesses that Stavrogin does not really love her although they have just spent a night of passion together. Stavrogin has false enthusiasm for life, but it *is* enthusiasm. By "false enthusiasm" I do not mean precisely what the term "gratuitous act" came to mean for André Gide.

From Stavrogin's model, Gide derived the gratuitous action of his characters, one of whom—Lafcadio—is a philosopher of the "acte gratuit." But the derivation was, as an independent idea, a misunderstanding of Dostoievsky's characters and their motivation. Lafcadio's is the *cult* of the gratuitous act; Stavrogin's is its *necessity*. So Gide's is the gratuitousness of the gratuitous. The clue to the marrow of this distinction can be supplied by psychoanalysis. Stavrogin's is the substitute act of a psychotic—the forced alternative of some secretly desired act, perhaps the Oedipus crime; herein lies the "absurdity" of his tricks, such as biting someone's ear entirely without "cause" in the rational sense. On the other hand, Lafcadio's is the esthetic act of an ethically confused person, a confirmed neurotic. Lafcadio throws a man out of a train window in order to experience the voluptuousness of criminal feelings; he is, of course, natural inheritor of de Sade's esthetics of sin and of Des Esseintes' experiments with artificial sensations, as well as an imitator of Raskolnikoff, who, like Stavrogin, found crime a "necessity" in the sense of inability to resist temptation. Since Lafcadio has no motives for crime (except carefully coddled ones) his criminal esthetic is virtually a psychological displacement; that is, in the intellectual realm, he has decided on the "made-up," the imagination, in preference to the "real," the actual, as a practical principle. But without moral inevitability (even though, like Raskolnikoff's, the ultimate motive be hidden), Lafcadio's is "displaced art." So he is in a position very similar to Verhovensky's; one might say, a vulgarized position. He "makes up" his crime, commits it, and "lives with it"; he cannot resist making the idea, the "word," into "flesh," knowing that in essence it is merely a word, a dictionary denizen and not a thing on anyone's lips or in his heart. Similar, indeed, is Quinette, Jules Romains' character, who commits crimes for the sake of showing (like a detective-story writer who imagines "the perfect crime" as subject for a novel) his ability to outwit the police. Yet at least Quinette's "displaced art" is more genuinely like Verhovensky's plot to exalt Stavrogin-Tsarevitch than is Lafcadio's crime—with one important discrepancy between the first pair. Verhovensky's climax to his "art of revolution" is indefinitely in the future, but by this art (however "absurd") Verhovensky means to transform reality; i.e., to create a society by legalizing the illegal. His instrumentality of "art" will accomplish an indefinitely postponed legitimacy of fact. His "false" enthusiasm for life is based on confidence in possibility; this enthusiasm is irrational not only because he exaggerates the power of the revolutionary movement, but because Stavrogin's reply to his proposition is flatly negative; nevertheless, Verhovensky proceeds, still "possessed" with his "made-up" man and hoping that Stavrogin will consent to be exalted if revolutionary Russia should be thrown at his feet! When Kirillov brands Verhovensky as a "false intellect," we unmistakably detect Dostoievsky's voice stigmatizing the revolutionary Nihilists. But, as history has helpfully informed us with its irrefutable data, Verhovensky's intellect, however smaller it is in genius, is no falser than was Lenin's or Trotsky's. Indeed, "Ivan the Tsarevitch," the false Stavrogin of Verhovensky's imagination, is a phantom no less "true" than the generic revolutionist or the uprising proletariat of Lenin's early days. The enthusiasm of the Russian revolutionists survived all kinds of failures, betrayals, and anti-climaxes till the hour of final victory. Verhovensky, after Stavrogin's spurning, believes in Stavrogin, and the vision inseparable from him, more than ever by virtue of the absurd. After 1905, and during Kerensky's pseudo-revolutionary regime, it was more than ever unjustifiable to "believe" in a "Russian revolution" except according to a logic of "the absurd."

The link between Lafcadio and Meursault, hero of Albert Camus' novel, *L'Etranger,* is obvious; both commit "gratuitous" crimes, although the common man, Meursault, is far from being an esthete. No, he is "existential"—i.e., his act of murder has no psychological motivation, no moral anticipation, whatever—it is as sudden as Stavrogin's seizure when he bites the ear; it is not philosophically, rationally, or esthetically, but "existentially" absurd. It *is absurd* because it *is.* This is a *reductio ad absurdum* of the absurd as it was conceived by the inspirer of existentialist philosophies, Søren Kierkegaard. Although he adjudged it the only true method of having faith in God, Kierkegaard could never believe, he himself asserted, "by virtue of the absurd." The prototypic act of faith Kierkegaard found in that of Abraham, who proceeded to sacrifice Isaac to the raising of the knife, secure in his confidence that God would somehow restore Isaac to him. Kirillov would say of this biblical myth that Abraham lied—that no angel appeared, and that he merely hallucinated the whole affair. Kierkegaard does not question the myth and yet he cannot have Abraham's faith. Yet if he had been, like Dostoievsky, a creative artist, one feels that he would have created a Kirillov: i.e., a man who would die because, the divine being a human "lie," faith is self-demonstrably absurd. Generally speaking, the realization of any kind of faith depends on the criterion for credible proof. But man alone creates the logical proof for a formal proposition of his own creation; religious metaphysics, for example, creates its own premises, hence its logic is foolproof.

Whether belief in the immortality of Christ as man, or in a socialist future of man be in question, the proofs are absurd certainly, in the eyes of all, if more than the self-evident (such as traditional myth) is deemed necessary for final conviction. Yet daily, at the present time, everybody with any enthusiasm for living lives a life of "absurd" belief in the reality of the mind conceived *as project,* as vision of the future. This vision of the future seems to grant us permission to live comfortably in the present, and only this grants it to us. Vulgarly, this state is to be termed "optimism." But we see how weak and wrong this term is when applied to Dostoievsky's characters, who are so unhappy and yet display such unfailing enthusiasm. The vulgar error of confusing these two kinds of optimism is due to the degradation of man as a society.

An engrossing question is the distinction, in legitimate values, between "false" and "genuine" enthusiasm. Again we must turn to the great grouping of Dostoievsky's characters: to certain of his women, so volatile, so mad for love, that they are no more than oddly civilized Bacchae, self-destroying in their inverted ardor; and also to Raskolnikoff, the brothers Karamazov, Myshkin and Rogojin, as well as to "the possessed," Stavrogin, Shatov, Kirillov, and Verhovensky. The most enthusiastic characters of Dostoievsky find some way of destroying or crippling themselves. Verhovensky is one of the few who "escape abroad," and doubtless Dostoievsky meant obliquely to indicate thus his inferiority to the others. Madness, suicide, or murder (as murdered or murderer) are the destinies of all of the novelist's most important characters. "Passion" is a term which has perennially served to denote the feelings of tragic characters. But Dostoievsky's art requires for them the compound term, enthusiasm-for-life, because his tragic art is uniquely a comi-tragedy. No other writer ever succeeded in manipulating the dramatic values of tragedy and comedy in such dazzling comminglement. The esthetic perversity of Gide's Lafcadio is tragedy done in the comic style— that is, Lafcadio's crime would be tragic if deeply motivated, but it is unmotivated in any dramatic sense. Pirandello's tragicomedy of individual personality results from a redundancy of human identities, each of which tends to cancel the other; all his protagonists are "possessed" by Stavrogin's dilemma of "not being possessed," without having Stavrogin's intellect; they have no determinacy, and yet are unwilling to endure "gratuitous," arbitrary, or irrational action. Stavrogin differs from the Pirandellian protagonist precisely because he can endure the gratuitous action, can intuit the positive value of moral experiment. And yet in the end, driven from crime to crime by the objective situation, he commits suicide through self-loathing. Crime of some kind is the token, therefore, by which the Dostoievskian "enthusiasm for life" is infallibly recognized. Yet the crime (of suicide or murder) is never escaped mentally excepting in one case—Shatov's. A "miracle"—the birth of "Stavrogin's" child by Marya—saves him. Shatov's failure is one of his own imagination, pure and simple: the negative instinct to lean on another *real,* rather than *imaginary,* person; he should be able, that is, to believe in "the god in man" without Stavrogin as a living, conscious, and individual example of it. So Shatov, while of greater pathos than Verhovensky, is inferior if regarded as an intellectual displaying enthusiasm for life. But the intellectual who displays enthusiasm for life *is the proto-artist, the visionary with a craft,* and that is what Verhovensky is. He is a "happy Pirandellian," realizing that his center (Stavrogin-Tsarevitch) is "elsewhere"—hypothetical, suspended—but driven on, "possessed," by a "Cause" that is Stavroginism, just as Paul's was Christianity. In being Stavrogin's self-appointed demon, his "Paul," Verhovensky indeed is possessed, but in being *possessed* by the real Stavrogin, he *possesses* the other, the fictitious Stavrogin, "Ivan the Tsarevitch," as Paul did the Jesus of Christian legend. In the same way, in the sexual realm, Dante possessed Beatrice, and Petrarch, Laura, as the false parts of real women. All the comic quality of Dostoievsky's stories arises from this definition of the absurd: the acceptance of a fiction for "the real thing," just as in *The Possessed* it is funny, and its consequences are thrice funny, that the governor's wife, Yulia Mihailovna, surrounded by a bevy of sycophants, schemers, fools, and scoundrels, imagines them an idealistic group of young people and "fanatically devoted" to her.

Dostoievsky wrote the comedy of all kinds of visionary beliefs into the tragedy of realistic frustration by providing a varied gallery of types for his novels. His remorseless realism, however, makes Verhovensky—a scoundrel by all conventional standards —into a powerful machine of sheer action. It is somewhat amazing to reflect, after the last page of the novel is read, that Verhovensky, despite the collapse of his immediate schemes, his utter loss of Stavrogin as a concrete hope following the latter's suicide, remains the only "successful" character in the book, in that he escapes with his skin and his revolutionary zeal alive under that skin; without Verhovensky, the whole plot machinery of *The Possessed* would be non-existent. Not only does he effect the catastrophe of Yulia Mihailovna's literary fete, but he has Stavrogin's unwanted wife murdered and throws Liza at Stavrogin almost at the same moment; he then arranges the "political murder" of Shatov as a potential informer, and dictates the "political" moment of Kirillov's suicide. So it is the very "falseness" of his intellect that makes his enthusiasm for life destructively triumphant; he does not care how many people *die* so long as his vision *lives*.

To Dostoievsky, this is comic because he usually gives us protagonists who place first the possession of *the real,* predominantly love, and, frustrated, drive themselves and others to catastrophe. Verhovensky is one who will grovel, when necessary, to make his dream come real, as he grovels to Stavrogin in their crucial interview on the subject of "Ivan the Tsarevitch"; to Stavrogin and Dostoievsky, the groveller is beneath contempt: a low comedian. Dostoiesky's lovers drive themselves to distraction from sheer pride; honor is the supreme moral keynote of all Dostoievsky's great characters, at least honor as conscience if not guide. From this is derived their tragic dignity.

Myshkin and Stavrogin are the two great abstainers from enthusiasm for life, so their talents for living, so large if unequal, are basically compromised; even though transiently, obliquely, Stavrogin seems to have false enthusiasm, and Myshkin genuine. And it is precisely these two who have the most ambiguous comi-tragic air of all Dostoievsky's characters. Stavrogin is even *above* *honor* in the conventional sense. He drives wild an opponent in a duel because first he makes him an abject apology, and then, when his opponent misses the final shot, fires into the bushes at one side. Eventually we learn that conventional honor is meaningless to Stavrogin because he feels profoundly, inwardly, disgraced. Likewise, Myshkin's instinctual, quixotic goodness places him in a false position in the eyes of society, for he too seems to lack conventional, manly feelings of pride and honor. Myshkin is an epileptic—hence mediocre society can excuse his odd lack of common enthusiasm on pathological grounds. We might say that the psychotic personality of Stavrogin is masochistic, since his aggressive acts are trivial, even absurd, and his one gesture toward redeeming his honor as conscience is to plan publication of his confession—divined by the monk, Tihon ("cursed psychologist!"), as an impulse to commit a deliberately absurd act because people eventually will laugh at it.

The mysterious Tihon is certainly a Freudian by instinct, and a prophet, for he points out that such crimes as Stavrogin's of seducing a child are really not so extraordinary, and people lay them to mental sickness and immature development; from the layman's view, they are easily forgivable. Stavrogin seems a stronger, more manly character than the tender-minded Myshkin, and therefore has not the spell of a lyrical personality, one of innocent charm and sweetness. The "gratuitous acts" of Myshkin are like those of Jesus: they proceed from a generic, deep-laid goodness that transcends individual relationships; therefore Myshkin brings catastrophe through his very charm and his messianic pity for the women who love him but whom he cannot love personally in return. Myshkin's "enthusiasm for life," by transcending individuals, seems to transcend *enthusiasm* itself simply because it does not seem concerned with private actions —with "the real person." But *the real person* in Dostoievsky is one with enthusiasm for life as based on direct personal relationships; this is genuine enthusiasm. On the contrary, a person who seems in a state-of-being related merely to himself (such as, for example, the ecstasy of the epileptic) or to a mere vision from which all others are excluded, is false to the main (or what the psychoanalysts would call the *libidinal*) drive of society.

With Myshkin, love is not intellectual, personal, but instinctual, impersonal: therefore it is without personal object while having a personal subject. With Stavrogin, love is, as with others, intellectual and personal, but in lacking any definite subject, any true giver, it is unique in that it is found only with objects. Every individual is rightfully a giver and receiver of love, an object and a subject of love; subtract one partner from this duality, or neutralize them through mutual friction, and you have a person ultimately without either false or genuine enthusiasm for life. By these standards the most pitiable of Dostoievsky's characters, Stavrogin and Myshkin, seem also the most moving and great.

With majestic implacability, Dostoievsky grounds his judgment of life on a recognition for the immediate (i.e., unsublimated) realization of the aims of the individual. It would seem that his contemptuous hatred for Turgenev, a genuine artist whom he caricatures as Karmazinov in *The Possessed,* is based primarily on Turgenev's conscious posture as a writer, an artist, someone with "mere visions." There peeps out in many instances through the pages of *The Possessed* its author's spontaneous prejudice for the Russian individual *qua* individual. Yet Dostoievsky's prejudice, even as that of the dilettante liberal, Verhovensky Sr. (Stepan Trofimovitch), is idealistic and a thing apart from his inevitable investigation of human impulse, its deepest sources and its wildest vagaries. To reread *The Possessed,* after a ten-year recess from Dostoievsky's art, is to be overwhelmed with the incessant expression of novelty on every page, as though every character were an inexhaustible reservoir of copious energy and unpredictable moves. It is the aura of an overall "enthusiasm for life" created in all precisely by but one thing: the vibrant drama with which social space is filled by the complex psychic shock of individual upon individual. Dostoievsky is pre-eminent before all writers in the theme of *human confrontation*. If Stavrogin is the "god" of the modern gratuitous act, he was crucified in his own story by a conspiracy of human presences who will not leave him in peace. The love and ambition of others are the two passions that make the contemplative solution of his subjective pain impossible. A split man, the idealized "false" personality given him by Verhovensky has symbolic entrance into the crevice provided; and it is, so to speak, his personality of Ivan the Tsarevitch—the one who might have committed everything to a great action—that sacrifices itself in his suicide; so finally Stavrogin becomes a synthetic sort of Christ: a combination of Verhovensky's, Shatov's, Kirillov's, "made-up" men in one.

The paradox of Dostoicvsky, that which makes him no artist's inferior, is that his greatest characters, of whom none is greater than Stavrogin and Myshkin, somehow remain outside the cosmic realm of dynamics in which his other characters blindly but confidently move, haunted there, perhaps, with anxiety and guilt, but ever hopeful of triumph in love, worldly ambition, or holy redemption. If despair is common to Dostoievsky's characters, none loses faith in the final, saving human presence of a man of God—either, like Alyosha Karamazov, in becoming one, or like others, in kneeling before one; none, save those capable of false enthusiasm by "making up" personal gods and "living with them." Dostoievsky himself believed in the "true God," having seen him in a vision early in life; hence, all worshipers of false idols—personal creations of the mind or "human gods"—must come to grief. In his role of "human god" and inspirer of Verhovensky's imagination, Stavrogin remains a mystery, because, mocking his past beliefs as a Slavophile, he renders ambiguous the origin of his own inspiration. A homogeneous air of the sinister is cast over all his activities prior to our meeting him, and when we do meet him, it is only to hear him deny all goodness, to observe him paradoxically incapable of positive motivation. Who is the only one, according to Christian logic, that would inspire *to* evil without being inspired *by* evil, that would do so merely because of what he *is?* Only the Devil himself: evil incarnate. Somehow I believe Dostoievsky has given us permission to identify Stavrogin's abortive "enthusiasm" thus. Even while, for his own purposes, the Devil may appear fanatical, he would not advance a "Cause" he believed had any likelihood of success. For if a general or "universal" cause succeeds, man tends to derive good from it, and so (at least for the nineteenth century) to attribute his condition to God as the universal source of good. And have we not leave to believe, from Dostoievsky himself, that Stavrogin was his personal devil?

4

HECUBA'S HIDDEN HISTORY

Persons of the conversation:

    DREW ORCUTT, dramatic critic

    JAY WALLACE, literary critic

    EMORY BECK, poet-essayist

Scene: Wallace's living room.

    ORCUTT: Whoever invented that ungodly institution, the dinner partner? But an even greater wonder is that it still survives —as you saw the other night at the Martins'.

WALLACE: Yes. I wanted to hear more about one remark of yours. You said Hamlet could not be acted. And then I remember a cloud of irrelevancies cropping up around you.

ORCUTT: Oh, that woman next to me, I forget her name, began to talk about the "uncut *Hamlet*"! She went back to Evans' dressing room, you know, and got his lowdown on the whole thing. Did you hear it?

WALLACE: I absorbed the sound, not the sense.

ORCUTT: Well, Evans' sense and her sound convinced me that *Hamlet* should always be cut.

WALLACE: Don't talk about cutting. I began to think of her throat as she went on.

ORCUTT: You know my peculiar professional peril, Jay! People go home and complain that I bore them by talking shop. I know of a specific case.

WALLACE: The point is they're overjoyed to get you into a spot to listen to *them*.

ORCUTT: "Overjoyed"? It's a lust. Like the itch of actors to do Hamlet.

WALLACE: Do you really think that the role is *unactable*?

ORCUTT: To answer you in one hundred per cent seriousness: yes. I've seen, I think, *all* the tryouts!

WALLACE: Bitter, bitter man! You mean you're disillusioned that the ideal Hamlet will *ever* come along?

ORCUTT: No. I think the ideal Hamlet is impossible. The role has no center; it lacks the very thing every actor has to have to act something: the meat of the matter to get his teeth into. That's my pet—er—conclusion.

WALLACE: Do you think Shakespeare was inept?

ORCUTT: Shakespeare was so mighty he didn't stop to care. To him it was a fascinating opportunity to exploit a legend. He reveled in Hamlet's feelings. But those feelings—has it never occurred to you?—are appallingly "incidental."

WALLACE: You mean you revert to the classic view of the sceptics that Hamlet's words don't amount to a character pattern; that we are never made to understand his motives?

ORCUTT: Does Hamlet understand his motives? You know, the writings of the professors have never magnetized me and my college education was acquired in a mist. But I *have* read Bradley's commodious essay because someone (I won't reveal his identity, you know him) recommended it to me years ago as the most reliable and illuminating. It may be so to the extent of casting serious doubt on all the classic interpretations, including Bradley's own, though his is probably the most plausible as he maintains. It boils down to something very simple: Hamlet is supposedly one of the temperaments: the Melancholic. Medieval, you see. That's easy for an actor, but not for an audience—if it's critical.

WALLACE: Fortunately for actors, audiences are not critical. But I deeply sympathize with critical scepticism about Hamlet because it's challenging. The Freudian hypothesis that Ernest Jones explored is probably, from the formal point of view, the most satisfying. But that relies on unconscious psychology and on the highly useful concept of ambivalence: a way of calling black, when convenient, white.

ORCUTT: Ah ha! Why not just say Jones' theory relies on psychology? Hamlet gives signs of understanding the incest motive pretty thoroughly. Don't you think so?

WALLACE: Why, yes: you mean the "bad dreams"! Dreams are even attributed to Oedipus, as you probably recall—then, there are Hamlet's self-accusing hints of the unmentionable: "I have more offenses at my beck—"

(*The doorbell buzzes.*)

—That's one of nature's more remarkable puns. I'll bet it's Emory—Emory Beck. I asked him over.

ORCUTT: You mean you "beckoned" him?

WALLACE: And also, of course, ". . . There are more things in Heaven and Earth . . ."

ORCUTT: Emory Beck. He writes poetry, doesn't he?

WALLACE: Yes, but I wanted to tell him I liked an essay he lately published—on Proust. (*Admitting Beck*) Hello, Emory! This is Emory Beck, poet and essayist . . . Drew Orcutt, drama critic extraordinary.

BECK: How do you do?

ORCUTT: How do you do? *I* know of *you* too. (*To Wallace*) Thanks for the "extraordinary."

WALLACE: Don't mention it. Sit down there, Emory. (*Pouring drinks*) Don't look now, either of you, but we're about to slip into a literary show this evening. We're well into Hamlet, Emory. Drew believes he's simply "unactable."

BECK: I wouldn't know. I've never seen him acted. Not even in the movies.

ORCUTT: You mean you've omitted to see *Hamlet* on principle?

BECK: That's right. I haven't dared to go. I've read and re-read the play—oh, I guess at least a dozen times since I was twelve or thirteen—maybe more times.

ORCUTT: You see, Jay, he probably feels the way I do but by an entirely different route. (*To Wallace*) How many "Hamlets" have *you* seen?

WALLACE: What difference does it make? I've seen a couple. There haven't been many, I believe, in our time. Except in England and when I was in England, I don't think it played. John Barrymore, over here, was a bit before my day.

ORCUTT: Not before mine. Though I couldn't have been much older than Beck when he first read the play. I recall a silhouette that flowed rhythmically and uninterruptedly from the actor's forehead to his toes and my feeling that Hamlet was somewhat exaggerating the reasons for his unhappiness. But no version of Hamlet I've seen since has given me so accurate an idea of the way Shakespeare, as I see it, wrote the part. Barrymore seemed a man escaping from his own Narcissism, which struck me and strikes me as a very logical portrait of Hamlet. Yet you don't fill a part—you don't act a character—by running away from it!

BECK: But suppose the character is a man who is running away from his own Narcissism?

ORCUTT: Then the dramatist has to do it simply. Shakespeare does Hamlet with unpardonable complexity. When I say "unpardonable," I mean unpardonable for the stage. We have no way of knowing how it was acted in Shakespeare's time, but I suppose it didn't make much difference—

BECK: It has made the difference of another essay to William Empson. Have you read it, Jay?

WALLACE: Oh, yes. Did you, Drew?

ORCUTT: No. Er—did you say "Empson"?

WALLACE: Emphatically Empson. A critic to conjure with. He is an able conjuror himself. In this new *Hamlet* piece he has risked some historical speculation based on God knows what, exactly, but anyway on the not unknown and sometimes palpable fact that Shakespeare would step in and revamp other men's plays or their notions about plays in general. The best known predecessor in the *Hamlets* was by Thomas Kyd and apparently this lost play (supposedly the first to introduce the Ghost) was a humdinger of a melodrama which, to take Empson's line, tended to be laughed off the stage till Shakespeare elected to delay the rush of absurdity with soliloquies by a hero brooding in high style on the action's plausibility. So the Swan of Avon did some swanlike play-writing and the result was the *Hamlet* we have.

BECK: I am highly suspicious of Empson's criticism. He's what I call a very sweet crank; very distinguished and flaky. Nothing seems real to him but the literary commodity, in which he deals with all the objective economy and tacit sincerity of an advertising agent.

WALLACE: You're hard on him, I think, but it's true that he writes as though he has paradoxes for breakfast.

ORCUTT: You mean I've been neglecting a famous source of literary cuisine?

WALLACE: That's about it. But *Hamlet* is a perpetual lure for those who like to settle questions or at least to contribute to unsettling them. Empson's formula is the linguistically determined *Hamlet,* Fergusson's is the dramaturgically determined *Hamlet.* You both know Fergusson's *The Idea of a Theatre*?

BECK: Yes. I think his essay on *Hamlet* very good and his reasoning very fair.

WALLACE: I do, too. His analysis is competent and fertile but it leads away from Hamlet the temperament, which is the prejudice of those now in the room. As for Empson's theory that Shakespeare made the Elizabethan Hamlet "serious," that would be hard to contradict in any wide perspective. One can imagine the breed of actors described by Hamlet himself doing the Kyd part, and that such a frivolous marriage of madness and reason must have offered Shakespeare the obvious temptation of "solemnizing" it.

ORCUTT: Then there's nothing in Empson's essay that can't be passed over?

WALLACE: Nothing that can't be passed over with a smile of polite acquiescence.

ORCUTT: That soothes my conscience. However, if you have the essay here, I'd like to borrow it.

WALLACE: All right. Remind me to give it to you. Though be warned: it's a sheer piece of academic rumination . . . bringing words up from that section of time's stomach where no one suspected they were.

ORCUTT: I see you *both* connect Empson with eating.

WALLACE: I had *Hamlet* when I was growing up on cereal. You forget my own father was a professor.

ORCUTT: What did you think of *Hamlet* at twelve, Jay?

WALLACE: I was fourteen before I read it but I didn't stop eating cereal till I was sixteen or seventeen. I thought it was wonderful—I mean I thought *Hamlet* was wonderful. . . . In the simplest sense, I justified everything Jones and the others have to say about the hero's infantile roots. I became Hamlet in his great "domestic" rebellion.

ORCUTT: Do you mean that—er—you heard in his speeches what might be called the sibylline voice of Freud's aboriginal family situation?

WALLACE: Yes, putting it that vaguely makes very precise what happened to me. But we are beating about the bush, aren't we? . . . Drink up, both of you. (*Replenishing their glasses*) I have a lot on my mind about Hamlet. All these years he's been, so to speak, my private increment: a kind of savings account working for me even when my thoughts were far away from it. The common truth, Drew, is that Hamlet, as you imply, is a conception so immense that anyone may read into him—well, let's put it pointedly and tritely—*himself* and succeed in finding a *true* Hamlet.

ORCUTT: But not *the* true Hamlet . . . ?

BECK: Aren't there degrees of truth? I can't believe Empson's essay has the least genuine relevance.

ORCUTT: Jay's right. *You're* prejudiced, too.

WALLACE: (*To Beck*) If you rule out archaeological ingenuity as relevant, then you're right. But Empson has a stimulating dialectical theme. He *would be* the one to suggest that the most subjectively tempered and complex of Shakespeare's heroes was the result (as we find him) of an objective contingency; a "mirror," so to speak, "held up to" the problem of communication.

BECK: Empson does not *honor* Hamlet!

WALLACE: Every man has his way of honoring Hamlet. But let's drop Empson's way, shall we? Look here: The problem of Hamlet's extra-theatricality, which Drew assumes as so absolute and insoluble, logically points, it seems to me, to his extra-*humanity,* in that his reflexes as a human being are too varied and multiple. He would then be a trope in human form of Shakespeare's "myriad-mindedness," wouldn't he?

ORCUTT: Do you support Eliot's theory that *Hamlet* is a bad play because the hero seems motivated by . . . his feelings seem based on . . . things undisclosed by the play's situation?

WALLACE: Do *you* support Eliot's theory?

ORCUTT: I am not an authority on Shakespeare criticism and its disagreements. I am only, as you charitably put it a while ago, a "drama critic extraordinary."

WALLACE: Come, now!

ORCUTT: But you're absolutely right!

WALLACE: Thank you. Eliot's criticism, Drew, is only a version of a pioneering psychologist cited by Ernest Jones in his *Hamlet* study, Van Croll, who refers to the disproportion between cause and effect in Hamlet's behavior and concludes that Hamlet was therefore "mentally unsound."

ORCUTT: Eliot doesn't conclude so, does he?

WALLACE: I think he betrays his *wish* to do so.

ORCUTT: Hm . . . Bradley, as I recall, can hardly prevent himself from saying Hamlet is "touched" a bit. "Melancholy" is the princely version of such things.

WALLACE: Exactly. All paths of logic, if followed far enough, take us back to Hamlet's psychology and its ambiguity. And *there's* the Minotaur that has to be killed. What the psychological critics have to contend with is the standard criticism of Freud's method of interpreting truth through dream analysis; namely, that in dreams, objects in their symbolic capacity are fluid and open to different "contents," they are subject to the modulation, that is, supplied by the concepts of *ambivalence* and *displacement*. The symbolic scheme is loose-jointed and can be twisted to suit diametrically opposed directions—

BECK: Yes, but didn't Freud warn us of the danger in interpreting isolated dreams, and fragmentary evidence, just for that reason? Didn't he say that dream interpretation can be properly practiced only in relation to a given individual, and all that can be learned about him and as many dreams as he can remember?

WALLACE: Of course! That's just what I was getting to. Freud believed that the "gestalt" of an individual exists: the whole truth of him without which no detail of his truth can be accurately known. But Drew says that Hamlet's gestalt—that is, Hamlet as a human individual—does not exist.

ORCUTT: I don't know if a stage character is actually the same as a human individual. I suppose a stage character is a human individual, some hypothetic individual, *simplified*. Ibsen's characters are ideal in that respect. Maybe Hamlet is *too much* of an individual; maybe, for all I know, he is only a projection of Shakespeare, with as much of Shakespeare's innermost being put into the role as could be got there.

WALLACE: So we could infer that, to get at the real truth of Hamlet's character, Freud would have had to analyze Shakespeare?

ORCUTT: I suppose so. It sounds fantastic, doesn't it?

WALLACE: Only if you imagine it as a fact. But I believe the truth of Hamlet's character is available by a different path. Now I'll confess. I was thinking of committing myself to an essay. Hadn't you guessed it? I think it is foolish to say that Hamlet has an Oedipus complex for it implies he is only a variation on Sophocles' hero. The incest situation never exists as a thing in itself except in Freud's prehistoric anthropological myth; its living meaning, its truth, can exist only in an individual, and every individual in the last analysis has his own complex. (*To Orcutt*) To take up your cue, the character, Hamlet, is a hypothetic individual (probably Shakespeare himself) with a Hamlet-complex. I would define the Hamlet-complex as the disillusionment of the divine king with his own function. Hamlet is therefore a heretic-in-spite-of-himself among England's kings—I say England's, of course, because it was Shakespeare, an Englishman, who visualized and conceived this "Danish" story. I was thinking of calling my essay "Hamlet as the Anti-Oedipus"; you see, the exact opposite of the character reputed to be Hamlet's prime and truest literary antecedent. . . . Hamlet may have dreamed of Oedipus, but Oedipus could never have dreamed of Hamlet—not merely because Shakespeare's character had yet to come into existence but because Hamlet represents something of which Oedipus never dreamed, either awake or asleep.

ORCUTT and BECK *together:* What was that?

WALLACE: I see I've struck fire.

ORCUTT: Well, put it out.

WALLACE: The moral rejection of the office of the divine king: *that* was beyond Oedipus' imagination! He was a true divine king; in fact, he was in the grand old mythological line of Zeus and his father Kronos; patricides and incest-criminals.

ORCUTT: Oh, then that would be the mythological basis for Freud's human history, no?

WALLACE: It is indeed that. The incest-parricide business had even gotten to have the status of a sin, or quasi-sin, for you remember that is the point of Aeschylus' drama about Prometheus, whom Zeus feared because he knew a "secret"—as I believe Bulfinch coyly puts it—"affecting the stability of Zeus' throne." Now what is all the pother about a "secret"? Prometheus, remember, is mankind's mentor: he even, according to the tradition followed by Aeschylus, "made men cease to live with death in sight." That is to say he made them, indirectly, "immortal." The divine king is symbol of this conferred immortality and in the harsh processes of mundanity he had to undergo Prometheus' own ordeal —the same, by the way, as Christ's—to "certify" its truth. What is primarily involved in the sacrifice of the divine king, you understand, is *racial* not *personal* immortality. Personal immortality was predicated on racial—at least in this mythological pattern. For this supreme gift, for Prometheus' knowledge which includes the faculty of self-reproduction, man had to pay the historic price of several sorts of pain. This pain, among other things, was the duty of the divine king, who in his role of social symbol was a scapegoat. In the antique "secret" sense, then, the foul crime in *Hamlet* is as *de rigueur* as is its purgation. Aeschylus has Force (another name for Hercules) attend Hephaestus as he obediently nails down Prometheus at Zeus' order. This is the force of history: the divine king is himself magically compelled. But what threads the intelligence of Aeschylus' Prometheus as well as that

of Shakespeare's Hamlet is the essentially *human* situation of
the biological descent: the passing of supreme power from father
to son and the son's assumed impatience to enjoy his inheritance.
Mythology, of course, is a hodgepodge of story lines, but the
parricide-incest pattern is usually present. The most interesting
element in regard to a "mythological" Hamlet is the moral ambiguity of the underdog son's Promethean technique. As a subjective Prometheus, Hamlet sometimes breaks his chains to act.
Now Prometheus—look at the text for yourselves—is a politician of guile; which is to say, the force of guile—the kind of
thing the Greeks did to win Troy. He advised the Titans to use
it against Zeus, and when they declined, went over to Zeus' side.
Isn't this guilefulness just what Claudius uses to win the Danish
crown and the Danish Queen, his sister-in-law? Ostensibly, Hamlet despises Claudius' *guile* as much as his *deeds*. But isn't Hamlet in the selfsame boat when he adopts his strategy of "madness"? Yes, he identifies his own virtuous cause with his father's,
but the play hints more than once that this identification leads
to damaging his father's virtue as well as his own, the chief instance being when he spares Claudius while at his prayers because, he says, Claudius killed his father "full of bread, his sins
broad blown." In this deep-rootedness of Hamlet's guilt, revulsion has been "father" to anger. He believes the whole sin pattern a degraded and dispensable thing, something which the un-
dignified aspects of his "madness," his personal filth and dis-
array, might well demonstrate. Consider this: one legend has it,
according to Sophocles' lost play, that the fate of Oedipus' father,
Laius, befell him because of a crime of kidnaping and sodomy;
the point is that "divine crime" itself is as traditional as are the
means for combating or escaping it. If Hamlet could have
brought to the stage a greater logic and knowledge than Shakespeare has allotted him, one can imagine the scorn he would have
heaped on that strategy of "paternal" Zeus, an incestuous patricide, in holding Prometheus in such terrible fee because Prometheus knew, but would not tell, from what direction—among

Zeus' multiple progeny—the patricidal attempt against him would come! Prometheus, apparently, knew something that was hidden even from the Ruler of the Gods: the prophecy that one of Zeus' sons by Thetis would overthrow him as *he* had overthrown *Kronos*. Hamlet, the great secret reasoner, has this tremendous intuition of his father's own historic-mythic guilt, and tremendously resents his own part in the usual conspiracy of obedient crown-idolaters. At heart, he's a super-Olympian; *King Hamlet* was only an Olympian.

ORCUTT: By that standard, isn't your Hamlet a super-Oedipus rather than an anti-Oedipus?

WALLACE: It's not my doing, you know, it's Shakespeare's. He could have had things merely that way. And he makes Hamlet, of course, the mouthpiece of the Renaissance man, "holding the mirror up to nature," by which is meant imitating the ancient idea of the cosmos—order and proportion in all things—and the position of man above the animals though below the angels. But in Hamlet as an individual we might notice that this advanced and ideal knowledge is something of a mockery. Never underestimate the Mocker in Shakespeare's private character: I'm convinced he had it in for the kings of England. He was too great a humanist not to be secretly bored to death with the mere mundane course of human history: the perpetual struggle for a throne on the part of Earth's Zeus-like children. Yet power fascinated him more than it did Hamlet. *Who* has more ways, or as many ways, of showing the vanity as well as the rewards of seeking the office of king?

ORCUTT: Nobody, I guess.

WALLACE: The value of being the King of England—I think it's a delightful ironic paradox—was damaged by nobody more than England's greatest historical as well as tragic dramatist. Nothing stimulates the author of *Coriolanus* more than cuffing the rabble or showing the king—as he did so often—wallowing

in the high exclusive privilege of the *tragic* end. Look what he
made of Mark Antony and that high-born strumpet, Cleopatra,
Queen of Egypt! *Antony and Cleopatra* is a sadistic comedy as
much as a tragedy. I mean the author is the sadistic comedian.
Like all the rest, Shakespeare had ways of flattering Elizabeth,
but his way of flattering her in Cleopatra was simply to show that
all the unpleasant traits to be associated with woman as "the inferior sex"—selfishness, petty cruelty, narcissism, cowardice,
carnality—could be majestic when raised to the aristocratic level.
But what really raised them to that level?—the passion of his
own poetic genius. What else? Shakespeare, I believe, showed
the limit of human possibilities in his noble characters, no matter
what their individual leanings.

ORCUTT: Cleopatra is an example of a wonderfully successful
character, possibly the author's most lucid female. At the same
time, I have objected in print to those ladies who act her merely,
in your words, as a high-born strumpet. She *can* be acted that
way, but—

WALLACE: You *would* say, wouldn't you, that since she is a
"character," the appropriate ways of acting her are finite?

ORCUTT: Yes, of course. She is far from having Hamlet's elasticity—that perilous elasticity! The thing that most strikes me
about the play's speeches is Hamlet's variability. And I was
noticing just the other day when I had the book in my hands how
obsessed he is with the subject of changeableness in things. And
always for the worse. It always ends with a skull or a worm or a
broken vow. He is convinced, I think, that everything in Denmark, which he calls "Hell," will come to no good end—at least,
while he is around. Yet meanwhile he identifies himself with
everybody: not only with Claudius as his mother's lover but also
with Laertes—you know the line, "For, by the image of my
cause, I see / The portraiture of his"—and even with Ophelia,
whom he finds a sister in enigmatic flabbiness. He brands both

her conduct and his own as whorish. He has a sort of *ambisexual* personality. . . . Then how peremptorily he dictates his mother's character—that is, gives it a moral shape—when he confesses her by force in the closet scene. He is a sort of universal conscience—I mean Denmark's universal conscience. He's "conscience on the loose." But, I ask, is he *Hamlet's* conscience?

WALLACE: If that's a direct challenge, I'll take it up. I have *isolated* Hamlet's conscience, and his only. What you describe is merely the compulsive gyrations of the "machine" Hamlet himself names as his intimate property.

BECK: Oh!—in the note to Ophelia, you mean?

WALLACE: Yes: "whilst this machine is to him, Hamlet."

ORCUTT: You see, even his private conscience is not his own!

WALLACE: I shall have to fall back on Hamlet's key trait, ambivalence, and explain more fully. Hamlet's real personality is at that level where the common uses of both gods and men, good and evil, self and others, have blended into an amalgam which acquires or lacks substance and differentiation according to the impulses of mental consciousness. Hamlet himself—I forget his exact wording—attributes truth to the thought that "makes it so." It is this that justifies the Freudian approach to him and also transcends it. I think that in one way or another Hamlet is always pointing to the powers of his imagination, those powers he shared with his author, and this is why the personal can so easily, in him, turn itself into the general, the particular into the universal, the self into the other. But observe the peripety of his paradox. In identifying himself with everybody, he identifies himself with nobody—

ORCUTT: And you still maintain he's a character?—

WALLACE: Yes, of a most prolix negativism and a most laconic positivism! A royal being to the bone, poor Hamlet lacked political self-interest. Think: he *should* have been overjoyed to

have escaped Oedipus' fate. He *should* have exulted that his
uncle rather than himself had accomplished the historic crime.
His was an ideal political opportunity where any normal tragic
hero of Shakespeare's—such as Macbeth—would have rushed
in where devils had not feared to tread, but where angels, you
see, *would* fear to. . . . Hamlet is an angel to the extent that he
rejects the traditional divinity of earthly kings. That is why he
rejects the role of revenger in which he is cast by the facts of the
case. His chains are those of humanity and superhumanity. It
is *he,* not the Ghost, who travels between the Here and the Beyond. The Ghost is only the imaginative convention on a heroic
scale: the incarnation of a truth which Hamlet—insofar as the
murderous role of Claudius has already been supplied by his
imagination—already knows. The Ghost is a projection of Hamlet's own psyche. Thus, in a sense, the play is what would happen
if one's secret thoughts could go abroad and talk. Hamlet believes in the sacred saw: Murder Will Out. He is destined to murder his father's *idea,* his spirit and not his body, and he knows
this cannot remain concealed. He has to behave toward the
Ghost as a news-bringer for the sake of appearances—because
he is scared by his own secret reaction, never wholly clear to him
in conceptual terms. So much in Hamlet, Drew, is protective
coloration. So you are on the right track. But it has a subconscious purpose made plain by the history of humanity's kings. It
would have been easy for Hamlet to have survived the Oedipus
guilt—surely as the *psychological* guilt it was for him—but he
could not survive another guilt, which was only the more real and
objective because negative. Some time before the rise of the curtain he has discovered, vaguely but certainly, that *morally* he is
not his father's son . . . he has not inherited, that is to say, that
impalpable power of a king duly transmissible to his son, a
primitive word for which is *mana,* but which is actually—to
parody Hamlet's words about his technical position in the revenge pattern—"the cause and will and strength and means" to
be a king. Though the origin of the idea of *mana* is in magic, it is

no more "magical" or "divine" than what we commonly call "genius." But it is power, no matter how occult or supernatural its supposed source. Hamlet has plenty of guts, to be sure, but he hasn't the guts to be a king! In this, his guts are as heavy as the dead Polonius'. This simple fact may seem irrational, even incomprehensible, but it seems to me a fact—not a subjective fact for Hamlet only, but an objective fact for everyone.

ORCUTT: You mean this anti-Oedipus guilt explains Hamlet's inner tumult and outer hesitation better than does the Oedipus guilt?

WALLACE: Yes. You cannot explain the behavior of a stage character by *entirely* unconscious motives. That is the reef on which the theories of Jones and the other analysts are finally wrecked. It is the rule for critics to assume that Shakespeare threw out the nature of Hamlet's original action—as seen in Saxo's saga and Belleforest's romance—as political motive, and substituted Hamlet's (or Shakespeare's) own private motives, whatever these are. But the case is otherwise; it couldn't but be otherwise. My argument is that Hamlet's "lunatic" strategy is primarily political in *content* as well as *form*. Yes, madness— yes, "dat ole debbil" madness—is the key to the whole thing after all. . . . But I'm getting breathless and you two have hardly had a chance to get out a sentence at a time. Hmm . . . Maybe I'm high on more than Hamlet.

ORCUTT: Don't be silly. You've hardly touched your last glass. Your theory does *tower*.

WALLACE: Thanks. (*Pouring*) I'll raise the spirits in your glass. . . . Emory, I wanted to compliment you on your Proust essay. You have an interesting reference to *Hamlet* in it. Are you entertaining a Hamlet of your own?

BECK: I'll admit it. I am. I even have some notes for an essay. But I'm afraid I'll have to do a deal more reading in *Hamlet* criticism before letting my ideas see the general light.

ORCUTT: Don't be embarrassed by me. I am, among other "extraordinary" things, an ignoramus!

WALLACE: Stop it, Drew. May I be forgiven for quoting myself? "The fear of repeating somebody else's ideas is an especially craven academic fear." (*To Beck*) Have the courage of your imagination and you're sure to be original. Like Hamlet.

BECK: Er—thanks! Only a contemporary surreal-symbolist, such as I, would think of it, I suppose. As this is a "Hamlet" evening . . .

WALLACE: Don't be shy. If it's outlandish, all the better for Drew's viewpoint.

BECK: As a matter of fact, I thought of it when I read a translation of the article Proust once contributed to *Le Figaro:* "Filial Sentiments of a Parricide." A friend of Proust's—actually a distant acquaintance—loses his father naturally and then kills his mother. It is very sudden and follows a pious correspondence with Proust, who has lost both his parents—naturally, of course. Jay, it was odd for you to mention the Ghost as a "news-bringer" because, while reading Proust's account of his sympathy with the ambivalence of a tender-hearted parricide, it occurred to me that both Hamlet and Oedipus receive news of a strange crime which they vaguely associate with themselves. Then I simply had a vision: I saw Hamlet as a poetic young man, a retarded poet of thirty, luxuriating in melancholia: only vaguely resentful of his mother's behavior and only vaguely resentful of his uncle's replacement of his father but automatically instigating himself— for aesthetic reasons—into rhetorical fulminations against them; "ornamental lip service" I was thinking of calling his soliloquies. He is enjoying himself. Nobody's grief is so exquisite as his. Let them be rebuked. In short, he is exploiting a "remembrance of things past"; he is living in a picture frame of melancholy and he is an image of grief. Then the Ghost intrudes like a cacophonous newsboy and spoils it all—you remember, among the satiric familiarities with the Ghost, Hamlet calls him "boy"? Hamlet has had dreams of an imaginary crime, perhaps, but this is a real one. And how can he refuse his father's spirit and fail to avenge his murder? He is vain, hot-tempered, high-strung, as irrational as any poet . . . and naturally jealous of his uncle. He lives, moreover, in a superstitious era. The guilt of an unavenged crime is supposed to have dreadful consequences for the whole state. He is terribly proud. He has to cut the right figure. Then the whole thing gradually sours because it is so repulsive.

ORCUTT: Eloquent. I like the Ghost as a newsboy—that almost vanished race—though I admit I've never seen it played that way!

WALLACE: Your notion is pretty—and pretty ingenious. Consistent with Proust's effeminacy, too. But where I *really* agree with you is in the assumption that this crime is entirely *in retrospect* with Hamlet. Regardless of how much he identifies himself with it, it has no future. It can only be a sort of plaything. With father dead and mother remarried, one's subconscious incest desires, one's vague dreams of violence, are apt to be lulled to sleep, perhaps for good. One is then plausibly tempted to "reconstruct the past." You mean that is what Hamlet is doing in the sight of all before he hears about the Ghost?

BECK: Yes. I think of Hamlet as having in him—as the active substance of "that which passeth show"—the germ of an elegy. Then he is ordered by the Ghost to do something bloody, something real. He is shocked out of himself: out of his own sense of reality. He calls on his manhood to live up to his duty as a king's son—and fails. Ernest Jones' essay, by the way, is one piece of *Hamlet* criticism I do know. He attributes to Hamlet what he calls a "syndrome," well known among cases of hysteria, and adduces persuasive arguments from a variety of sources, including Hamlet's own behavior. It seems plausible to assume, among other things, that Hamlet is promiscuously bisexual in the impulses that stem from the incest situation of childhood; Jones says that Ophelia is not merely a substitute for the attractive object of his mother, but also for the attractive object of Laertes, in Hamlet's feelings.

ORCUTT: You mean that Hamlet is to be thought of as a repressed homosexual?

BECK: I don't say so myself: it isn't necessary to my theory. Nor is it necessary, I think, in analyzing the personality of the narrator of *Remembrance of Things Past*.

ORCUTT: But why shouldn't Hamlet—among other things as you say—be a homosexual? And why shouldn't he have been a woman? I sensed such an odd epiceneness about Barrault's notably virile Hamlet—perhaps owing not to Barrault but to Hamlet. Didn't someone actually claim that Hamlet was a woman?

WALLACE: Yes . . . a man named Vining, I think. That right, Emory? I believe Jones quotes it.

BECK: I believe he does.

ORCUTT: There you are!—"Myriad-minded" implies myriad-sexed and myriad-aged—Hamlet is "the thing": not the *play* and not the *character*. At least, not a "playable" character. But, do you know, I've heard it said that Hamlet is a foolproof part, that no actor can utterly fail in it. I invert that opinion. To me, the role cries out for a character key and receives no answer—unless an arbitrary one. Let me tell you a little anecdote: I have a teacher friend who once induced me to view his college production of the play. The young man acting Hamlet had inwardly decided—on no one's authority, I imagine, not even his own—that the Prince is a petulant fellow. I happen to know my friend had not directed him that way, but something made him, once before the audience, impart a tinge of petulance to virtually every speech. So his performance, while monotonous, gained a certain coherence. But the truth is, it does not basically contradict anything basic in Shakespeare's writing. I went over the play and imagined the stage direction, *Petulantly,* at the head of each of Hamlet's speeches—*and it worked.* Yes, it worked. Then I varied the adverb. I thought of *Ironically* and *Solemnly:* you'd be amazed how those hold everything together, not in a responsible sense, but—(*To Beck*) That's why I'm suspicious of this "hysterical" Hamlet of Jones'. Wouldn't *Hysterically* also work?

BECK: You're mocking Shakespeare.

ORCUTT: If I am, it's only because there's some Hamlet in me.

BECK: Let me add that that isn't all my theory. It fact, it started as something different altogether.

WALLACE: Something different? Out with it!

BECK: This other conception isn't so far from yours, Jay: I mean Hamlet as an abortive Hercules, which I suppose would make him a "Prometheus." I thought of blending the neo-Proustian parricide, the infantile neurotic, with the triumphant "child player"—a Hercules in recitation.

WALLACE: Ah! Will you forgive me if I interpolate a thought that has occurred to me?—it's in your behalf and Drew's.

BECK: Naturally—go ahead!

WALLACE: In the critics' argument over the correct interpretation of Hamlet, I would be not for each interpretation cancelling out the others, as Bradley presumes they must, but for each one serving to supplement the others. A *definitively* correct interpretation would signify the critical genius for synthesis. Your concept, Drew, insists on an element of Hamlet, *fluid elusiveness,* which in point of fact is quite integral with my own. One aspect that appears to me at the moment is that the region of variability, ambiguity, and elusiveness so orthodoxly ascribed to Hamlet is, indeed, a rhetorical reference to what psychology calls the unconscious, that uncertain realm where Freud marked out the dream-world. At the same time, we must recognize both Hamlet's words and his deeds as explicit, daylight action; even if, as Emory thinks, it is *dreamy* action, the action of a man morally committed to words, ideas, and visions, as a poet would be. In a way, I have identified Hamlet with Prometheus and, in an approximate sense, he is to be so identified; and so too his identification with Oedipus, though both these identifications are distinctly ambivalent. The rock to which Prometheus is chained represents the base part of all existence; of his mother, himself, of all men. The same generality is true of Hamlet's insistence on human clay: that "bunghole" stopped up with Alexander's remains. Thus Hamlet's covering himself with filth as part of his "feigned" madness is not merely, as Jones contends, something typically infantile and bound up with universal childish rebellion against the parents, but also something attaching itself to myth—and to religion. Hercules had to clean the Augean stables. Man has to conquer the mire: it remains one of his ordeals. . . . But what struck me like lightning, a moment ago, was that the melancholy which Bradley identifies as Hamlet's private temperament was, as melancholy sunk in sloth, the sin of *accidia* in the Middle Ages, and that Dante in the *Divine Comedy* shows us its perpetrators immersed *in mud*.

ORCUTT: Did you say "lightning"? *That* was a quick flash.

WALLACE: Forgive me, Emory! Proceed.

BECK: After that, I'm glad my next move is to quote the play. (*To Wallace*) May I have your copy?

WALLACE: (*Moving*) Just one thing, Emory—I'm not trying to scuttle you, really!—Did you know that Hamlet as a dreamy, poetic youth is one of the hypotheses duly eliminated by Bradley in his retrospective of the critics?

BECK: No. But I'll bet he didn't quote evidence *for* that hypothesis.

WALLACE: Chalk up one for Drew. Some might maintain you can prove anything about Hamlet by quoting him. (*Handing him the book*) But proceed.

BECK: Thank you. . . . There's one phrase in the play that gave me a definite clue to the Proustian element in Hamlet's nature. . . . I think it's at the end of the Third Act. . . . Yes. He has just glimpsed Fortinbras' army on the march. Hamlet speaking:

> Sure he that made us with such large discourse,
> Looking before and after, gave us not
> That capability and godlike reason
> To fust in us unus'd . . .

"Looking before and after"—that is one of Shakespeare's great insights about the use of the mind. It's the aesthetic Present that Proust was dedicated to living in. It's a sign for Total Recall.

WALLACE: But Hamlet is thinking about the opposite when he speaks that way! He is thinking of the mind as efficient reasoner. I think the "before and after" applies to logical inquiry, not to time; to the facts of the matter. Hamlet knows all the facts —and yet he has not acted on them.

BECK: I'm offering Total Recall, I admit, not Total Proof. But let me quote you the passage I started to. . . . Remember that the city theatre of the troupe visiting Elsinore has been closed because of competition from the child players? Hamlet and Rosencrantz are speaking; Hamlet asks if the players have declined through rustiness and Rosencrantz answers:

> Nay, their endeavor keeps in the wonted pace: but there is, sir, an aery of children, little eyases, that cry out on the top of question, and are most tyrannically clapped for it: these are now the fashion . . .

HAMLET: What, are they children? who maintains 'em? How are they escoted? Will they pursue the quality no longer than they can sing? will they not say afterwards, if they should grow themselves to common players—as it is most like, if their means are no better—their writers do them wrong, to make them exclaim against their own succession?

And so on. . . . Then:

GUIL: O, there has been much throwing about of brains.
HAMLET: Do the boys carry it away?
ROS: Ay, that they do, my lord; Hercules and his load too.
HAMLET: It is not very strange; for mine uncle is king of Denmark, and those that would make mows at him while my father lived, give twenty, forty, fifty, an hundred ducats a-piece for his picture in little. 'Sblood, there is something in this more than natural, if philosophy could find it out.

This last speech, no doubt, has many facets. But isn't one certainly a metaphor—and I should say a potentially "Proustian" one—encompassing the dead king as Hercules, of whom both the son Hamlet and the brother Claudius are images "in little"? —that is, as child to man? What so much strikes Hamlet about the theatrical situation is that the children have had a triumph. One might notice that Shakespeare is always presenting Hamlet as struck with the competence of "examples" which should "exhort" him to act in his given task. But in this particular case there is a real subtlety—a hidden dimension of involuted reality reflected in metaphor. Hamlet, as one speaking lines of poetry, is also an actor, and as shown in the graveyard scene, he is very jealous of others' ability to "mouth." . . . "An thou'lt mouth, I'll rant as well as thou," he says to Laertes . . . Also notice the connection between "making mows" and "mouthing." Hamlet is more than eager to believe that his courtly speech is a perfect instrument in which to express himself. He keeps a notebook, too; piously, like a conscientious schoolboy. There is an-

other case for Hamlet's Proustian nature, though salted with
what you called Shakespeare's mockery. Let me find it for
you. . . . Here: "Remember thee!" Hamlet exclaims when the
Ghost has hastened off:

> Yea, from the table of my memory
> I'll wipe away all trivial fond records,
> All saws of books, all forms, all pressures past,
> That youth and observation copied there;
> And thy commandment all alone shall live
> Within the book and volume of my brain . . .

He then invents the "smiling villain" moralism about Claudius
and takes out his notebook to copy it down, adding to the page
the Ghost's last words to him. That is, Shakespeare has used the
notebook incident with pointed irony to damage the validity of
the oath Hamlet has just sworn in such noble language: to "wipe
away all trivial fond records" and replace them with the Ghost's
"commandment." Shakespeare here initiates us into Proust's
principle of *memory* and *desire:* a single mental reality. The mind
instinctively retains what it holds "fond" however "trivial" it
may be. That such a thing as Hamlet's oath implies an artificial
and imposed cleansing of memory is shown by the use of the
notebook, which exists to remind us of what we may forget.

ORCUTT: I think you have illuminated that passage very well.

WALLACE: Yes, though yours is a rather "precious" line, as
you well know.

BECK: But notebook or no notebook, Hamlet is always doing
just as the child players do—"cry out on the top of question." It
is his favorite occupation. The embarrassing thing is that the only
one who can "tyrannically clap" him for it, if he is to gain a
"triumph," is the Ghost. Thus more or less directly Hamlet is
always calling upon language to achieve an end it cannot achieve.
In the soliloquy about the player's speech he has a line concern-

ing the passionate use of language to "make mad the guilty . . ."
This is why he is so delighted at the success of the speech he in-
serts in the play; it does not cause Claudius to confess, as he had
hoped, but it does make him "mad," it sends him off in a panic.
Now when Hamlet hears of the "Poetomachia," the struggle between the poets, and the "War of the Theatres," the struggle between the actors, he associates himself, as somehow a "boy,"
with those child players who presume to exclaim, as he says,
"against their own succession," since when adult, they may become the common players they now oppose. I ask: Isn't this
situation an image of the royal prince's typical, though not always
overt, contention with his father? The very word "succession"
is from the technical vocabulary of kingly rule.

ORCUTT: That's most interesting. You are quite an analyst.

WALLACE: It *is* very interesting and I don't see why, whether
completely original or not, it isn't a genuine contribution to the
play's understanding.

BECK: Hercules' name, let me add, is mentioned in two other
places: when Hamlet says that Claudius can no more be compared to his father than he to Hercules, and when Hamlet says
in the graveyard scene—I know the couplet by heart—"Let Hercules himself do what he may, / The cat will mew and dog will
have his day." He and Laertes are the mewing cats—competing
in language—and Claudius the dog-king having his day on the
throne. The reference to Hercules, in the speech I read, signifies,
say the scholars, a sign of Hercules supporting a globe, which
stood before the Globe Theatre in London; so when "the boys
carry it away," as Rosencrantz confirms they have, they are per-
forming a Herculean task with their tongues. And *this* is the only
Herculean task Hamlet believes himself fitted to perform successfully: language, rhetoric. In honor of Proust, I have even read an
erotic motive into the conversation of Hamlet with Rosencrantz
and Guildenstern. The children are mentioned there as "little

eyases," that is, *eaglets*. You remember it was Zeus who as an eagle kidnaped Ganymede, a young boy, so Ganymede can be conceived as an eaglet. Maybe, Jay, there is some connection to be established between Laius' abuse of a young boy and some such aberration by King Hamlet as Hercules-Zeus . . .

WALLACE: Now, Emory, don't spoil your case by carrying it too far. Even Hercules could have failed at some things.

BECK: Well, if the child player can usurp the position of the common player, the boy usurp the man, then it means, in the structure of the whole complex of the metaphor, that love's Herculean task was to make Zeus yield to Ganymede as Mars yielded to Venus. Maybe Hamlet felt his father did not return his love—

WALLACE: You sound like Stephen Dedalus in *Ulysses!* Come now, Emory, admit—as he did—that you don't believe your own Hamlet theory!—at least not as much as *I* believe it.

BECK: Well, I wouldn't defend the Ganymede-Zeus figure in regard to Hamlet but I would defend it in regard to his author. Anyway, it's plain that Dedalus is ironically insulting Eglington when he says he doesn't believe his own theory. I remember that passage.

ORCUTT: I have an idea you're right as I recall it. I must look it up. Joyce was terribly *méchant* and I think he poured the accumulated spite of his life into Dedalus the son.

WALLACE: (*To Orcutt*) Thank you for the exact cue! I think Shakespeare poured the accumulated spite of his life into Hamlet the son. But the son was father to the most atrocious thoughts. Here—I'll give you my abstract proposition in the nude. Hamlet's dominant quality—the thing that does not change amid all the changes he rings with it—is intellectual irascibility. It's his note —his musical motif—and the true key of all the arias of the soliloquies. Drew, I'm not daunted by what you call the stage-direction key; my adverb is *Irascibly*. This irritability, as more generically it might be termed, is the supreme nerve of Shakespeare's sensibility exposed by Hamlet as a medium. I mean that sensibility which appears *benignly* in *The Tempest,* but *malignly* in *Timon of Athens* and *Hamlet.* Now why is *Hamlet* so much more interesting than *Timon of Athens?* Because it is less abstract and conceptual, infinitely more natural, a play. When Shakespeare discovered the Amleth legend in the Danish saga, he undoubtedly saw something that appeared to him in a rare, very rare, aspect. Unquestionably he saw the incest pattern, but what fascinated him about his divination of everything *lying under* the behavior of the ancient Hamlet was the fact that the whole historical picture, as represented in the theatrical conventions of his time, was stereotyped and shallow. Don't forget that the seventeenth century was already launched when Shakespeare wrote. He would make the historical picture profound and alive by showing everything in it that contradicted or mocked the cultural ideal: the reality as enmeshed with the ideal. I don't mean that others may not have had this particular angle on *Hamlet;* I'm giving it, as they say in billiards, an "english." My own english. Shakespeare's great irony and his great esthetic feat, then, was to exhibit this picture—this quasi-divine game of harvesting crowns—with everything concerned in it showing in the prism of a single ironist: an individual hero who would be universally misunderstood, who would be a living paradox incapable of being "read." This is the Shakespearian hero that Drew claims is unactable. In any case, he seems to me Shakespeare's supreme act *as an artist,* as an intellectual craftsman who invents. He would not leave out any of the emotions, no—but they would all be insulted by having them imitated through a kind of *madness,* a most *special* kind of madness. And the medium was made privy to the device of the master. Hamlet knows Shakespeare's secret: that is what "passeth show" in him!

BECK: Jay, you're being *too* grand: you're *crushing* my Hamlet under yours.

WALLACE: Emory, it makes no difference. Forgive me if I am, but it makes no difference to *you*. In your heart, you will always carry your Hamlet and his globe of "Herculean" poetry, even though my Hamlet should be cried from the rooftops of the universities, which he won't be. Yet you are present at the birth-pangs he is occasioning. . . . All the while I've been talking this last minute or two, something was maturing in the back of my mind and I just then realized what it was. . . . When you mentioned Hamlet's soliloquy about the player's speech, Emory, something popped into my mind once again: an allusion in the same speech that had awakened an echo in me, but one that pointed nowhere. I kept thinking that Hecuba—you know the line, "What's Hecuba to him, or he to Hecuba"—was linked with something significant *in another context*. I know what that context is now and I also know why it so bedeviled me. . . . It takes place in the *Ion* when Socrates casually refers to Hecuba as one of the characters in Homer—you remember the *Ion*?

ORCUTT: Er—let me see . . .

BECK: Ion is a rhapsode, and Socrates demonstrates that he is "possessed" when he recites. (*To Wallace*) True?

WALLACE: True. Now what is the peculiarity of this "possession" of Ion's? It is *unique*. Socrates claims, and convinces Ion himself, that acting is the art of being possessed, even of insanity, because it happens that Homer, and Homer alone, is capable of inspiring Ion to his eloquence that sometimes, in moving his audiences, reaches a frenzy . . .

ORCUTT: Jay! Your breathing indicates you're approaching an "Ionic" mood.

WALLACE: Maybe so. I intended to get out the *Ion* and show you but I'll do it later. Ion cannot explain to Socrates *why* Homer uniquely possesses him, and neither of course can Socrates explain: that is the point. Plato wants to call the actor's inspiration —and by one remove the poet's too—a *lunacy*. It is made quite clear that Ion is reasonable about everything else—reasonable, that is, or bored, for the works of all other poets bore him. Now: as to Hamlet and *his* Hecuba . . . Hamlet becomes concerned because, while listening to the player recite his speech about the death of Priam, King of Troy, he himself has been so detached; indeed, in degree if not in quality, as detached as Socrates listening to Ion. Both Hamlet and Socrates are esthetically moved while Hamlet is moved also in another way. It's all very clear: *Hecuba* is the link between vagueness and precision in Hamlet's "detached" emotion. What is Hecuba to Hamlet that she is *not* to the player? Gertrude, of course, his mother, *another* queen whose husband has been murdered but who, unlike Hecuba, has become party to the crime by marrying his murderer. If only Hamlet could experience pure grief as the player does—but to do this he would have to be as *peculiarly* detached as the player is. Ion and the player are peculiarly detached because they are quite open to the identification; the esthetic feeling of which they are the media is monolithic and pure. It cannot be such with Hamlet, however, not just because it is mixed with reality, but because the reality itself, for him, is so complex, so intensely mixed up with ambivalence. The player's invocation of Hecuba's grief incites Hamlet to perceive in a white-hot light, so to speak, the truth of his relation to Gertrude's grief: he can slough his grief as she did hers, so that Hecuba is nothing to Hamlet and his mother in a way in which she is not nothing to the player, who represents "Ional" emotion, "Ional madness." So Hamlet's outcry, "And all for nothing. / For Hecuba!"—Shakespeare made the phrase "For Hecuba!" occupy a single line—has a peculiar truth applicable entirely to himself. Hecuba is nothing to him exactly because she is also everything; in other words, pure ambivalence. The madness of inspiration regarding her is present through default. And Hamlet's default is far deeper than his mother's; his "nothing" includes the whole Denmark feeling-complex of which Gertrude, in her Hecuban capacity, is only a part. Hamlet cares no more for Denmark's historic destruction than for Troy's, and yet while the player's Ional exhibition is purely gratuitous, his own would not be. Hamlet is neither Machiavellianly nor Ionally mad but impotently mad. The anti-human, the anti-historical at last becomes the anti-real emotion. Yet some law, quite above or unconsciously deep, in him prevents his escape; the inevitable condition then is only what we constantly witness in the speeches, that of the toweringly irritable self-critic, sparing neither world nor self. Think of the many ways, not only that Hamlet under-lines the indignities of man in having so perishable a body, but also that he mocks and stands aside from all the uses of greatness. Where honor is at stake, he defines greatness as "greatly to find quarrel in a straw" and he terms the very heart of political power —territorial acquisition—an "egg-shell"; both allusions are in the speech that Emory quoted, the one that mentions "looking before and after." Hamlet is an untiring critic of mundane ambi-tions up to the moment when he knows he has lost all relation to them: when he is dying.

ORCUTT: Now, Jay! You yourself called Hamlet a "prism"— isn't he just exercising one of his moods in the speech you men-tion? Isn't he as noble as they come? Isn't he everything even an Elizabethan could want from a "glass of fashion"?

WALLACE: Oh, yes! Shakespeare played very safe, you may be sure. Hamlet would be no toad, but a toad's reverse, a god. Otherwise, his author's ironic project would not have its keen and perfect point. Hamlet has to be obviously, apparently, super-ficially fit in every way; otherwise his tremendous apostasy—I call it his heresy, his historical heresy—would not be the superb thing it is. He is designed as a great deviate in a stiflingly conven-tional world. Remember that Shakespeare is also one of the great lyric poets; one of the great picturers of the erotic as of the other passions. He can be soft as an angel, and so can Hamlet. Doesn't Horatio's tiny elegy, "Good night, sweet prince! / And flights of angels sing thee to thy rest," almost stun you with its exquisite obviousness? Yet it is just right. In my thoughts, I have compared

Hamlet with Myshkin because his sympathy is so quick, so intelligent. Doubtless Freud, Jones, and the others are right: there is a pathological structure in Hamlet as a human being; he could not have risen to his plane of transcendence unless he had been free from real commitments in the absolute sense—as free from them as Myshkin was. But, then, Hamlet is an idiot of a kind distinctly different from Myshkin and all other comparable characters. He is superhuman because—this is my special paradox—he is *anti*human. He carried his hatred of the smallness of kingly aims to the criticism of that divine presumption that mythically kings have always had—and that remained vestigially with the kings of England, who had (if we read the historic records properly) their own way of being divine sacrifices. It was the divine presumption that Oedipus had. But the moral of Sophocles' tragedy is that divine incest is not as human incest—there is a malign element in human incest that carries danger to family and thus to state. Zeus got away with murdering his father and marrying Hera, who was his sister. But humanity has a weakness, a limitation that tells; it cannot get away with its family crimes as can the gods—if only because of human vengeance which tracks them down. This is only the historic interpretation and it seems foolproof. But Hamlet is a "fool of history" who would criticize not Sophocles' principle of human-divine relations, but the "madness" of King Oedipus which could accept the absurd proposition that the human individual, as king, can successfully mediate between god and people. In this, Oedipus was quite naïve. He believed implicitly in the sacred doctrine that the king should keep the state unpolluted and that success in this was possible. The moral of all Greek tragedy was *not* that human failure is inevitable but that the gods punish human crimes. Remember, it was Apollo, not Zeus, who devised Oedipus' punishment, in that Apollo's oracle foresaw the crimes. In the Greek hierarchy, Apollo is the symbol of reflective wisdom and the patron of the arts. If Oedipus had been more truly "Apollonian," if his wisdom had not been so practical—his guessing of the Sphinx's riddle has the practical consequence of winning Jocasta and her throne—he might have been able to escape his destiny. The relevance of Emory's interpretation is that Hamlet *is* truly Apollonian; he is capable of genuine and inspired reflection; indeed, it is a kind of sin in him, for its chief function, I would claim, is its exploitation of that supreme irascibility, that subtle operation concentrated in the soliloquies, by which every moral and emotional value dear to man is carefully "resolved into a dew" and the nothingness at its heart uncovered. Anger, incoherent anger, at the nature of all things: this is Hamlet's secret response; this is his "madness." The irony of the famous soliloquies is in their bare statements as made: anyone who can juggle the subjects of life and death, spirit and body, in such a masterful way is simply making them interchangeable with each other and thus, intellectually, absurd. Esthetically, the concept of ambivalence may be very beguiling; psychologically, it may be very useful; but morally, in any decisive application, it is absurd. That Hamlet remains a corporeal body after such a sublime philosophic display as the "To be or not to be" speech is only an integral part of the irony. The whole meaning of the play is in the overwhelmingness of the soliloquies, which are placed throughout as instruments to crush the significance of anything that Hamlet could possibly "do" in the sense of physical action. So you see, even Empson may be worked into an enlightened critical inquiry. I think you have a sound intuition, Emory—Hamlet demonstrates the kind of time in which he lives by means of the soliloquies, and this resembles the eternal present of Proustian time; at least, to me, it is anti-historical, metaphysically *beyond* the time and space that throne-chasers have adored, while physically *in* it. So you have my anti-Oedipus. Not such because he is not involved morally and emotionally with all that Oedipus was involved with but because he made an absolute *and absolutely contrary* judgment of the ultimate significance of killing his father and marrying his mother, which in his case as in Oedipus' was of *royal* significance. History, or fate, or whatever one wishes to call the invariable life-force, placed Hamlet in a peculiarly strategic position; he was someone spared by Apollo from committing the divinely sanctioned crimes of incest and parricide. He took such advantage of it as never before was known in Earth or in Heaven—

ORCUTT: That "in Heaven" is good, Jay! The gods would be the last of all to mock and devaluate human history as you claim Hamlet does. They started it.

WALLACE: Exactly. Hamlet is criticizing the precedent allegedly set by the gods. Today we can be sophisticated and interpret the pagan gods as projections of human ideals: nothing more. Freud may be right in that the human race always suffered from the conscience of a crime committed against itself, against its immediate flesh and blood, and worship of the departed spirit of the murdered would be a form of repentance and propitiation. I would not for a moment deny the depth of the meaning of the Ghost's appearance to Hamlet. Hamlet's feelings are vastly profound. He is hypersensitive, yes! He is quick on the trigger to perceive the exact pattern of chivalrous behavior, the very image of the noble response, and he cannot resist falling in with it, but like a terrible vengeance comes its mockery riding the crest of that idiosyncratic, blind "irritability" of his. He is helplessly clairvoyant. He sees far too much actuality. And he has the arrogance of all this consciously superior knowledge. "Oh, my prophetic soul!" he cries triumphantly at the Ghost's "news." He means this self-congratulation in every fibre and never forgets it. He has magic power—but it is not mana in its positive, but in its negative or taboo, form. His anger against his father is not private, but public. His mana is taboo not merely because it is potentially, psychologically, historically incestuous and parricidal, but because it entertains superhuman vision for its own sake; yes, it is —Drew, you also are right, I think—curiously narcissistic. It is the mana of the medicine man, the fitful medicine man, not of the father-king, Hamlet, who is sober-sacred. That Shakespeare preferred medicine men to kings, I think, is proven by the existence of Prospero, a king who is a magician in the highest and purest sense. Hamlet is not a magician in that unsullied sense. Otherwise, he would not have his malign, his taboo, anger. Now he is simply an amazingly talented person, a genius, if you will; a lay philosopher and poet appointed by Shakespeare to be the embarrassment of history and all its ethical complacence regarding human ambition.

ORCUTT: Oh, Jay, you've taken my beautifully vague and unactable Hamlet and made him a master-mind, a kind of Nietszchean dreamer. I prefer him as the yearning romantic, the melancholy youth of a few thousand tall words. *So* ruffled, *so* frustrated—and doomed, among other ways, to be slighted by his impersonators.

BECK: As for *my* Hamlet, your Hamlet has just devoured him —right under my eyes.

WALLACE: You both flatter me. I've only tried to show what Hecuba was to Hamlet! And I presume that I have virtually identified her as Clio, the Muse of History. Gertrude perforce appears to him in that mask; or rather, she was the literal mask which interpreted the historic features of Hecuba as actually Medusan and in this way betrayed Clio's mask. Can't you come in under History's wings even if the image is not lovely?

ORCUTT: You are painting history as a Last Resort, aren't you? Anyway, I for my part still have to digest your Clio image.

BECK: Your images are fine. *I'm* curious about the *Ion*. I haven't read it for years.

WALLACE: (*Moving*) Help yourselves to a drink. I intended to read you the *Ion*. It's wise to stick close to sources in sceptical company.

ORCUTT: If I may strike a gloomy note, Jay, your theory— persuasive as it is—is not apt to prove popular. You make Shakespeare's motive in creating Hamlet so *ulterior*.

WALLACE: Genius delights in the arcane and the secret, nose-thumbing irony. Shakespeare, I think, was a normal genius. Geniuses who try to be too *obviously* communicative are showing their Achilles' heels.

BECK: "Achilles' heel"! That makes me think of your theory. Isn't Hamlet, according to you, the Achilles'-heel of history which Shakespeare was ironically anatomizing?

WALLACE: (*Putting down a copy of the* Dialogues *which he has just opened*) Good Lord! That reminds me that I haven't explained still another link that led from Hamlet's Hecuba to Socrates'. And which, as a *link,* just this minute, I swear, occurred to me! Originally, I planned to end my essay by identifying Hamlet as an incarnation of the Socratic daimon of all kings; that taboo, negative, and ironic element in the crowned head which says "No" to the projects and impulses that enter it. Such a daimon, isolated and incarnate, would mean anti-history, wouldn't it; that is, the tendency that prevents "things getting done"? It would involve all kinds of moral scruples and private complexes—just as it does in Hamlet's character. Tell me now, do you each think this clinches my argument as a formal proposition?—Hamlet's daimon *opposing* Clio?

BECK: I always prefer a striking poetic image to clinch any argument.

WALLACE: Yes? What about this: Shakespeare wanted to frustrate, with a dose of poison, the tide of history rushing through humanity's veins? So he chose the poison with which the fatal rapier is capped and the poison which is put in the drink. But really—and this is *exactly* in the spirit of my interpretation—Hamlet is the thrombosis of history, that clot in its bloodstream that is fated to stop its heart.

ORCUTT: That, Jay, does give me a jolt. I believe that maybe, *there,* I can detect Hamlet's own voice! It's strange it took that to make me really see your angle. You may be right. If I think about it enough, it may wean me away from my Hamlet-worship, in which I revel no matter what the performance is like. All I want to see and hear is some more or less young man doing his utmost—as Hamlet did—to accomplish the impossible.

WALLACE: I see you don't take my theory seriously for an instant. Because, you see, Hamlet *did* accomplish the impossible. He submitted himself to history! Sprawled out at last, he lies with Clio's death mask on his features. Isn't that the point of his very messy, but definite, demise? You've probably noticed that I've been mixing the present tense with the past in speaking of Hamlet's doings. That isn't merely a tribute to the Total-Recall Hamlet. Somehow I think the action of the play *was* an historical event, although one of the most scandalous.

BECK: Read us from what isn't an historical event, the *Ion,* which I think is an eternal conception of inspiration. Don't you?

ORCUTT: Yes. We'll imagine Ion as *your* Hamlet—who would be, no, an Anti-Rhapsode?

WALLACE: Yes *and* no.

5

PROUST'S AGONY OF PROLIFERATION

In the simplest sense, an object is that which exists independently of a subject. But how can objectivity in art be considered pure? —a thought which brings in question the puristic claims of the non-objectivist category of painting. How can any work exist independently of its creator? The school of fictional naturalism essayed a certain kind of impersonality and fidelity to concrete details at the expense of psychology. Nothing, however, can remind us better than the "social" novel of Marcel Proust that the failure of the naturalist school as such was due to the declassification of human personality into animal being. In objectifying the social self-consciousness of his characters (seen through a scientifically intense lens) Proust created the subjectivity of objects:

the Parisian society of his time. One never doubts, in the work of one who is as subjective in spirit as any creative artist who ever lived, the objective existence of his subject matter and its extreme identifiability.

In the unexpectedly recoiling, almost invisibly subsiding and reviving narrative themes of Proust, we become aware of a distinctive motion, a type of duration in the Bergsonian sense, that passes from the author into what he is writing about as an object and back into him; this is a process which seems perpetually to increase the intercourse between subject and object, and to transform them equally. As the subject (Proust) goes through a constant process of objectivization, the object (or the subject *matter*) goes through a constant process of subjectivization. In his fundamental moral attitude toward the world, Proust is certainly scientific: interested in investigating the nature of objects. But he is a specialist only in that he is interested in the processes of sensation —that sensation intuited as a common experience of human society. This sensation is wholly positive and thus without the negative qualification of scientific method, which divides the object lifelessly. To Proust, the highest object in the world is the human individual, whose sensations are virtually, to him, sacred. It is not that Proust assumes the existence of a moral conception of social impulse, such as that embodied in Jules Romains' theory of *unanisme:* a magnetic attraction of the spirit. It is entirely in the sensibility that Proust's organizing and unifying principle is lodged—his own sensibility which was attuned to the most fragile "wave-length" of emotion he could apprehend in others.

Proust was *the artist* in that he did not presume that the action of his esthetic principle depended upon the conscious or unconscious moral consent of the group (of which he was a member) to be a group, to be socially unified. If objects—that is to say, people and things and scenes—appear so vivid in Proust's pages, it is because of their power to woo him, the artist, and leave their impress on his sensibility independently of their desire or conscious intention to so affect him. As to inorganic nature—the sea,

flowers, buildings, the moon—these objects could have no desire
to affect him; and indeed, it was often the case that human beings
not only lacked the desire to produce an impression on Proust
but were totally unaware of doing so. He, the spectator, ab-
stracted the element of self-consciousness from the intermittently
self-conscious object and enshrined it in the esthetic action of
the pure sensibility. This placed the object in a form of being of
which the essence was the principle of communication; it is the
speed of this intercommunication that creates its radical esthetic
nature and that suggests the impatience and anxiety of a neurotic
sensibility. The symbolism of Mallarmé caused that writer to say
of a painting of a river scene by Monet that it recalled the smile
of the Mona Lisa. This is an association with all the psychological
connectives omitted. Proust tends to reveal such psychological
connectives, which become an architecture of sensibility, and
(being in this sense more "literal" than Mallarmé) may be called
impressionistic rather than symbolistic. As in Mallarmé's comparison, the subtle secret of Proust's method is in the illusory
interchangeability of the animate and inanimate among objects.

Proust's attitude derived from his infallible instinct to regard
everything as a work of art—that is, whether church, girl, or
hawthorn bush, as something fixed permanently for his endless
and arbitrary contemplation. A concrete object to Proust was the
same as an ideal object to Plato. Psychologically, this condition
in Proust's nature, having its pathological structure, stood for
a great original unwillingness to relinquish a simple pleasure, one
imagined as completely and permanently identical with his happiness. We find this clearly established by the opening section of
his work, the "Overture" of the first volume, in which the chief
theme is his almost insupportable anxiety to receive his mother's
kiss every night before going to sleep. The obdurate objectivity
of the world soon taught the child Proust that he was doomed to
be robbed of the concrete realization of such essential desires by
the organic movement of nature, which occurs in time. Hence
among his first instincts (one clearly, in the most refined sense of

the term, of *self-preservation*) was that of estheticizing; or registering images in the mind as things of beauty, and thus things to be indefinitely recalled. As a result, Proust's life (and here is the psychological origin of his hospitality to disease) was a continuous "ascetic" preparation for the act of recalling (as a grand climax to having been deprived of it by time) all that had given him pleasure; and this "act of recalling" was no less than the entire work of *Remembrance of Things Past*. Yet it was by no means merely the action of will, a formal conception of his fate, that drove Proust to the sublime procedure of making a desk of his deathbed—it was, precisely, sensation: the automatic registering of his secretly willful instinct to reproduce in himself pleasurable effects. Thus he finds, when he dips the madeleine in the tea, that this act recalls with visceral sensationalism a past pleasure with which it has been associated. So arises his remarkably saturative conception of metaphor, that it not only implies the simile, the term of similarity, but also contiguity—the term of spatial association in the more concrete or visible-tangible sense and of temporal association in the more complex and intellectual sense.

It is at the place in Proust's novel (in the volume, *Within a Budding Grove*) where the narrator discusses the painting of Elstir that he also discusses the metaphor. In fact, he only introduces mention of the rhetorical term because of Elstir's painting. Although the word "impressionism" is not mentioned, Elstir is obviously an impressionist, and Proust describes the nature of impressionistic painting better than any critic has done it. Elstir's canvas, "Carquethuit Harbor," is described as representing everything in its area of paint as having illusory identity with something else, so that an endless continuity is established. The sky is part of the sea, or vice versa; the ships seem part of the town buildings; and men and women appear to walk or rest indistinguishably on the wharves or on the ships. Thus, not only is the "objectivity" of every natural object curiously transformed, but the picture seems bathed in an element which is not precisely any single element in it, while it partakes of them all as an organic synthesis. It seems that here Proust furnishes us with the most important key to his method: a super-flexible impressionism, reinforced with all the literary devices of symbolism. The gracility of his style, its octopuslike ability to imprison an object in its tentacles and free it with all the undulant, sensual, and unpredictable rhythm of the sea itself has been established from the first page, and here the esthetic principle is formulated.

Proust is a word-painter who extends the visual principle of metaphor instanced by Elstir's painting to embrace the temporal and psychological principles. In the poignancy with which not only can he originally feel a sensation but also recall it to mind and form it in words, he reaches a norm of emotional intensity, and consequently destroys the distance between moments of time as Elstir did between points of space—an intensification to which an enlarging perspective is alike necessary. Always, of course, as the associations of a certain image were enriched by experience, the potential recall of that image could carry a greater charge of instantaneous pleasure, or at least a larger number of units of pleasure for disposal at various times. To the normal person, many pleasures, though temporarily keen, are easily exhaustible and steadily fade in the limbo of time-perspective. But it was just such pleasures that seemed inexhaustible for Proust. He was a sensuous battery that learned the art of storing up pleasure-units omnivorously and indefatigably, releasing them finally only when he undertook and completed the composition of his great work. And, of course, this was when he needed it most.

This was when he was sickest, and so least competent to seek organic experiences to replenish his esthetic energy and exercise its faculty. Hence, there was an early, divine intuition in Proust's organism: a sublime foresight of its profoundly lurking weakness, and all his life, in a sense, was a truly medical preparation for a cure in the form of compensation. Of no human being could it be said more truly that his doom was written, not merely on the surface of his face and languid body, but beneath that surface, in

the nerves that made a sort of excited and extravagant callig-
raphy. The aspect that must occupy us as to Proust's triumphant duel with pain is his pain's mercurial relation with his
pleasure. It is on the pleasure-pain antithesis and synthesis that
his revelation of the metamorphic nature of the metaphor rests.

The little Marcel discovered that as he approached a moment
of pleasure (for instance, his mother's kiss, or much later, the
sight of Albertine), his pain of longing was in direct proportion
to the anticipated pleasure of realization. This is a familiar phenomenon, and also familiar (transposed to general experience)
is the fact that it came about in his further development—his
obsession with Gilberte and his exhausting romance with Albertine—that he ritually observed, pleasure gradually becoming a
"habit," how the sensation of realization dwindled in ratio to the
increasing number of times such moments of pleasure were
achieved. Basically, the moment of pleasure was not as effective
as its anticipation. Not only does Proust say this literally. More
significantly, he has given us leave to understand it symbolically
when, for example, he lurches at Albertine for their first embrace
and, to his astonishment, she rebuffs him. As a matter of fact,
the young Proust is astonished merely at her unwillingness to
grant him the favor. Consequently, his reaction is merely polite,
since he expected her to behave according to the "etiquette" of a
mechanism—a thing, a submissive creature for his delight; that
is, he expected her to "behave" like a work of art. He not only
has learned that anticipated pleasure, if very intense, is usually an
exaggeration of the "real thing," but that both pain and pleasure
begin to merge and become one when subject to esthetic recall.
Already at this point in his life, his adolescence, he had secretly
established the basis for recalling those intense hours of his anxiety that his mother might not implant her good-night kiss on his
cheek, and recalling them specifically as "hours of delight." So
he knows also that whether Albertine gives in to him that night in
Balbec when she asks him to come to her room in the Grand
Hotel, whether on the whole it is a painful or a pleasurable ex-

perience, whether she disappoints him thereafter, whether she repeatedly gives herself to him, whether he loves her to the end or gives her up at some point, it is virtually (i.e., in its "eternal" aspect as art) all the same: he has in him that faculty that will convert all pain into pleasure with the medicine of art. To use a Proustian sort of metaphor, Proust's pain was like a deadly venom contained in snakes and taken, properly concentrated, as an antidote for their bite or a narcotic to relieve intense pain; throughout his life, he patiently extracted this essence from his experience in order to be able, when he was prostrate and hopelessly entrapped in his disease, to produce it in the exquisite vial of his sensibility, and inject it into his nervous system by means of the most sensitive needle ever to transmit such an essence.

To the artist, the world is an object, and the relative "subjectivity" or "objectivity" with which he conceives it would seem to depend basically on the aggressiveness or passivity of his desires toward it. Pain, either in its higher brackets of spiritual suffering or its lower brackets of physical suffering, is to a large extent the result of the refusal of society or nature to co-operate with the instinctive desires of the individual, which are, as the organism develops, primarily aggressive. His needs must be fulfilled for him to grow and live in comfort. Nature and society must show a reciprocity to his spontaneous gestures, his instinctive aggressiveness. We see in Proust's case how sharp a basic antagonism may be set up between the individual and his own nervous system, his physical body. These things may be primordial mysteries: at least, they are shrouded in the mystery of human birth and infancy. We know that nature failed Proust in a certain vital way, that is, a certain aspect of nature failed him, but we also know that another part of his nature, expressed by his ego, rose valiantly to his defense. In Proust's fluid sensibility, an attack of asthma became more or less interchangeable with an "attack" of desire, that is, an attack involving the "infliction" of pleasure. We may turn to that scene in Jupien's brothel, where we learn of the sado-masochistic pastimes of Charlus, and find in them simply a variation of Proust's impressionistic version of pleasure-pain. Proust's relation to society has a supreme aggressiveness modified only by an innate weakness that made him instinctively reserve his capital energy for a final ordeal. It is the omnipresence of nervous hypersensitivity that seemed to crowd out the cruder —and more physically intense—form of sexual sensation in Proust's life. But abstinence from physical expenditure in sex was the only denial that Proust seems to have practised in his social period. As is shown, even at the end of his life, by his indefatigable efforts to verify and amplify his early memories, all his senses, and their repercussion in memory, remained vitally alive.

Moreover, we realize through Proust's majestic portrayal of human beings that these beings held an intense charm for him, and that a tireless passion imbued him to please and succor them; Proust himself speaks of his curious ability, at the slightest suggestion, to forget some frantic obsession and impersonally conspire to satisfy a casual wish on the part of a friend, who is unaware that he stands in the way of Proust's own satisfaction. This fluid law of ambivalence illustrates the fundamental reversibility of pain and pleasure in Proust's system, and shows the extremity to which his contrivances for foiling his nervous system could go —to the extent of giving up his identity without second thought. When Proust talks of Norpois, of Bergotte, of Elstir, he identifies himself with their unattractive defects as much as their attractive virtues. The moral change in self he could transfer to the relations of objects (animate and inanimate) which, as in Elstir's painting, gave up their identity to each other. The implicit ideal is a state of perfect reciprocity. Only the inevitable flux and surge of time's waves carried Proust from the objects and experiences that he continuously sought, something instinctive and highly emotional: his fateful limitation as a solitary ego. Every vignette, every portrayal no matter how small, has an air of nostalgic intensity, as though Proust left the subject not out of will but out of some obscure and specifically unwilled necessity, as if he were carried away by an errant gesture of the ocean of time. In this way, objects, persons—such as that indelibly fleeting milkmaid viewed from a train—became concretized projections of Proust's desire to cling to a life that was too short for him to live.

Proust is a realistic idealist, who took as his whole subject a Parisian society dominated by something at once interchangeably and ceaselessly in movement—an ideal and a fact: the fused hierarchies of rank and fashion; he nominated himself as the elegist of the fact if not also of the ideal. That the fact could be dissolved in the ideal is plain in the leading character, de Charlus, in whom sexual inversion exists as an inside, a subject, desirous of being objectified, but perpetually thrown back upon itself, rebounding from the object of society. Sexual inversion is a "fact" inconsistent with the "ideal" of rank and fashion, and yet Proust richly demonstrates how Charlus' nature ideally synthesizes this contradiction in his struggle as an organism against the "fact" of social ideals, not only in the Faubourg St. Germain, but in himself. Proust finds on the beach at Balbec a kind of group-life which he compares, in a biologically simplifying metaphor, to a zoöphyte (Portuguese Man of War). This is the "little band" of girls among whom he first sees Albertine Simonet, but there is a reason in his sensibility for the emphasis given the unitary nature of the band; Marcel is so much attracted to each that he later confuses one with another in his memory and declares he could never be sure if it was Albertine or someone else in the group to whom he had been *originally* attracted. So it is with every history of individual human desire. The love of a certain society is somehow organically connected with love of an individual in it, and love of a human type with love of a subtype and a particular person. Proust's impressionism is the esthetic judgment and formulation of the secret, more or less invisible, and fluttering single root of desire—that intuition of the sameness in variety of which Elstir's painting is a literal expression.

II
STRATEGIC WITHDRAWAL

6
HAMLET'S CELL

*Hamlet, Oedipus, Kierkegaard, Axel, Melville's
Pierre, Gide's Lafcadio, Ophelia, Des Esseintes,
Igitur, Fabrizio, Julien Sorel, Tate's George Posey,
Camus' Caligula, Breton's Nadja, Stavrogin, Mysh-
kin, Rimbaud, Proust, Pirandello's Henry IV, James'
Gray Fielder*

The cell of pure contemplation

The Hamlet-being created by Shakespeare was destined to be repeated by many a hero of fiction and many a hero of fact—not
in the round, of course, but in the detail whose compass needle
invariably points Hamletwards. I mean something besides the
platitudes of neurotic introspection and the incest obsession,
though these are thoroughly valid; something, too, besides the
philosophic distemper which, after all, appears in a wide context even in Shakespeare. The incest obsession and the Ophelia-
diversion are found in clear enough tones in Stendhal's portrait
of Julien Sorel. I mean rather, for closer example, the resurgence
before programmatic action which is the peculiar philosophic pre-
occupation of Kierkegaard, whose reasons for refusing to marry

his fiancée, Regina, are rooted in his concept of repetition. Yet an element still other than the neuroticism and the incest obsession in Stendhal's heroes seems to me also part of the Hamlet-being. This may be termed the Cell of Pure Contemplation. In Shakespeare's tragedy, this cell is formed by the black walls of the great soliloquies.

The Cell of Pure Contemplation, in the psychic life of heroes, is not always the logical climax of the physical life which it was for (to take a nineteenth-century hero) the Durtal of Huysmans: the sensual man who becomes spiritual and renounces the world. This Cell is not always material and does not preclude worldly behavior; it is a more or less floating metaphysical unit which may function at any time as a judgment against worldly affairs or even as a preparation for them. It is the philosopher's chamber, yet it is more—and less.

As we find it mentioned by Richard Chase in his discussion of *Pierre* in his deep and able book on Herman Melville, it is an objectified self-image, a presage of the hero's own ruination, being a monstrous rock which is identified by Pierre with the fallen titan, Enceladus. To this isolated image, Pierre is accustomed to retire as to a totem that is also taboo. Chase's exhaustive analysis of Melville's novel concludes that it offers a judgment by the author on his own adolescence: "it is the product," says Chase, "of a great intelligence in the act of affirming its maturity by disburdening itself of a great insanity." But this conclusion makes out Melville's art as confessional in the bad sense, as "clinical" —a purgation before it is a creation or an affirmation.

At the end, the hero (whose name signifies "stone," or earth) is left a suicide on the floor of a prison cell: an intentionally awful symbol of individual failure. The symbolic scheme is rightly read by Chase as containing motifs identifying Pierre with Hamlet and Orestes as well as with other mythical and semi-mythical heroes. Pierre's father, whose legend he worships, is dead; his mother remains his idol and he is engaged to Lucy, a pure girl, with whom he experiences the most lyrical transports.

However, a "fatal woman," Isabel, enters his life, breaking up his engagement and causing a serious rupture with his mother. Going to the city, then, he seeks fame as a writer and a solution to his continued problem of sacred and profane love, for both the women in his life accompany him. But Pierre is destined to find creative mastery neither in his work nor his life. His idealistic drive and noble sentiments are foiled, confused, and dissipated by both internal and external struggle (he is poor), till a wild impulse makes him shoot his cynical cousin for having slurred Lucy's honor in a letter.

The novel is packed with allegorical symbols and overtones and has a patently unrealistic yet poorly integrated style, its intonation never being quite convincing. Astonishingly enough, it is about as artificial in substance as *The Pilgrim's Progress,* a fact which makes its application to the artist's life fantastically inept. The secret of its failure lies precisely in the fact that Pierre is a frustrated author whose life and works form a sentimental parody of Melville's own self-consciousness. Here the Cell is a writer's den clogged by Christian dread and the compulsive emanations of a rabid inferiority which, if it is a caricature of Melville's own trait, is still a literal measure of Pierre's titanic freakishness. Chase terms Pierre a "false hero . . . because he tries to derive consciousness and morality from absolute values." And he further says that another statement by the novel is "that the act of making absolutes and taking them for final truth is the act of an adolescent mind."

Form will determine the final nature of content. The all-importance of the integral form, or *context,* lies in the consideration that Melville must have been unaware that Pierre was a "false hero," otherwise he could hardly have expended so much energy telling his story; and no more could he have realized, objectively, that Pierre's failure is specifically an adolescent failure. Art does not exploit one's failures, frustrations, and immaturity unless it is itself an abortive act. Art is successfully parturitive; it exhibits one's objectified consciousness—or it isn't art.

The "statements" allegedly made by the novel cannot really be consubstantial with those Chase makes because they imply a deliberation and understanding which Melville did not have.

It is interesting, moreover, that while these statements *are* objectively true, as Chase applies them specifically to *Pierre,* they are not true of artistic experience in general. If we turn to the context of reality beyond Melville's experience in this novel, as it relates in turn to Pierre's fictitious experience, and go—let us say—to Rimbaud's real experience, we see that adolescence, if it has enough genius, is a high form of illumination, and that "absolute values" are the media of this illumination. In this light, it appears that *absolute values* is itself a vague term: the specific adolescent, if he chooses absoluteness, must choose its specific values. If it be argued that, in the biographical perspective, Rimbaud after all is a self-confessed failure, an adolescent titan of poetry rather than a mature artist, the question might be waived for further argument. But what of the cases of Mallarmé and Valéry, who adopted poetry as an experience identifying the hero as a hermetic, quasi-Hamletian being, and even as Narcissean? Think of Hamlet, and consider Valéry's apophthegm: "Man is a closed animal. He cavorts outside of himself."

No, we cannot accept the authors of *L'Après-midi d'un Faune* and *La Jeune Parc, Hérodiade* and *Narcisse,* whatever be our final judgment of them, as—in Chase's terms—"disburdening" themselves of "a great insanity" of adolescence unless in a most positive, constructive, and assured way. For Mallarmé, as we find in *Igitur,* adolescence is a threshold inseparable from the corridor of manhood; its most trivial *folie* proves to be that on which manhood grows the leaf of future wisdom. M. Teste, Valéry's autobiographic reflection, is a literary amateur. In relation to the fluidity and specificness of reality, Valéry found literature inadequate, an "amateur's" pastime. But this very consciousness bespoke his maturity. Professionalism is no gauge of intellectual mastery.

The final solution of the problem of Pierre's meaning is that he is a *fictitious* hero insofar as his purported experience, as allegorically sound, is humanly false. If we take the Cell of Pure Contemplation as a philosophic-moral moment harboring a judgment of worldly action—preparation *for* it or *against* it—we might take Pierre's version of it as a degradation of that moment; a cell whose inhabitant is trapped, from which no escape is possible (though desired) and into which no illumination finally can enter. While his father's ghost *ejected* Hamlet from the metaphysical cell where his standard already fluttered, the spirit of Pierre's father *shuts* him, at last, in a moral cell where he faces nothing but his own metaphysical impotence.

The Cell, in Pierre's case, is a symbol of intellectual immobility which plausibly puts the literal quietus of death on its subject; figuratively extended, it is a magician's chamber in which the artist, the cell's user, is not the magician but the magician's victim. Neither Lucy ("Light" and "Virtue") nor Isabel ("Lust" and "Sin") can transmit to Pierre the power which the Firebird gives the questing prince of the legend in the noted Russian ballet: the power to destroy the father-surrogate, the elderly enchanter. Pierre becomes, according to the motive ascribed to Melville by Chase, like the stone of his own habitation, the mere human fragment that has come, both in essence and form, from an earth to which it must return. His prison cell, therefore, is quite different from the Cell of Pure Contemplation, and just as different, in its implicit metaphysics, from the Ivory Tower as a legendary vessel of the individual's maturity.

Variation: *The ivory tower*

The mythical ivory tower of Alfred de Vigny, which Edmund Wilson was careful to distinguish from Axel's castle, lends more strength to the Cell of Pure Contemplation than does the extreme image of esthetic retirement from the world instanced by a real hero, Proust. The sealed room of that great esthete, with its magic light and medical dimness, is too easily oriented to a certain street in Paris. The Cell of Pure Contemplation—whatever the worldly fate it directly reflects—is always somewhere in the breast, echoing the palpitations of the heart, ventilated by all the pores, and feeding the adventurous paths of the brain.

The revulsion from society that the French Symbolists experienced made a group gesture which crowded Mallarmé's salon, where the ivory of the tower was literally smoke from the master's cigarette, something, as he said, to "put between the world and himself." The decisive fact about the esthetic status of the Cell is that it has a precise dramatic value as spiritual awareness. It may emerge in quantitative fact as isolation in the actual world: a monk's cell, Rilke's Duino and Muzot castles, or Proust's bedroom; it may be primarily only a tremendous point of tension, as it was in Hamlet's biography. Always, it is the sign of a metaphysical victory, an "election" in the personal politics.

Villiers de l'Isle Adam's work, *Axel,* chose for its fable an absolute severence from society, which the young and elegant Count Axel hates as the betrayer and slayer of his father, and which he strives to forget in an ancestral sanctuary. It is striking that the ghost of a wronged father should station itself, however implicitly, over a battlement frequented by a noble hero created nearly three centuries later than *Hamlet,* and that this hero, while passionately in love with the miraculous creature who eventually dispels his woman-hate, should veto the idea of marriage in order to persuade his lover to join him in the sublime rite of a double suicide; striking, because a parental overhanging and a paradoxical misogyny also governed Hamlet's course toward an early death.

Villiers' artificial romance makes one thing clear: the ideal nature of the Tower, which is an insulation of the will. It is a magic premises where every intruder is helpless under the pure enchantment of an idea. Axel is a Rosicrucian mystic who chooses annihilation as soon as love and marriage appear on the natural agenda. Like Hamlet, he is filled with so much horror at the idea of contributing to the race's perpetuation that he denies himself and Sara even one night of passion before they take their lives. Yet Hamlet did not disdain the logical factor of love and procreation except inside the bounds of dramatic necessity; certainly, being a man of the world in the strictest sense, he did not place himself above procreation *esthetically*. That the Hamlet-being in Axel is a brilliantly presumptuous adolescent is proven by the romantically ideal character of his suicide, echoing as it does the premature love-deaths of numerous young heroes of nineteenth-century literature, among them Shelley's Laon, whose love for his sister also motivated a double suicide.

The Tower as an intellectual fetich, however invested personally, insured that it would contract about the intimate properties of the ego. Its genuineness is richly lucid in Rilke, for whom the Cell (though it, like Axel's, echoes grandly with the centuries) was a necessary material refuge in carrying out his greatest literary project, the *Elegies,* and at Muzot, was likewise the harbinger of his death. Mallarmé left Paris and his friends for solitude in the country. In this physical echo of the esthetic symbol, he proceeded to write the dread *Igitur,* whose sole spokesman is a Hamlet-being with the immensity of his ethical dilemma converted about him into the emptiness of the void.

Mallarmé started with the magic formula, *Héros = Hymne.* Hero is Song. The poem is the beginning and end of the spiritual self, and within it must be contained the drama of creation and annihilation, life and death. While Huysmans' hero, Des Esseintes, attempts to harness all the world to the sensations of the self—the sensual subject—Mallarmé tries to absorb not only the world, but also the vacuum which interlards and drenches it, with the absolute faculty of consciousness, not the continual consciousness of human experience, but the specific consciousness of a poem. In the Mallarméan soliloquy, the hero not only *speaks to* himself, he *engenders* himself.

Igitur is an ikon on the wall of the Cell of Pure Contemplation. It is the concept of drama narrowed down to the smallest possible physical dimensions. In the terms of this drama, a fabulous toy theatre, the hero shrinks in bulk as he grasps more surely the totality of consciousness, as he matures and achieves immortality in the womb of the vacuum. Indeed, his is a *worldly* act of self-maturation as much as anything else; it is the immurement of the self in a cry of revolt from whose splinters the adolescent pieces together his manhood.

The poem saddened and awed Catulle Mendès, one of its first readers, who attributed its apparent pessimism, rather vainly, to Mallarmé's abandonment of his Paris circle. Igitur's experiment with death in life—immortality seized in a moment of pure self-consciousness—is in direct contrast to the madness of the Romantics to unite with everything. But despite the hermetic spell of Mallarmé's hero, we can see with its help more inner poetic sense to the personality of his classic progenitor. The outer poetic sense of Hamlet is found, positively converted, in the occult yet aggressive estheticism portrayed by Huysmans in his great dandy, Des Esseintes. *Against the Grain* is a virulent challenge to cultural stupidity, busy at Huysmans' door accumulating wealth to spend on seeing the world and "doing everything."

Huysmans' exquisite young hero, being freed by wealth to do everything, himself creates the isolation of a hermit in all the indulgences of a super-rake and insatiable esthete. The untrammeled sense of invention is invoked against the sovereign conventions of mediocrity, which seeks only the large public fetiches of art and nature to graze on their resistant surfaces. Without stepping from his fabulous seclusion, Des Esseintes can enjoy in his dining room, which duplicates a ship's cabin and is equipped with theatrical devices, all the sensations of a sea voyage. He experiments ceaselessly with love and his perverse saturations of emotion force him to herculean extremities, till he employs a female ventriloquist to mimic a jealous husband threatening to break down the door while he makes love to her.

Des Esseintes impoverishes the imaginative resources of man to gain a new feeling—but this feeling must obey one law: that of illusion. However, as this hero of fetichism learns, nothing is so quickly exhausted as conscious illusions, those things which in the theatre must be literally repeated every night to a different audience. Conceiving society contemptuously as a desert or a madhouse governed by reason and commerce, Des Esseintes drowns himself in its midst by inventing an artificial oasis of the senses. Not fed by nature, this oasis runs dry. But is not the whole subtlety of Huysmans' conception that nothing is meant by his hero but what shall pass away from his blood and his brain in the performance? To Axel, more noble, more Hamletian than Des Esseintes, the mirage of the senses, however privately fomented, is as repulsive as the world's attempts to exploit anything else; briefly, it is a trifle bourgeois. Axel decks himself with a supramundane insolence toward the private property of the earth and the ages as well as of the individual. In the same mood of metaphysical intransigence, Hamlet disdained all the material advantages of a sovereign prince for a few weeks of deadly sport.

Cadenza: *Axel, Graham Fielder*

Like a mocking shadow of Des Esseintes' positivism is the refined, gentle, and wholly negative agony of Graham Fielder, Henry James' expatriate hero, who suddenly is called back to America to inherit his uncle's fortune, but has not the least idea of what to do with it. Of course, both time and national temperament divide Fielder from these other heroes, and perhaps it is his imbedded puritanism that makes him more like Axel than like Des Esseintes. But Gray Fielder remains urgently of their company, and especially Axel's, through a specific device. He also acquires, on his return to his native land, an ornamental ivory tower, the symbol of his European culture; here, *transplanting* has created the ivory of the tower. In one of its set of drawers, the valuable carving contains a mysterious letter which, if not another financial bequest (we never learn if only because James did not finish the novel), is probably, since it comes from another millionaire who has a daughter, a "financial hint" involving marriage.

This hospitality of the Tower to such an untouched secret reminds us that similarly Axel declined to make use of a great treasure, inherited from his father and concealed in the castle, because gold represented the reality of the world he despised, and that not even the desire of the beautiful woman he loved induced him to make use of the treasure. Beneath the floor of the Cell, according to Igitur, its inhabitant deliberately hoards only one kind of gold: the secrets of the abyss.

In making Des Esseintes an ethical sensationalist, Huysmans was determined to make him a purely esthetic one. Des Esseintes has the same metaphysical mechanism as does Hamlet: the subjective residuum which grows the flower of consciousness without requiring its fertilization with the continuous quantitative, or real, aspect of experience. This exhaustion of novelty from outside means a superabundance of esthetic capital within. It also means a reduced emphasis on worldly program: a lack of faith in the dialectic of real experience.

We perceive the enduring motif of Hamlet: an accurate fiction is better than an inaccurate reality. Des Esseintes' ethic is a conscious stage management, a kind of theatre which he installs as a king would private theatricals: in order to live *their* life rather than his own. Before the end of his story, we learn that Des Esseintes has a soul—he closes forever the home of his desperate adventure and lays his curse on the world whose co-operation in living he has tried to eliminate: "—Society, crash to ruin! Die, aged world!" Huysmans' hero has suffered the involuntary martyrdom of a Christ of Estheticism, his spirit selfishly rather than charitably having perished on the wrack of a base and blind culture. His ultimate horror is the horror that drives the Durtal of Huysmans' novels to espouse religion after the gutter, to live for a while in the drama of silence that is the cathedral, and then to retire into a strange monasticism.

When Hamlet, in one line of blank verse, builds about him the cell of the soliloquy, he populates the air with the dense ideas of moral philosophy. It is an agitation far, indeed, from the trance of a hermit saint or the raptness of a humble novice murmuring his prayers. It has the ache, the heat and hustle, of the world in it; it has the wrenched, arabesque muscles of dramatic doing. In Hamlet's mirror, Igitur saw the repudiation of further experience not as the dramatic anticlimax of the moral life, but as the last detached function of the mind in the drama of human consciousness: *willed nothingness*. This is why objects die in their identities before his eyes, like animals presuming to control their destinies. This is why Mallarmé afterward wrote the word "Waste" on his manuscript. But it is an aspect of the Cell also to write, as Mallarmé wrote in *Igitur* itself: "Le Néant parti, reste le château de la pureté." The "château" is absolute space, whose purity man vitiates by his relative presence, his transient nothingness with the compromising sides of a cell.

Mallarmé's Hamlet was one of the first vivid indications of that isolation of the individual which has seemed clearly, since Kafka's writings, the tragic inheritance of the supremacy of the individualistic idea in Occidental ethics. A hero of Jean-Paul Sartre experiences a rather middle-class incident suggesting Mallarmé's experiment with *le néant*, but appropriately the Sartrian metaphysical reaction is on a visceral plane: nausea. Not long after *Igitur*, Paul Valéry, in *Le Cimetière Marin*, expressed much the same technical definition of alienation as Mallarmé did. Valéry addresses the noonday sun, a symbol of complete balance and thus of the absolute:

> Tête complète et parfait diadème,
> Je suis en toi le secret changement.

Though in this poem Valéry has some of the tragic sadness of *Igitur,* his acceptance of death is essentially lyric, optimistic, and serene. His strategy is the ancient poetic-mythic one of resurrection through dissolution: reincarnation of the person in the end-less variety of the cosmos. The poet prepares for this future by imitating the cosmic imagination as closely as possible; conse-quently, his prospective step from life to death seems paradox-ically sweet and anesthetized when related to the trauma of spir-itual birth and death so acutely delineated in Igitur's mind. Valéry's patient ritual of consciousness, ideally achieved in soli-tude, is a development of the ivory-tower idea of hermetic indi-vidualism, but it is a far cry from Hamlet's own Cell, inundated as that is with the public conventions of the tragic stage.

Pierre's titanic rock-totem, which anticipates his fatal isolation in, and identification with, the prison cell, has two most interest-ing if disjunct parallels in French fiction. Julien Sorel, during his affair with Mme. de Renal, has repeated occasion to retire to isolation in nature, particularly to the "little cave" where as a boy he has meditated on how, like Napoleon, he will be a conqueror. The little cave is a precursor not only of his cell in the monastery, which he abandons, but of the prison where his dream of worldly success expires in the shadow of the death sentence. In the stories both of Fabrizio del Dongo and of Julien, the seminarist's cell and the criminal's cell are malign and benign aspects of the same moment of philosophy: the Cell of Pure Contemplation.

In *The Red and the Black,* Julien is finally driven from the little garden-paradise which he has shared with his incest sur-rogate, Mme. de Renal, who is wife and mother and whose chil-dren's tutor he has been, and automatically takes up his former ambition to conquer "the world" (Paris), where he duly begins an affair with the girl who incarnates the Ophelia-diversion, Mlle. de la Mole. Julien's worldly nature as a rising clerical is tri-umphant when fate intervenes to throw him back to the incest mood. His prospective marriage wrecked by Mme. de Renal's testimony, Julien visits her with the hate-ambivalence he has already practised on his fiancée, and in this storm he shoots his former mistress, only injuring her, with the familiar result: their quasi-incestuous love extends its consummation in a prison cell. Julien has carried the Ophelia-diversion far, only for fate to drive him back to a paradigm of the sinful garden of pleasure: his pseudo-incest. Julien's severed head (the object which, carried by Mlle. de la Mole in her lap, dominates the book's closing pages) is a literal symbol of incest: the head of the newborn emerging from the mother. It represents their now impossible "son."

Fabrizio of the *Charterhouse* has lovers corresponding to Julien's incest surrogate and Ophelia-diversion. Clelia's supreme charm is psychologically inseparable from the chasm between his cell window and her aviary. The plan of escape from prison means to fulfill the plot of abandoning the incest surrogate (the Duchessa, whose lover he has been) and consolidating in reality the Ophelia-diversion. Stendhal meant to finish the novel with Fabrizio at last in the arms of monastic solitude; that is, the prison cell would have helped to teach the ardent spirit a philosophic value long prepared for him. Greater philosophic evidence, of course, exists in the later novel. Fabrizio has a religion of superstition based on an early association with a teacher, Priori Blanès, who is eighty-three when Fabrizio pays him a last visit following his humiliation at Waterloo. The juncture of the church and the *campanile,* where the astrologer Blanès has his observatory, is a sign of the poetic magic which even in Leonardo's day in Italy had been thought "black."

This magic was severally insight, prophecy, art. As a seer, the poet foresees and claims his destiny in advance of its incarnation as fact. He is always the recipient of a transcendental knowledge as was Hamlet through the medium of the Ghost.

Variation: *Oedipus, Hamlet*

Oedipus, Sphinx-wise though he was, was blind to his destiny. Sophocles' irony was extremely simple in its ultimate poetic pattern: the blind seer, Tiresias, sees what the unpoetic king,

Oedipus, cannot see. When the revelation comes for Oedipus, it is too late to have prevented the tragic action; the poetic justice is for Oedipus to inflict, as he does, optical blindness on himself as the agent of blind emotional purgations (incest and patricide). As Francis Fergusson has pointed out, Oedipus is prosecutor at a trial which he does not know is his own. Therefore most of the play's action is a "reconstruction of the crime," a review of past events.

The tragedy being inherently an accomplished fact, no wisdom is available to Oedipus to save himself. Hamlet, however, does not labor under this negative handicap. His tragic irony is that he has been deprived of the Oedipus tragedy and knows it. In *Hamlet,* too, in another sense, an essential tragic action has preceded the opening scene and hangs over it. Personally, Hamlet remains outside it, but metaphysically he is its Cupid, whose blindfold comes off at one touch from the Ghost. Reinforced by the Ghost's communication, Hamlet perceives, as the full-blown poet-seer, the absurdity of a revenge plot which is redundant to the family tragedy in which he was the predestined Oedipus-hero. In this aspect, the Hamlet drama is an indirect travesty on all the dramas of blood and their self-righteous avengers. Guilt abides in thought, and in suppressed thought, as well as in deed. Tourneur's unexpectedly ironic end to *The Revenger's Tragedy,* in which Vendice and his brother, in an ecstasy of the blood lust, celebrate their revenge by revealing themselves as the old Duke's murderers, is an automatic confession of guilt no less than a boast of cleverness.

The Hamlet-being in Fabrizio is not Olympian; it must sit without inner conflict at the feet of the father surrogate, Priori Blanès, if only because in the tale of action to which, like Julien, Fabrizio is committed, the Oedipus pattern is blindly imitated if just as clearly there as in Julien's case.

The hero's transcendent illumination must come via the consultant of the heavens, who even so must be cryptic. Fabrizio is warned that he will endure a prison "far different in its austerity, far more terrible" than the one he has experienced already. This will be followed by a trial that will determine his future, no doubt the second judicial trial which takes place, but also an enlarged trial of the spirit. ". . . if you will resist the violent temptation which will seem justified by the laws of honor," says the Priori, "your life will be most happy in the eyes of men . . . and reasonably happy in the eyes of the sage . . . I have seen only that after your prison, I do not know whether it is to be at the actual moment of your leaving it, there will be what I call a crime; but fortunately, I believe I can be sure it will not be committed by you. If you are weak enough to involve yourself in this crime, all the rest of my calculations will be one long error."

The interpretation of this prophecy in the light of the subsequent events is very complicated, but its large rectitude, I believe, is proven. What is "the violent temptation which will seem justified by the laws of honor"? This would seem Fabrizio's escape from the great prison at Parma, an escape planned by both Clelia and the Duchessa; it is *honorable* because Fabrizio has killed in self-defense and therefore has been unjustifiably condemned. Yet his prison cell is the milieu of the love that will free: indeed, it liberates by its very condition of being without access. Clelia, visible to Fabrizio at given periods through his cell window, is more available than the absent Duchessa, in whose love Fabrizio feels guilty because it is love for the incest surrogate, and a deception of the benign father surrogate, her husband the Duke.

The remaining problem in regard to the Priori's prophecy is: What is the crime that will take place on or about the moment that Fabrizio leaves prison? Has Stendhal furnished a decoy, or is it Fabrizio's hair's-breadth closeness to stabbing General Fontana, who has come to save him, not kill him, during the poison attempt? It seems to me likelier that Stendhal, in the overall design, has made Priori Blanès the Tiresias of Fabrizio's ambiguous destiny: the "crime" is the *escape itself* which Fabrizio conspires in only passively, and which he redeems by his later voluntary surrender and legal exoneration of murder.

Following the Duchessa's successful negotiation of the trial, Fabrizio triumphantly becomes Grand Vicar. His destiny as a religious personality is now sealed and his last days foretold in Stendhal's intentions. The fact is that Fabrizio, in the way that human nature often behaves, has proven the Priori's prophecy both right and wrong. What is essential is the skeletonic design of fate woven by the Priori like an artist in the air of his observatory. Fabrizio, passively, *has involved* himself, and yet his complementary action has rectified the "one long error" into which, the Priori warned, the "rest of his calculations" would be converted thereby.

Fabrizio, terrifying Clelia by his apparition in the cell window after his escape, signals to her that he has given himself up only to see her again; i.e., being theoretically unavailable at liberty (since her father is compelling her marriage to a rich man) she is more available to Fabrizio at the window of her aviary than anywhere else. Is this situation not a mechanical duplication of the true milieu of the Cell of Pure Contemplation? It is this *idea* by which the Priori has judged Fabrizio's life, and in thus assigning that life's philosophic value, he has placed a magic imprint on his pupil's heart.

Fabrizio's worldly phase as the Grand Vicar, during which he woos and wins Clelia's flesh illicitly, is the result of his naïveté: he is imitating the action of natural passion automatically imposed by liberation from the cell; this is an apostasy to the wisdom that the Priori's grace shed on him in the starlight of his recaptured boyhood. In the perspective of the Hamlet-being, it is the useless submission to the Ophelia-diversion. Fabrizio's story imparts that the secrets of the Cell shall not be known outside it except as a tragic idea or a tragic unfoldment in action. Pure contemplation is a charm against the act of sin as well as the ideal embrace of its transfigured image. *It is the seer's privilege, the poet's profit, and the hero's labor.*

Variation: *Hamlet, Orestes*

That to which Hamlet committed himself was a false restitution of moral justice. When Hamlet feigns madness, it is the way the play feigns being a revenge tragedy, the way the Player King and Queen feign being the real ones. It is the esthetic usurpation of the drama by the melodrama, corresponding to all the usurpations (such as Laertes' at Ophelia's grave) of which Hamlet has appointed himself the esthetic critic no less than the avenger.

The classic example of nemesis in the Orestes tragedy is plain enough. Matricide does not wipe out matricide; at least blood, in terms of the vendetta, leads only to more blood. When Vendice tells Antonio that it was for his (Antonio's) good that the old Duke has been murdered, the living Duke replies: "My good! Away with 'em: such an old man as he! / You that would murder him would murder me." Hamlet's pseudopatricide and indirect matricide are obviously a travesty and a perversion of Clytemnestra's and Orestes' sincere passional crimes, as well as a lurid mockery of propriety in Hamlet's metaphysical view. The point at which he is hopelessly trapped in the main action is crucial: Laertes casts doubt on the supremacy of his love for Ophelia. Everything about Hamlet—and he is the first and best to know it—is Olympian, and that his capability in natural passion, or as Freud would term it, libido, should be questioned is a mortal insult, the more so as it comes as a challenge from Ophelia's brother: it is his father's *brother* who now possesses his mother. What also touches the quick is Laertes' boast of his love, which savors of literature, and seems to Hamlet a parody of himself as poet, even as the Player King and Queen, at his own initiation, have parodied the lips of true royalty. "An thou'lt mouth," concludes Hamlet in his defiance, "I'll rant as well as thou."

In Fabrizio, in Julien, in Flaubert's Frédéric Moreau, in Rousseau, as in Balzac and certain of his heroes, all who fix on the maternal mistress as incest surrogate, and in Hamlet, too, we must not forget the natural capital of the libido, which is accumulated possibly not to be spent altogether in the pursuits of pure contemplation or of the symbol dwelling in perhaps vicarious flesh. But any such extra expenditure is apt to take the shape of dalliance, of sport. The duel with Laertes, with whom Hamlet has an instinctive sympathy ("by the image of my cause, I see / The portraiture of his"), is a *false* sport. In the last scene of *Hamlet,* exactly when everyone participates ostensibly in the action as sportiveness, the deadly frustrated force of life comes to the surface in wine and capped rapier. Murder will out. The effigy of *play* will be crucified.

Cadenza: *The actress's lovers*

The consolation sought by the disappointed lover in nineteenth-century fiction frequently took the form of an affair with an actress. Fabrizio has killed in self-defense Giletti, the outraged lover of the little mummer, Marietta, whom he has secretly seduced in the spirit of dalliance. A strange note of frivolous vanity is sounded in the action of the fight with Giletti, itself so much like a piece of Commedia dell' Arte: After successfully stabbing his assailant, Fabrizio loses no time in begging a mirror from Marietta to learn if his face has been marred. It is spectacularly a circus rider to whom a hero of Balzac's applies, not for genuine consolation but to front as, impersonate, a mistress; for this empty service, the lady consents to accept an allowance. Her employer's purpose is to avert suspicion from the woman he really loves but whom, during the story, he never manages to make his mistress. Balzac observes that such touching romantic fidelity is commoner in life than one would suppose. It may well have been.

The actress-mistress is not merely an immediate substitute (as she is for Lucien de Rubempré, for example, when frustrated in his marriage plans) but also, as one whose regular occupation is impersonation, an open symbol which may accommodate the vestigial reign of the mother image, and thus be a blind form of the incest surrogate. Surely it is unnecessary to rehearse the nature of Balzac's own psychology or that of Frédéric Moreau, the hero of *A Sentimental Education,* who devotes himself to the hopeless love of a married woman older than himself. Berlioz was one who loved an actress with singular passion, and Chopin, in loving and marrying a woman who went in masculine dress, indicated the hermaphroditic aspect which, in the abstract or concrete, the incest surrogate may assume. This kind of impersonation, as psychoanalysis if nothing else has revealed, registers countless variations in the imagination and motives of incest feeling. Such a variation takes place in *Hamlet* when the Prince says to his stepfather: "Farewell, dear mother."

> KING: Thy loving father, Hamlet.
> HAMLET: My mother: father and mother is man and wife; man and wife is one flesh; and so, my mother.

The bisexuality of the soliloquist's imagination, as well as its theatrical instinct, receives light in the pages on Des Esseintes' fleshly exploits: He falls in love with a brawny circus acrobat, hoping that her masculinity will prove a brutalizing joy in which he can quench his own effeminacy. She reveals herself in intimacy, however, as all too feminine: vulgar and silly. Another illusion wrecked! The amazon wears a false mustache, the effeminate a wig. After all, it was left to the lofty romantic art of Gautier to define, in *Mademoiselle de Maupin,* the ideal of the living hermaphrodite.

Certain of the above remarks are not psychoanalytical statements about real persons (though they have that potential validity) but only a part of reading the extensions of the Hamlet-being as these appear in fictional and factual imagery. Kierkegaard is not an imaginary man unless we wish to call his literary pseudonyms "Hamlet-beings." His metaphysical arguments, seen against his actual relations to the fiancée whom he finally rejected, tie imagination in with fact and present fact-fiction amalgams. The main thing here is the human pattern, indiscriminately embodied by formal writings or observed, conceivably, across a room.

Kierkegaard's magic engagement

When Kierkegaard wrote his long essay, *Repetition,* he felt that the essence of his idea contradicted Hegel, but the fact that he used the term "dialectic of repetition" is significant. He offered his dialectic to replace mediation. The word "mediation" in this sense pertains to the dialectic of a marriage of opposites—i.e., Hegel's formula. Kierkegaard unquestionably saw in Hegel's formula a direction oddly parallel to the materialist dialectic of Marx; he saw in it the marriage of two human beings ("thesis" and "antithesis"). In *The Aesthetic Validity of Marriage,* he refers to Aristophanes' image of love in *The Symposium:* the two halves of a divided being seeking to reunite. He saw his own logic of repetition, on the other hand, somewhat as Proust regained his lost time, for in *Repetition* he makes a distinction between the "pagan life-view" and the "modern life-view" which might be taken to justify, among other recent views, the distinctive processes implanted in memory by Proust.

"The dialectic of repetition," wrote Kierkegaard, "is easy, for what is repeated has been, otherwise it could not be repeated, but precisely the fact that it has been gives the repetition the character of novelty. When the Greeks said all knowledge is recollection they affirmed that all that is has been; when one says that life is a repetition one affirms that existence which has been now becomes. When one does not possess the categories of recollection or of repetition the whole of life is resolved into a void and empty noise. Recollection is the pagan life-view, repetition is the modern life-view; repetition is the interest of metaphysics, and at the same time the interest upon which metaphysics founders; repetition is the solution contained in every ethical view, repetition is a *conditio sine qua non* of every dogmatic problem."

There are several arresting associations at large in this passage. For one thing if Kierkegaard wrote of "the aesthetic validity of marriage" it was to satirize his own logical masquerade, to provide a formal *conditio sine qua non* for the dogmatic problem of love anticlimaxed. He might as well have written above: "Love is the interest of marriage, and at the same time the interest upon which marriage founders." The necessity of repetition or recollection to a meaningful life refers to a conventional law of psychology, that of recognition; if there is no positive identification in the content of intellectual sequences (or consciousness), these sequences tend to fall apart; there is no rhythm or reciprocity in apprehended reality. Like certain more recent writers, Kierkegaard is interested in that which is the *same* the more it is *different*.

Surely this is also the underlying real affirmation which Hamlet felt in his contradictory life: the Ghost's program of action while dynamically logical would tend not to repeat but to change a fundamental reality of Hamlet's own. Hamlet wishes to remain in his metaphysical cell. But he dare not disobey his father's ghost. At the same time he does not accept the Ghost's report of the crime implicitly. Why so? Not, assuredly, because he doesn't believe it, but because he wants an excuse *to repeat its circumstances*. "The play's the thing" for this, trumpery as it must be in the outward form. The play that will "catch the conscience of the king" is a link in the compromise between the Ghost's program and Hamlet's true desire. In this scene of decision, Hamlet plays the naïve, choleric son, which indeed he constantly prompts, goads, himself to play. At first, Hamlet says that he must hold his tongue (I:II:159), and then he finds reason (III:IV:73 *et seq.*) to hold his arm. But the play goes off on schedule.

"Repetition," says Kierkegaard above, "is the interest of metaphysics and at the same time the interest upon which metaphysics founders." Why this paradox? Because of extensible time in ordinary duration. The objects of contemplation may be "eternal" but there are limits to the possibilities of concentrating on them. The absolute monastic situation may give an illusion of their uninterrupted reality, but this will prove boring because it is without opposition. The saint is bored through the absence of dialectic, through the monotony of his ideal time. Doubt rescues him. Invention rescued Kierkegaard. His "experimental psychology" is the pseudonymous occupation of a play-actor. In this, he is oddly like Hamlet, whose father's ghost, if it had not appeared, might well have been invented by the son. Being a character in a play, Hamlet can transcend the decisive action, in which he is once for all imbedded, only *metaphysically:* yes, through the stained-glass windows of the soliloquies. It is as a metaphysician that Hamlet advances toward us from the black-and-white page to head his contemporary company. But Kierkegaard, as someone without dramatic determination, was always faced with an alternative: the repetition-metaphysics straight or dramatized. His chief "ethical life-view," his "dogmatic problem," was whether or not to imprison himself in the "repetitive" circle of a magic engagement ring. This is his version of the Cell of Pure Contemplation.

Cadenza: *Ophelia, Regina-Cordelia*

Hamlet refused to marry Ophelia. Kierkegaard refused to marry Regina. This comparison is not so facile as at first it may seem. Consider, in the light of Hamlet's relations with Ophelia, how Kierkegaard presents himself in *The Diary of a Seducer,* the imaginative form which he gave his courtship of Regina Olsen. Walter Lowrie, the Kierkegaard translator, observes in his introduction to *Either/Or,* Volume II, that Kierkegaard's discourse on marriage "was written in part at least before he fled to Berlin from the scandal of his broken engagement, therefore during the two months of agony when he was employed in trying to induce Regina to 'break it off,' pretending that he was a scoundrel."

Recall Hamlet's description of himself in Act III, Scene I, quoted above, and compare Kierkegaard's "Seducer" enumerating the qualities by which he speculates Regina-Cordelia is being "tempted": "my pride, my defiance, my cold ridicule, my heartless irony." The diary tells us that, despite this technique of wooing, Cordelia develops a "naïve passion" for him. Kierkegaard has the ardent language which Hamlet likewise has at command as well as more than a touch of Hamlet's ambiguity. But after winning Cordelia from her recognized suitor, and possessing her heart and consent, if not certainly her body, the Seducer takes sudden and irrevocable leave of her.

Though it is relatively difficult to piece together the Hamlet-being from Kierkegaard's numerous writings and his constant balancing of fact with fiction, such an image emerges with nude eloquence to show him clothed in the philosophic negation of Shakespeare's most memorable thinker. Lowrie observes the irony that precisely when Kierkegaard was about to renounce the "happiness" of marriage, he wrote of its beauty "in glowing terms." Yet Kierkegaard did not withhold evidence in *The Aesthetic Validity of Marriage* that he was willing to see a fault in the marital agenda.

"The truth in this whole exposition, the real esthetic element," he wrote, "consists in the fact that love is represented as a striving, that this feeling is seen fighting its way through opposition. The fault is that this struggle, this dialectic is entirely external, and that love comes out of this fight quite as abstract as when it entered into it." The moral is clear: Why go through so much struggle in marriage if love is to come out as "abstract" as before? Kierkegaard had Hamlet's paradoxical habit of speaking in "feeling" (esthetic) terms only to mock them. Moreover, like Hamlet, Kierkegaard feared that marriage, whatever its "esthetic validity" might really be, would be morally disastrous to love.

It is customary for critics to take an author's work in one lump and try to discern there, if possible, a consistent pattern of the logical type. But when Kierkegaard's works are subjected to such an inquiry, it should be remembered that his "philosophy" was a perpetual self-investigation in terms of more or less fictitious postulates: the pseudonyms and such antagonistic character-types as Don Giovanni and the Knight of Faith, in each of whom he dialectically incarnated himself.

I am not interested so much in whether Kierkegaard included the incest-motivation of the Hamlet-being as in the philosophic refutation of programmatic behavior that is common to both their natures. Kierkegaard has supplied, to my notion, the indisputable proof of an artistic thinker *malgré lui* that his concept of repetition was based on his desire to preserve his love for Regina as an eternal object, finished and pure without marriage. This particular proof does not occur in his pages discussing Regina by name even though these pages have a way of suggesting Proust's analytical revival of sensibility.

Kierkegaard relates that he experimented with the element of repetition by going back to the residence he had had in Berlin to find if he could renew his old experience there. Of course, all seems different for him. But the most important difference, which he records without interpretation, is one manifested by his host, who "proceeded to prove the aesthetic validity of marriage. In this he was extraordinarily successful—just as he was formerly in proving the perfection of the bachelor life." Kierkegaard means that ordinary people esthetically rationalize (and often idealize) whatever changes they have made or propose to make in their lives, whether morally vindicable or not; that is, they live naïvely in the emotional or "esthetic" flux without reference to the moral philosophy of repetition. Kierkegaard himself would join this esthetic flux, but by no means naïvely.

Part of Hamlet's dogmatic problem, too, was the prospect of marriage. It was easy for him to estheticize and to dramatize his love for Ophelia, as shown in the scene by her grave. Most probably, he could have murdered his stepfather, consigned his mother to a nunnery, and reigned over Denmark with Ophelia— if he had cared to do things that way. But this ideal, anti-tragic esthetic method of regulating programmatic behavior, a way of "setting things right," he unalterably did not choose. He did not choose it *because the Hamlet-being is as much obsessed with repetition as Kierkegaard was.*

Hamlet's over-all problem, "to be or not to be," was complicated by the fact that one horn of his dilemma was split. To have chosen, in preference to the simple affirmation of repetition (which would have absented him entirely from the infelicity of the plot), the "happy" side of the split alternative would have been to deny the metaphysical value of repetition *positively;* to have chosen, as he did, the "unhappy" side was to deny it *negatively;* in brief, the latter subchoice, the one made, showed the denial of repetition as a *tragic* act, an utter dissolution of subjective reality rather than the optimistic execution of a program of subjective change. Both sides of the split alternative were *fictions* of the moral life, and neither provided the integrity which Kierkegaard denotes by repetition. Here is a radical philosophic idea by which Axel's behavior too can be explained.

The idea hangs upon a conception of fate as "the single individual" which was central to Kierkegaard's beliefs and which Shakespeare anticipated in the creation of the Hamlet-being. *To question the unquestionable:* this is the tragic hero's pride and punishment. Hamlet was Kierkegaardian in that taking this orthodox pride and bending before the orthodox punishment, he did not do it like the usual tragic hero, with profound naïveté and amazed after-knowledge (as did, for example, Lear and Othello), but with assuredly profound knowledge from beginning to end.

Under the star of the Hamlet-being

Kierkegaard was a Christian genius without being a saint, without retiring from the world. His life was dedicated to showing the dramatic values of a mundane Christian fate: he found through Mozart's opera the Christian dread of Don Giovanni, and in the Bible the pre-Christian faith of Abraham, without being able to duplicate either. His drama, his comedy, his tragedy, was to understand without being. He understood everyone: the merman who seduced the maiden, Faust who ruined Marguerite, everyone but the hero of the paradox of faith, Abraham—the one who was not tragic. His own being was concerned with a profound melancholy based on the Christian conception of sin. The paradox of this being (and his writings are riddled with logical paradoxes) was that his sense of guilt and sin flowed inevitably from his father's Christian teaching and yet was part of his individuality, something for which he aggressively assumed personal responsibility.

"The concept of guilt and sin," he wrote in *Either/Or*, "posits the single individual as the single individual. There is no question of any relation to the world or anything that is past. It is a question only of a man being guilty, and yet he must become guilty by fate, by that therefore of which there was no question, and that therefore he must become that which precisely annuls the concept of fate, and this he must become by fate . . . Every individual is himself and the race and the later individual is not essentially different from the first."

What is the interpretation of this passage with regard to Kierkegaard's own life? The individual, created in earliest childhood, has no distinct past even of his own, because everything in later life is "repetition." The past constantly "becomes," is an eternal present. Experience does not essentially change the inherent factor of personality, which only adds to itself as time adds to time, only rediscovers itself by having to contradict its opposites. "Genius," wrote Kierkegaard, "is immediacy as such, with the subjectivity preponderating . . . Genius displays its primitive might precisely in the discovery of fate and thereby in turn displays its impotence." This seems most clear. Could not this idea of repetition apply also to Don Quixote and authenticate the windmill as the dialectical device to exalt the Don's idealism? Fate is the perpetual rediscovery of a moral constant through the act of negating whatever be alien in experience and yet at the same time profiting by the alienation. Thus, Kierkegaard's breaking of his engagement was to recognize, through the "discovery of fate," the "impotence" of his genius—and in this case his genius expressed itself through loving Regina as her fiancé; that is, as one assured of the inveterate novelty of love as expectation. In this he was a "scoundrel" because Regina did not possess the same sort of genius but wished, like any other woman, the consummation of marriage.

Kierkegaard explicitly states that the guilt of an individual is not determined by "original sin," that is, by some distant act of the race previous to his own lifespan. In this rejection he seems heretical, and yet he defined his lifework as the redemption of Christianity from its false appearances. His conception of guilt and sin remains dramatically, one might say *dialectically,* Christian. Nothing demonstrates this better than the dialectic of tragic drama itself. And no dramas apply so clearly in this demonstration as Sophocles' *Oedipus* and Shakespeare's *Hamlet.*

Kierkegaard wrote: "The concept of guilt and sin does not in the deepest sense emerge in paganism. If it had emerged paganism would have foundered upon the contradiction that one might become guilty by fate." The sense of the last sentence becomes clear if one emphasizes the word "become." If an individual be guilty in advance of action through an inherent feeling of sin, there is no need to commit the crime defining his guilt, no need to *become* guilty since he is already convicted by his own individuality.

Freud's interpretation of Hamlet's character by way of Oedipus' serves a compact function here. In this light, both heroes have a secret established long before the rise of the curtain and even, in the logical domain of psychoanalysis, long before manhood. Oedipus discovers his guilt only through action (that is to say, through the quasi-courtroom drama that is a verbal rehearsal of action), and this necessity determines the form of the tragedy. Oedipus did not feel guilty when he killed Laius and married Jocasta because he did not then know his relationship to them. Thus, he had the dramatic aspect of being two individuals, or identities, rather than one: his supposed identity and that of Jocasta's and Laius' son. But in the Kierkegaardian-Christian or modern sense, this is impossible. Here, as in the Freudian system, fate is predestination; it does not become, it *is*, or it "becomes" only in the Kierkegaardian sense of the individual's continuity dialectically revealed. The unconscious or semi-conscious memory of childhood which, in our day, forms the substance of the Oedipal guilt-feeling, or of whatever experience is linked to our living symbols, was not near enough to the surface, in paganism, to have presented the problem which Kierkegaard defines: the "contradiction that one might become guilty by fate."

With regard to fate, the psychology of Hamlet begins where that of Oedipus leaves off. It is the psychology of achieved self-revelation; after this revelation, however much its image veers away from the surface, it may be perceived whenever the mind faces flush to the depths. Hamlet, from the beginning, is self-convicted of a crime which he might have committed, not in terms of a conscious program but in terms of identifying himself with the action which has begun with his father's murder and continued with his mother's remarriage. Claudius has taken over Hamlet's incest-fiction and, making it real, has brought it within reaching distance of Hamlet's instinct even if it was not already there. The past action, when the curtain has risen, is a repetition *a priori* in the Kierkegaardian sense, for it has concretized in objective form the emotional content of Hamlet's incest-impulse which, as I have said, existed as a vague blueprint in his heart. It refers both to what preceded it in Hamlet's experience and what (because and in spite of the play's action) will be preserved (i.e., "repeated") in Hamlet's experience.

The genius that is Hamlet (beautifully represented by Kierkegaard's phrase "primitive might") discovers fate through its "impotence." Fate, that is to say, ordained that the incest crime would be actually committed not by himself but by a surrogate. This substitution, of course, was made possible by the tardiness of the potential Oedipus. The action of Shakespeare's drama, then, can be for its central figure only a needless exposure of his own impotence-repetition: by killing his pseudo-father, as it falls out, he indirectly kills his mother and without actually having possessed her. Oedipus is made impotent under the sway of fate through the imposition of a crime; Hamlet is made thus impotent through the imposition of a criminal thought.

Why, in the motivation of Hamlet's character, has this thought, after all, a "fate" to be materialized in still further action? Only because of the very element which was part of Kierkegaard's genius: the subjection to father-tyranny. Kierkegaard wrote in "A Personal Confession": "From a child I was trained in obedience, in absolute obedience . . . From childhood on, I was in the grip of so prodigious a melancholy that its depths can be measured only by the equally prodigious skill which was given me for concealing it." With Hamlet, too, the father-tyranny necessitates an imposture, i.e., the appearance, in relation to the Ghost, that he is a dutiful, immaculate son. The Ghost interrupts the closet scene as an advent of filial conscience bringing Hamlet back to this imposture, for in excoriating his mother, he is only indulging his private sin. ". . . even as a child," continues Kierkegaard, "I was laid under the weight of an impression laid upon me by an unhappy old man who was himself crushed by it."

Hamlet's guilt, as well as his father's death, makes him, too, "melancholy." And what makes him subservient to the Ghost's command is guilt no less than the pure admiration which a large, philosophical nature could give the unhappy spirit of a noble, murdered father. Yet this filial obedience, demanded with such overwhelming urgency, is just what makes the carrying out of the play's action so onerous to Hamlet. The tragedy is a fraudulent exhibition of its hero's repetition-sense, a perversion of all sense and dignity in the metaphysical consciousness. Hamlet's ability to go through with it is the spectacular display of a genius for fiction, here the *actor's* genius.

Kierkegaard, too, projected his assertion of repetition in consciously and ironically fictitious forms: the pseudonymous spokesmanship of his various moral ordeals. He wished to hazard his bark—he seems to have done so compulsively—between the Scylla of metaphysics and the Charybdis of real dramatic crisis. This is what Hamlet also did. It is likewise what Raskolnikoff, who invented a theory of the superman and committed a murder to test it, and even later "author-heroes" did: Pirandello's Henry IV, who appropriated the life of an historical character, and Camus' Caligula, who parodied the art of the drama with productions more frivolous and mocking than *The Murder of Gonzago.*

The life which is led by the hero outside the Cell tends increasingly to be, in that time historically shared by real heroes and fictive, more and more a matter of programmatic pain or antiprogrammatic folie *and* néant.

The oracle and the "acte gratuit"

Human terror is fundamental to the enterprise of the individual, who faces life immediately after the womb as a symbolic desert with arid burning wastes, a symbolic jungle with labyrinthine fecund growths, a symbolic arctic architected with varieties of ice; the wind on the cheek, the crust under foot, the opacity that claps freezing hands on both eyes. What child does not discover, soon, the ineffable closures of animal warmth as well as fire and ice? After the first experimental steps and strategies, plotted by parents with increasing care as planetary life has unfolded, the individual consciously seeks guidance, comfort, an oracle to explain, reassure, and foretell. It seeks the specific for that oddly intrusive terror, and meanwhile feeds its hungers as best it may.

It seeks as well as possesses mother, father, teacher, the hidden instinct, the official mystery. It calls for Apollo, and before Apollo for the sun which became his flaming ensign. It calls for the Magna Mater, the female whose aggressive universal ascendancy D. H. Lawrence resolved to escape. It calls for any preternatural source supposed by man within any natural source. It asks always a warning of danger, a guarantee of success, or a recipe of compensation. It solicits from an authority as immediate as possible, literally at the elbow, or a centrally oriented shrine to which one may rush as Orestes to Apollo's temple or the miracle-seekers to the crypt of Our Lady of Lourdes. It clutches alike the devious dogmas of the Cabalists, the hieroglyphic in a lover's eyes, and that fluid incalculable of the individual's depths—so like the natural abysses—from which may be scooped nausea and melancholy, the idolization of the ego, self-extinction, hermetic philosophy and hallucinative art, indefinite suspense, and murder. It preserves, at whatever cost, what is necessary to its life or, at equivalent cost, may revoke the living necessity. The individual, merely narcotized by reason, administers this self-fate in a web of natural terror.

The fates of Macbeth and Oedipus were foretold by extrahuman prophecies; the fate of Hippolytus was decreed by a deity whom he declined to honor by tribute or example. The psychological connection between these two molds is simple: in both, the individual is visited with superhuman nemesis, the curse of the gods. What is the "crime" which makes gods and parents alike curse? Disobedience. Hippolytus' fault was to cheat the whole nature through neglect of the erotic. This nuclear fact is what causes Racine's *Phèdre* to seem so radical a conversion into terms of his own age. A reasonable Frenchman of Racine's time could not imagine masculine chastity (outside the religious calling) a plausible virtue, and hence in *Phèdre* Hippolytus, as though he were in the movies, is supplied with a secret love affair. Oedipus disobeyed the tribal law through a familial crime, and Macbeth's familial pattern seems clear enough: he is the infantile husband driven by a masculinized, maternal wife to an imitation of the incest-crime of patricide; Macduff is the father-surrogate who ultimately chastises him. Here the manifests of filial disobedience are princely chastity, royal assassination, incest, and patricide. Hippolytus, technically obedient to his father while remaining chaste, is still disenfranchizing the human law of love and procreation, and therefore on the transcendent level of the tribe, he offends not only the female authority of Aphrodite but also the paternalism of the state.

That Kierkegaard could not produce a father-authenticating faith is revealed by his essay, *Fear and Trembling,* where he explains how much he idolizes Abraham, the hero of a fable of supreme faith, yet cannot himself produce faith in the sort of paradox instinctively comprehended by Abraham: that in sacrificing Isaac, as God had ordered, he would not thereby lose him. The moral issue with Oedipus is the same as with Kierkegaard, even though the dramatic form of Oedipus' story precludes direct filial disobedience. The gods require implicit human faith in everything they do and are. Oedipus is impure in their sight because, as proven by his triumph over the Sphinx, he possesses a demonic wisdom. This is individualistic presumption, a survival of primitive magic. But magic is the prophetic instrument of the artist, whose primary function and desire is to learn his destiny through private divination. Socrates' dictum, Know Thyself, and his direct communion with his *daimon,* defined his curious apostasy toward the rule of the gods, and branded him with the stigma of individuality and abnormalcy which eventually ruined him. Socrates is the historic prototype of the knower drawing substance from a mystic withinness or from the evocations (such as "Diotima") of the personal imagination.

The temperamental affinity between Hamlet and Oedipus is

of the utmost importance. Both are proud, haughty, egotistic, and impulsive. Hamlet stabs Polonius with the same heedless, imperious rancor with which Oedipus kills Laius. No psychological gift is withheld from them; no man is so naturally favored in their eyes as themselves. The Ghost's revelation is only a confirmation of Hamlet's insight, which is therefore that of the seer. Concocting portentous charades is as much child's play for him as guessing deep riddles is child's play for Oedipus. Such stupendous "guessing," however, was an affront to the antique gods as it was a necessary challenge to the parental and divine authority of later times. Like Hippolytus, Oedipus has a token filial obedience in that, as the adult father-king, he acts to preserve the city by hunting down the criminal responsible for its taint; in short, he does exactly as his father would have done. Nevertheless, his is a mundane, political obedience toward the spirit of his father, rather than deference to the fathering presences of the gods, whom he has angered with two kinds of "knowledge": demonic wisdom and human crimes. Tiresias is the emblem of the supernaturally fathered insight which Oedipus would have needed to have avoided his human crimes.

Slaying one's father is an inversion of the tribal logic of the blood feud, and however clear-sighted the logic of personal innocence or justification, it remains a social crime. The Ghost directs Hamlet's dagger to its logical target, King Hamlet's slayer. This simple role of the Ghost makes him a paternal oracle supervising the ordinary continuation of the blood feud, and in Hamlet's day, its role was inevitably allied with absolute patriarchal religion.

Shakespearian critics have been mistaken to conceive Hamlet's special pathos as that of the father-deprived son. Prince Hamlet's ambiguous pathos is that he must acknowledge a father, not only outwardly in terms of the mourning he is thought to overindulge, but inwardly too, as King Hamlet is to him an admirable and guiltless man. The murder has been instrumental in giving this vital, dialectical image of his father into Prince Hamlet's keeping. Nobody but the living Hamlet, however, can see the inward relation to the outward, and this condition (which is his through private genius) is what confers his self-aware superiority over his contemporaries.

The same rebellious filial pride (for Hamlet both knows and feels more than his father, or anyone) belongs to Kierkegaard, who consciously dedicated himself to redeeming with his own genius the Christianity which his father had imposed on him with inadequate wisdom but crushing effectiveness. Indeed, Kierkegaard speaks of the bestowal of this patrimony exactly in the words with which Oedipus declares that Phoebus Apollo has disclosed to him his "doom": it has been "laid upon him."

Yet neither Kierkegaard nor Hamlet nor Oedipus is without personal guilt. Oedipus' sense of it increases with every pulse beat of the play as his self-righteous anger rises. Why is guilt not lacking even to the Sphinx's conqueror? Because of that superstition still commonly held as childhood's most powerful legacy: that father, mother, or a surrogate appointed by them—such as God, the supreme surrogate—knows best. Nemesis, the guardian angel of guilt, becomes essential to the functioning of the Oracle, symbol of traditional wisdom external to the individual. The Oracle has pronounced Oedipus' doom. Thebes groans under the plague. The wings of Nemesis on the birds of Tiresias overshadow the scene. Still the voice of Oedipus is heard, trembling between guilt and innocence.

We have seen how, in the contrasting cases of Melville's Pierre and Stendhal's Fabrizio, the role of the oracle may be successful or unsuccessful in shaping the future happiness of the individual. Blanès, the father surrogate, sets a beneficent star in the firmament of Fabrizio's spirit, while Pierre's innate guilt is too great to allow the benign aspect of the dual parent authority to exert oracular weight. Melville's novel is a reflection of modernity in its sense of complication in the family pattern: the breakdown of religious authority through violent contradictions in the family unit. *Pierre* involves precisely that puritan tradition which made order triumphant in *The Scarlet Letter,* but which in its own case succumbs to a quasi-pagan, eclectic chaos of godhead summoned from the titanic depths of the individual. Melville's hero, as Richard Chase analyzes him, is Promethean, and thus his terrible fall derives from presumption toward the gods.

Cadenza: *Individual and being*

In the depths of the Cell of Pure Contemplation (which is primarily the image of a mutating psychic complex) may lie the superstitious fear that the oracular source is outside rather than inside, and that, for some reason, it will not support and respond to the individual's need and demand; hence, the drastic intensity of such an effort as Mallarmé's, in *Igitur,* to measure the infinite by the model of the unaided individual consciousness. If it appears here that the Cell—and even *Igitur* provides no exception—is almost invariably haunted by some form of the Oedipus-complex, it is to situate the symbol, and to understand it as a dynamic function, at a level where the ghosts of the individual past and the ghosts of the tribe and the racial life help to define each other as primitive and precise energies.

"Precise"? The term may be questioned in this context. It is valid because it conceives the dramatic role of an isolated abstraction, the Hamlet-being, as it uses man to incarnate the artist as seer of the individual, self-contained fate. A glance at the occult tradition of knowledge whose trail is as never-ending as that of the stars, suffices to assure us that Pierre, the symbolic name of Melville's hero (stone), Hamlet's psychological obsession, hermaphroditism, and the "single individual" as a fate, are closely connected in that common bourne from which man draws his dreams and his philosophies. In a study of the *Hypnerotomachia,* Francesco Colonna's fifteenth-century dream of a love-trial, Linda Fierz-David observes: "Adonis is the fruit of an incestuous union, and incest plays a leading part in the symbolism of the philosophers' stone, the self-begetting of which is often represented by an incestuous union (brother and sister, father and daughter, mother and son). Adonis is a symbol of the philosophers' stone, just like the rose whose reddening corresponds to the stage of the *rubedo* which, in a large number of alchemical treatises, is the Great Work's goal. The red rose indicates that the labor is accomplished and also that the stone, like a risen god, has been born in ultimate purity out of the impurity of its primeval state. In actual fact the rose is a female symbol; in association with Adonis, it gives the impression of a union of male and female such as also occurs in the alchemical symbol of the hermaphrodite which is itself a synonym of the stone."

In this place, however, there is no intention of alchemical symbolism or technical dependence on occult knowledge. I am entirely concerned with the living individual as he may appear to the imagination as a hero, and irrespective of whether he lived as a character of fiction or as an organic phenomenon. Here the real and the fictive are equally "organic." This essay must be inevitably, in part, the history of a human effort which is, in a term, *the individual,* and if it be suspected that the moral agency of the individual is to pass away finally as an illusion identical with a phase of the social process on the planet, then this essay will have provided, at least, a gauge of that illusion's present viability.

The fame of the latter-day *acte gratuit* must be inflected through Dostoievsky's Stavrogin back to the Hamlet-being as its chief instigators. Stavrogin applies to the monk Tihon to be confessed, and finally informs him that he wishes to publish his confession of the child-seduction, and its dénouement, as an act of penance. The subtle monk surmises that this would not be a true act of contrition and humility before God but something done to satisfy what now would be termed a masochistic impulse. He tells Stavrogin that his pious wish to publish the document hides a desire to commit an absurdity so as to be laughed at by everyone.

Stavrogin is certainly one of the most indecipherable characters in all fiction, and since he abdicates life even before he actually commits suicide, it seems extravagant to be positive about the power he may have reaped in the Cell of Pure Contemplation. The very term which I have been crystallizing seems a little suspect in contact with this feverishly restive, remote, all-betraying, fantastically high-horsed hero. But can he escape the traditional circle of the Hamlet-being, where the Cell is symbolic of an arrogant self-sufficiency, an inexhaustible mockery, a personal withholding that is a kind of sterile, proud pleasure, a cruelty toward men and women, and a decisive rejection of love; not to mention, of course, the authorship of a document more profoundly mock-heroic than Hamlet's speech-writing?

Where could Stavrogin find the sheer personal stature to play the coward and the clown—as, like Hamlet, he is supposed to do "madly," irresponsibly—if not in the same elusive spiritual closet where Hamlet dealt with his undeniable gifts: a closet of infinite mirrors? Moreover, as the Ghost wants Hamlet to be the hero of the Danish melodrama of revenge, Verhovensky wants Stavrogin to be the hero of the Russian romance of revolution. Each hero nevertheless makes the prescriptive form into something different. And if, unlike Hamlet, Stavrogin absolutely declines the honor of the program selected for him, his previous interests and qualifications have eminently designed him to be the savior of Russia, as Hamlet, had he chosen another kind of strategy, might have been expected to be the savior of Denmark. Both heroes, however, die of a self-imposed, private guilt, and carry the secret of the Cell to their graves.

If Hamlet commits himself to the program of justice dictated by filial duty reinforcing the law of the vendetta, he acts, however knowingly, with a self-confidence and propriety which cannot be claimed for Stavrogin. The latter spends the night with Liza for no reason but that Verhovensky has arranged the incident with melodramatic impact and timing. Stavrogin loves Liza, apparently, in the same libidinal vein in which Hamlet loves Ophelia, yet Hamlet is too wise and gracious to risk a fiasco with Ophelia such as Stavrogin's night of passion turns out to be.

It has been suggested of Stavrogin, as of Kierkegaard, that sexual impotence was a determinant factor of their behavior. This would be symmetrical, but the physical datum is not essential to judging the spiritual function. Stavrogin's negativism has a more terrible beauty—as, let us say, the castration of Eros would have—if we think of his passion as all too physically achieved and spiritually anticlimaxed. Kierkegaard's theoretic impotence of sex would seem in a more beautiful pattern, too, if we assume he was convinced of it without putting himself, with Regina, to the test. For in Kierkegaard's elaborate moral fictions was imbedded a celebration of psychological impotence that would make a mere failure in bed look as planned and masochistic as Stavrogin covered with the public illumination of his sexual crime.

Among the "possessed" of Stavrogin's story, all the chief laymen are possessed by him or some vestige of him. He remains "unpossessed," or at least possessed only by ideas, and this is the crux of Dostoievsky's great intuition of philosophical being, the continuity of Hamlet's metaphysical line which has so impressed artists in the novel, especially Gide. The tragedy needs Hamlet but he does not need the tragedy; nor does Stavrogin need any of the complex reality which his own existence has largely created.

Dostoievsky's fable of revolution invokes the wild thrust and shattering image of the political program dedicated to social transformation. Stavrogin has been an oracle of this movement in Russia, and his logically unexplained abdication of his function upsets the lives of his followers and disorganizes the maturing plot. The hardest to discourage is Verhovensky, the individual possessed with the political image of Stavrogin as the revolutionary "Tsarevitch," Russia's proposed savior. This man smashes everything out of pique that Stavrogin, essential to his program, will not assume its leading part. From being an "oracle," Stavrogin has come to understand that in some momentous way he is still a "child," the oracle's counterpart, and yet he will not yield the oracular function to anyone or any force. All that Stavrogin will do for the world is marry a mad woman, a deed consistent with Tihon's estimate of him that he wishes to be buried alive with ridicule. If Hamlet had lived, and Ophelia, he *too* would have had the choice of marrying a mad woman.

Cadenza: *Mad Ophelia*

Ophelia goes mad from a mixture of grief and disappointed love. Her fate is a common legend of the romantic age of European man. Perhaps the most famous of classical ballets, one of the few still performed in entirety, is *Giselle,* called for its heroine, a peasant girl who goes mad and dies after discovering her noble lover's engagement to a woman of his own class. In one aspect, this fate is the malign alternative of the Cinderella girl, found in undeserved obscurity by a prince who later betrays her, and in still another, it is the misfortune of a noble lady of feudal times, imprisoned by an ogre or an evil knight till rescued by a champion of virtuous love.

The Cinderella-Sleeping Beauty theme is the dominant erotic motif of the tenth-century Japanese classic, *The Tale of Genji,* where it is orientated strikingly to the incest theme. Madness may be the result of long isolation and neglect as well as of sudden shock; in *Genji,* neglected women tend to go mad from jealousy. Historically, female lunacy is associated with the frenzy of the Dionysian revel, and thus is a clear symbol not only of woman's sexual aggressiveness but also her sexual availability. In Euripides' *The Bacchae,* Queen Agave, in a Dionysian spell, slays her son under the delusion that he is a lion. Then there are the fantasies of Dylan Thomas, running throughout his poetry and prose, concerning the sexual charm of madwomen.

The spell of André Breton's heroine, Nadja, is that of a madness ideal for poets, for Nadja's impulses and temperament, her whole instinct, are actually but the recipe of a Surrealist poet for a woman whose femininity is a constant bath of the gratuitous essences he admires. This is a pathology advancing along a way catalogued in the textbooks and indexed by names in hospital files, but for Nadja's lover, it is a freedom from that practicality of female nature which can be so oppressive even to ordinary men. Like a bird, Nadja always says "Follow!" and creates the unseen path of a magic forest in the familiar environs of a city. As Renaissance poets incarnated the spiritual stability of the universe in the image of woman, Breton incarnates there the universe's spiritual instability, and when he kisses his heroine, he sucks the breath of her certain escape into his own depths. Here the gratuitousness is that of a leisure of contemplation, a timeless time of watching the beloved, and as it were, watching *by* the beloved the invisible movements of the mutual destiny ultimately divided by madness.

Technical madness—that is, the permanent rather than temporary absence of reason—makes the possession of woman, sometimes, an easy matter; indeed, in the pathology of masculine desire, it constitutes female attraction on the lowest possible level. But what is its purely moral connotation? Madness is that state where ordinary taboos are lifted: the subject is "unpossessed" of consciousness and is therefore an "open" quantity. Agave's hallucination is the technical phase of converting subjective violence into objective violence; incest is directly equated with murder. Madness is the moment for crime in the night of the senses, for possession of the unpossessable and the deed's automatic consignment, if possible, to oblivion. It is freedom without fate, action without consciousness.

Stavrogin's act of marrying a madwoman is not meanly pathological but lies on the metaphysical level of his character, where it signifies the baleful emptying of the true program in the very midst of the act: a kind of symbolic self-castration whose thread seems to knit Kierkegaard's abortive engagement with this vain marriage of Stavrogin's, repeating the horror and senselessness of the child's seduction. The "madness" of Stavrogin's other acts, notoriously biting an older man's ear and pulling another one across the room by the nose, is symmetrical with the theory of general castration-motivation in him. But what is notable is the *parody* quality of this symbolism, its formal absurdity, which has the same esthetic charge as Hamlet's more calculated absurdities, chief among them the play he stages.

Ironic playfulness which conceals grim sincerity: this is the common *emotional* trait of Hamlet and Stavrogin; and surely it is echoed in the bizarre pseudonyms decorating the desperate homilies of Kierkegaard, and especially the title of the first part of *Fear and Trembling:* "Preliminary Expectoration." Formally and technically, this trait substitutes automatically for moral seriousness, for that ordinary zeal the individual has in prosecuting his worldly ends. But "personal success" is the last attribute one would associate with the lives of our heroes. Their acts are a way of cloaking a vast mundane emptiness, a chasm fitting in extent and ominousness the public grandeur of their supposed or expected roles.

The mystery surrounding many a hero of the conventional romantic novel of these times, and making him a real or apparent scapegrace, perhaps a "beloved rogue," invariably exploits an irrational nature, putting him in the light of a puzzling champion of gratuitous action. Often his behavior is that of one on a routine "secret mission," but where this is true, it is merely the artifice to justify the romantic enigma that must be his façade. This hero-trait in novels is a standard part of all real criminal motivation wherever the tragic sense, or the least concern for character, exists. The hero of Allen Tate's novel *The Fathers* is a figure with qualities strikingly suggestive of Stavrogin's, as though somehow George Posey were Stavrogin's descendant, as Stavrogin is Hamlet's.

Variation: *George Posey*

Allen Tate has rendered his hero the more enigmatic by creating him through the eyes of a boy into whose family he marries, and who somewhat reluctantly and uncomprehendingly adores his strenuous unconventionality. A definite culture, that of the old feudal South, is the program which George Posey fundamentally rejects and mocks, without having the will to make his escape or retire into himself. He lacks the metaphysical rage of the true Hamlet breed, but being "a very powerful man of action," he provokes from his environment the half-bewildered, half-meek toleration sometimes accorded the exceptional individual. Posey is strong-willed, high-tempered, and incisively unrestrained or humorlessly dry when his feelings are aroused. Plainly, he regards the mock-chivalric conventions of Virginian society (he is a "stranger" from Maryland) with impatient, scarcely concealed cynicism. This appears when he must endure the formality of asking Susan's hand from her father, and even more patently when, winning the right of the victor in the knights' tournament to crown his lady, he tosses into Susan's lap the wreath which custom requires be placed on her head.

The title of Tate's novel signifies the oracular voice of the parent which Posey obeys to the end, though not without an ambiguity and moral hesitation whose motivation is only gradually made certain. Even Posey's dominant practicalism is ambiguous: he, like his father-in-law, is for the Union in the historic dispute, but a military coup plus their position as a native family compel them to take the Secessionist stand. Posey's incidental wail echoes, if faintly, that of the Hamlet breed: ". . . they think of nothing but death and marriage and the honor of Virginia." It is striking that while Posey's drive, unlike Hamlet's, is *away from* the Cell, he is trapped into the same sort of ambiguous protestant acts as Hamlet.

His is the cry of the titan against the rule that seems unworthy, unviable. The course of Secessionist action to which Posey must commit himself is subjectively a *gratuitous* course. But at least the power of the military struggle is real, while not so the etiquette of the personal duel. Like Stavrogin, also challenged to a duel, Posey tosses his gun away, canceling the ancient rite. To Stavrogin, form and substance alike are gratuitous, but since for Posey only *form* is, he decides the issue of substance by knocking out his opponent with a single blow to the jaw after proving himself a crack shot with the pistol. Posey feels too sensible to waste life; his principle is that, however unavoidable, war is an *absurd* waste of life, just as the Secessionist stand is absurd because it divides the national strength.

Posey is very much aware of the meaning of "disunion" because of his personal secret: he is a bastard, and remains, as his author reminds us, "a man without people or place." If thereby his character, as the novel shows, renders him prophetic of the advance of reason, toleration, and economic progress, he tragically remains, as observed by his young worshiper, Lacy Buchan, "the mother's boy." George Posey is therefore among the heroes disinherited by a fate they can neither help nor comprehend. When his creator explains, through the medium of Lacy, that "while the world he could not recover . . . existed, its piety, its order, its elaborate rigmarole—his own forfeited heritage—teased him like a nightmare in which the dreamer dreams a dream within a dream within another dream of something that he cannot name," we sense the profundity of the Cell's inwardness without the Cell's metaphysical shape, its centripetal power.

Not being naturally contemplative, Posey can know nothing of the Cell. Yet he is a son deprived virtually if not wholly of a father. Though he accepts and admires his father-in-law, how much he rings of Hamlet by boycotting his mother-in-law's funeral and then, as Lacy recalls, making "a terrible joke . . . about . . . cutting up cadavers." In the three qualities which his creator insists on for Posey, "power, secrecy, violence," we find the curious, proud, inveterate withdrawal from the expected, the conventional, and the programmatic that characterizes Hamlet's breed through Stavrogin. How can we ignore the fineness of a design which needed only these words to make it perfect?— "George was infuriated. He was infuriated because he had been charged with a definite responsibility by somebody else: he had been told what to do. It was too much for him." Posey will not uphold "the white man's honor" by killing his mulatto half-brother even though exhorted by his wife to do so. In the black of the Negro is found the color of the abyss which Tate means by the title of his novel's final section and which here is a bottomless, obliterative guilt. In the Cell, on the contrary, black is the color of the fountain where the soul is washed pure again and again.

By his actions themselves, by the spirit of his actions, and even by the color of his cloth, is the gratuitous hero made *one* in all his manifestations. Hamlet's black is the color of the unconfined abyss and the blind alley. The Cell is the fusion of this abyss and this alley in the blaze of a secret insight. This insight is the hero's tragedy which he must make his triumph. Essentially, it is oracular, but its wisdom is made available to others only *through the gratuitous act*. What is Kierkegaard's long disquisition on "the aesthetic validity of marriage" but a gratuitous act? What is the Seducer's "seduction" but gratuitous? And what will Fabrizio's freedom mean to him but the consummation of a libidinal fate (gaining Clelia) that will be gratuitous in the light of his monastic destiny, of which his prison cell is the fluid prophecy and the material symbol? Stavrogin lives in a metaphysical cell whose walls are proofed against time and experience, and which the grotesque clamor of a public confession could never reach; it is only the gratuitous, "worldly" Stavrogin who can be punished by ridicule . . . or thrilled by it.

The greatest oracle of the *acte gratuit* is Mallarmé's Igitur, whose pronouncement is that death must be the finally elected act of gratuity. In *The Fathers,* Tate chances upon a wonderfully revealing epigraph from Poe: "If man may die utterly it is only through his own feeble will." Mallarmé may well have seen this motto and understood it: only the feebleness of the will is to blame for death without self-conferred immortality. In the vacuum of the idea of death, gratuitousness encounters its repletest incarnation. The ideal artist-seer is an aristocrat such as Mallarmé, who dies a metaphysical death before the biological one, or Hamlet, who allows himself to be killed in a redundant tragedy. The suicide of Stavrogin is somewhat sentimental and bourgeois; consistent, indeed, with Gide's emphasis on Dostoievsky's superman-heroes, as misled beings in whom thought steadily paralyzes action.

Variation: *Christian and superman*

As the case of Raskolnikoff seems to indicate, the mesmerism of action by thought is by way of earning a disaster, if not an irretrievable one. But the moral is that action which is only the result of the individual's reasoning must be bad; destructive, not creative. Nietzsche, the formulator of the Superman who acknowledges no authority but the individual's, is for Gide another victim of the Stavrogin kind. Perhaps. But our ethical judgment is not necessarily that of the Christian philosopher Dostoievsky, whom Gide takes to be the chief Dostoievsky. There is a sense in which a great creator's inventions have a life of their own. Stavrogin belongs more to the genealogy of the Hamlet-being than to the creator of Zossima and Alyosha Karamazov. He is an idiosyncratic mood of the artist-seer, if not that seer's intellectual triumph.

One might think, to read Gide's praise of Dostoievsky's Christianism, that the test of a great hero's life is whether he is happy, or whether, at least, he learns the secret of happiness before he dies. If the spectacle of a great novelist's work is to provide a programmatic lesson, then Gide is right to emphasize that Raskolnikoff's beatific reformation in Siberia leads, both in chronology and the logic of idea, directly to the otherworldly serenity of

Prince Myshkin on the doorstep of the Epanchins. But momentarily Gide forgets, I imagine, that Myshkin was an epileptic—and that Dostoievsky was a dramatist before he was a Christian even if he essentially became a Christian *through* drama.

Gide would have it that the moral choice in Dostoievsky's novels is between anarchy and the Gospels. That is true if, again, fiction is merely the imaginative conversion of philosophic and ethical dogmas and if every "modern" hero is a Christian in John Bunyan's sense, someone for whom program is a "progress." Dostoievsky never landed a major hero in what could be taken for anarchy unless we somehow are to think him unfortunate. But if there is one "lesson" which antique tragedy has for us today, it is the reverse of a judgment of human existence by its capacity to yield rules of moral hygiene. If D. H. Lawrence, for instance, could have given society the sexual health on which he continually harped, we would not have had the emotional drive of the novels. Moreover, Gide would not hesitate to agree that the artist is not the reformer. Why, then, do we find him writing, with needless unction, it seems, that Dostoievsky's works "point," not to "anarchy," but "straight to the Gospels"? It is the moral experience, not the moral conclusion, that matters to man; the height and the depth of the drama, not its abstract ethical coefficient. If to the reader I seem to recommend the Cell of Pure Contemplation because it is a haven after storm and suffering, that is an error of interpretation; I recommend it implicitly because it seems one of the ethical beginnings by which tremendously man may meet whatever end.

My point as to Stavrogin is that he is historically real as man, and relevant now. When we turn a page of Mann or Gide, Kierkegaard or Bernanos, or even Cocteau, we must not expect to be overwhelmed with a sublime heroic idiocy or to note the redemptive step from crime to lyric edification. No, we sense the undisciplined demonic individual in throbbing and detailed operation; we see—as though "God's antagonist" were more important than

God—the distinct lineaments of the esthete of the *acte gratuit*. We cannot observe even the pretense of such heroes, in terms of Christian politics, that the Devil's Party is not in the ascendant, socially and individually. After the "straitness of the gate"—the "counterfeiters" and the "immoralist," after "Joseph"—the Devil's partner. The Faustian bargain of Mann's André Leverkuhn hardly needed to be made explicit. Again, if a crime is committed in some moronically rapt absence of mind, as happens with Camus' Meursault in his novel, *L'Étranger,* the culprit endures no soul-overturning revelation but instead chases the priest from his cell, where, awaiting death, he wishes to be lost in a contemplation that is pure insofar as it is remarkably blank. If we glance expectantly in Kafka's direction, we see a world which might conceivably have been enthralled by the Devil, but which Christ has not the least power to reform.

But perhaps I hammer the point. From the beginning of this essay, my assumption has been that God is simply one of the oracular symbolizations: the deepest, the widest, the most elusive and most protean; in other words, in these pages, he is a moral and psychological invention rather than a true identity. The stratification of the divinity-fiction has become very evident in Pirandello's *Henry IV,* where the Roman Pope is the metaphorical shadow for the oracular parent at the back of the uncrowded cell.

The hero of Pirandello's play is a contemporary Italian who lives an historical charade in a remote castle: he imagines he is the eleventh-century German Emperor, Henry IV, who had to humble himself in the snow before Gregory VII at Canossa. In this situation, the hero has gathered quantitative existence into the premises of the Cell, and expanded it into an artificial stasis of time where he waits and hopes and ostensibly sues for the amnesty that will save his soul. The fiction here, having the objective form of a physical theatre, repeats the pattern that is part of the present theme: an immobility before the prospect of action which secretes a philosophic negation of all program.

Henry's insanity, which has lasted for many years, has resulted from a fall off a horse during a pageant in which he impersonated the German Emperor, and in which the woman whose love he could not win impersonated the Duchess Adelaide, his "enemy" whose intercession with the Pope he had to beg. The accident has arrested the moment of imaginative projection, and this contemporary man remains, in his own mind, Henry IV. Pirandello's hero easily aligns himself with the Hamlet-being. He is known to his friends as eccentric and passionate and, while constantly staging "tableaux vivants, dances, and theatrical benefits," has the reputation of being "a jolly good actor." When we actually meet him, he is ironic, moody, spiteful, and creates on others the impression which Hamlet creates.

Technically, he has reversed Hamlet's impulse to frustrate the programmatic invention by entering into it as though it were a repeated theatrical performance, but the fact is that the programmatic invention itself is of the opposite kind from that which is laid on Hamlet; it implies perpetual postponement because this facsimile of Henry IV, naturally, will never achieve Canossa and the Pope's audience. It is significant not only that Henry protests that he would have repudiated his fiancée to please the Pope, but also that his whole delusion is a full-scale projection of the same simulacrum of truth which Des Esseintes amused himself by staging, *in camera,* as a form of the *soliloquy.*

Pirandello's art, of course, is based on the unreliability of the very formula which I have taken as the metaphysical substance of triumphant judgment in the cases of Hamlet and Igitur. But his Henry IV in this light tends to compass the anticlimactic fates of Raskolnikoff and Stavrogin, for whom the concretely projected metaphysic harvested only messes and the mutiny of moral meaning. But what of it? Hamlet's experience took *the form* of a mess and such a mutiny; Igitur's drained the world of its teleological function and secretly substituted the plasma of the absolute. The real heroes who are Mallarmé, Melville, and Villiers live on after the diverse deaths of their respective characters, the fictive egos. Remember that the integrity of the Cell is not put in question *in reality* except where a worldly program encroaches, where the dynamic lure of action opens a way for the renewed quest of the libido.

Henry's friends, including Donna Matilda, his old love, call on him with a psychiatrist and invent a plot to trick him back into sanity. The portraits of himself as Henry and Matilda as Adelaide, which hang on his castle wall, come alive through the agency of Matilda's daughter and her fiancé dressed to imitate them. Though he has kept the fact hidden, Henry has gradually recovered from his insanity before this visit, and apparently has been availing himself at leisure of the Cell's entertainments. But when the portraits move and the dialectic of illusion and reality is thus suddenly recalled to him, he is struck anew with madness and rushes precipitately to that abstract spot of self-extinction chosen with such exquisite finesse by Igitur; and there he perishes, unlike Igitur, embracing nullity in the shocked sight of the world.

The ironically perpetrated fiction is the gratuitous act as initiated by Hamlet while carrying out the Ghost's injunction, Stavrogin's marriage to the mad Marya, and Henry's adoption of the humiliated Emperor's identity. All these courses imply disobedience to a parent or a parent-surrogate, sometimes in the midst of seeming to obey. Their norm is that prodigious revival of an undying situation of childhood or adolescence which appears in its purest form in the thoughts of Igitur, willfully turning away from his admonishing mother toward the symbols of death in the cemetery; or, in substance, *back to* his mother where he lies, playing or dreaming, on the immense white bosom of *le Néant*.

Variation: *Igitur, Oedipus, Rimbaud*

Mallarmé's adolescent, Igitur, became adult precisely through a formulation of the gratuitous act. This formulation is *le hasard,* the "throw of the dice" which is absolute gratuity because **it** brings up its gesture from the newborn absolute aloneness. This is the emotion which Mallarmé orchestrates as Igitur fixes his abandoned intelligence on the tombs which symbolize the rebirth of an old freedom. The gravestones among which he preferred to play as a child become the monolith of time and space, and touching them again as a man, they faithfully emit that *bruit de folie* which is nothing but the music of the *acte gratuit*.

The truth is that the oracle of the parent or the parent-surrogate makes no sense just when it propounds no conundrum; it is all too incomprehensible in its plainness when the innermost desire does not echo the command. What made the words of Phoebus' Oracle interesting and acceptable to Oedipus was not their literalness but the seeming irrelevance of their application to himself; he considered them only a warning. From them he took self-interest, and his self-interest led him to the blind gladness of Jocasta. Oedipus consciously disbelieved while fearing the Oracle. In the act of conscious disbelief or disobedience, superficially only negative, may lie the very altar of desire, aflame with intimation of the self. Therefore the formidable juncture of parent and oracle may create for the child that mad impasse where contradicting the oracular is an infinite *Néant* in whose luxury he finds his parentless, imperishable ego.

If the endless possibility of gratuitous acts is the same as pure infinite space, *a kind of prison,* this does not discount the impulsive sensuality of the will which, getting lost in nonaction, erects the flesh of all action on the irreducible bone of being. One does not have to be Nietzsche's Superman, but only nature's Rimbaud, to discover the last authority which is manhood. All the rest, after that, is just growing gray.

But this crowned adolescent figured with the prophecy of manhood in the very act of reverting to infancy—is he really an "artist"? Is he not, as Axel, say, or Hamlet himself, a dilettante? Certainly not. He is sometimes, as Proust or Des Esseintes contrastingly were, a great amateur of the senses; or merely gifted in presence or intellect or both, as Fabrizio and Henry IV and Stavrogin; or a demon of precocity, as Rimbaud. Might one insist that Des Esseintes is a dilettante with a vengeance? And what a vengeance. It is uniqueness of consciousness that makes the seer, and Des Esseintes' confrontation of his exotic flowers filled their chalices with challenges, mortal and unforgiving, for there he expected to find the secret of beauty, and thus of truth. The Cell of Pure Contemplation is not big enough for Truth and Beauty to enter together except compressed as one simple being. Every soliloquy of Hamlet is a symphony of warring forces ordered with the arabesque of a formal art of the truth. Within a few lines appears the dynamic intuition of cosmic time and space.

To the modern professional sense, an artist is one who produces something or other every week or year and earns thereby a reputation if not a livelihood. This indeed might be near the truth if perennially so many individuals engaged with the arts did not comply with these requirements and yet fail to be artists.

The inhabitant of the Cell, on the other hand, is capable of anything which speaks to us in a pure voice, unsoiled with self-advancement, whether it employs a little verse or a diabolic charade. The timeless ethic of the artist is a creation first of self; then, of works. These works repeat and contradict the self and enlarge the repetition through the contradiction. Valéry, in believing that works only poorly "repeat" the self-created poet, indulges in a snobbery contingent on too much success within the Cell. Valéry is not tragic, as Mallarmé was. Is the *Divine Comedy* then, a "repetition" of Dante? Well, what are its labyrinthine chambers of universal attitudes, its perspectives of black fire below the earth and blue fire above it, but one highly calculated setting for the portrait of Beatrice?—and an ideal life-history of her adorer? But art is *not* gratuitous. Nor is it always achieved. Nor is happiness always achieved.

I have been speaking all along not of art but of the hero in art, or I should say, *of* art: the clairvoyant whose insight into the Cell is an anticipation of a fate denying him the drama of the man who learns the easy way to be a hero: the utter commitment to an action, regardless of the consequences. But it is the *action* which must dominate in the latter case, and the action may lift one up or bear one down: one follows with his soul and his soul can only whimper or laugh as he does. That is all. This is the theory of action as inevitable: the ideology of tragedy which sees in fate an unformed blend of character and deed that issues in a single and new product of reality. This is the hero's experience which organizes the final face of existence under the lightning and the light of artistic intelligence.

It is all very well. Yet this is not the *hero's* "repetition"—according to Kierkegaard—but the *author's*. Sophocles had captured and mastered all the oracles of his plays; it was only Oedipus and others who were very clever or very moral who came to such grief. The inhabitant of the Cell is a proto-artist who comes to a grief he knows too well in advance, and all his happiness can be is the wisdom that joyfully survives each throw of the dice banally, bit by bit, designing his ruin. This is Hamlet's motif, the motif of the artist-hero committed to a redundant program; it is the pith and skin of the perverse tragedy.

It is the gratuitous act on the level of necessity, where anything that happens is "necessary" just because it is anything, something, for *the thing* will never happen anew. It has already taken place, this unwinding mechanism of the enigma, and the gratuitous hero surrounds it as an oak tree surrounds its original seed. When action is comprised *only* of alternatives, anything done will produce the same (negative) result, which is gratuitous, and no dynamic future can arch over such a prospect. For the Hamlet hero, even art itself is gratuitous, if quite possible. Hence Valéry's subtle repudiation of his work; hence Mallarmé's slow, conscious, painful advance toward the blank page.

Stavrogin, when we meet him, is a hero without a dynamic future, and Lafcadio, Gide's hero, is a teen-age imitation of Stavrogin on the basis not of morality but of esthetics and the newspapers: Lafcadio's is the opportunism of gratuitousness, a quasi-esthetic practice in which the seer is diminished to the common craftsman, in which the mere criminal plot appears in the midst of philosophic futility and the poetic inspirations of folly and fraud; that is to say, there is a *program* to the very gratuitousness. Gide's story clearly demonstrates this. The dilettantism of the *acte gratuit* is where the will is directed not *against* the act but *in favor of* it. The gratuitous act is never the truth but only the transparent mask through which, as in *Hamlet,* the truth is seen.

Variation: *The false hero of gratuity*

Lafcadio, the pupil of the criminal, Protos, is like an overgrown Oliver Twist, a masochistic post-adolescent whose habits and impulses, if not whose language, are those of the big-city hustler before his final initiation. One speculates if Gide actually knew what he was doing beyond deliberately playing with the fantasy for which he has shown such a taste—the anarchy of the corrupt adolescent. Of course Lafcadio, in resisting the persuasions of Protos to enlist himself in crime, tends to seem wistfully "pure." The genuine hero of the *acte gratuit* has reached the age of discretion, whatever his quantitative years, and this discretion is just what gives him the power to essay the gratuitous, the absurd, the last futility beyond which is neither "profit" nor "salvation"—nor even satisfaction of any kind unless it be "repetition."

Lafcadio's crime on the train, the gratuitous murder of the old man with its grotesque echo of the Oedipal crime, has the aura of film melodrama, and the later scene, in which the novelist Baraglioul discusses the motiveless crime as motif for a hero, is a travesty whose insipidity Gide might have avoided even for a novel intended to be *chic*. The gratuitous act is exactly not what Baraglioul proposes: an idea for a novelist to exploit, for thus it becomes an end in itself. If Gide's own surrogate in the novel had been Lafcadio rather than Baraglioul, he would have understood better Dostoievsky's device making Stavrogin's written confession an aftermath of his deed, not an esthetic program for it. Stavrogin's crime begins as an immediate need whose power never deserts him and which generates its pitiless ghosts barbarously exposing their trivia. Not his crime but his confession is gratuitous.

It is the sensed disparity between the *individual* and the *quality of his act* that establishes the gratuitousness; between the remote motive for biting the ear and actually biting it. Stavrogin's need, whatever its nature, is not trivial, and he is the more genuine than Raskolnikoff in not having invented a program for *his* crime. Lafcadio's significant need, however, cannot be assumed from the tone of his personality nor the atmosphere coloring the text of the novel. One feels that the older he grows, the more credit he will want as a disciple of Baraglioul's idea, provided he retains the wit to understand its relevance to himself. Here, it would seem, is a fictive hero to prove that a hero need not be grand but only grandly trivial. That is a fatal error for a novelist to make. Even Lafcadio's spontaneous rescue performed in the burning building has the unconcealed thin air of something in a movie. The *acte gratuit* cannot be an ingenious apology for adolescent criminality nor a valid way to get the corrupt adolescent, however charming, to come of Rimbaud's age in the era of gangsterism.

It is exactly when the hero of the *acte gratuit* is allowed to think of his deeds as such that he ceases to be the "artist" and becomes the "dilettante." But it seems necessary to improve the idiom here. The seer, correctly speaking, is the amateur of gratuitousness. And when we mark the distinction between the dilettante who is the would-be, or might-have-been, professional and the amateur who is the anti-professional, we have in our grasp the superb amateur status of, at once, Des Esseintes, Henry IV, and Hamlet. The genuine work of art, not the mock work of art, is the only act of the amateur of gratuitousness which can evade the conscious absurdity and futility of the gratuitous

life. The transcendent irony is that sometimes, as with Kierkegaard, the fictive hero-personality incarnates that very absurdity
and futility.

When, as Gide remarks, the assumption of the nonexistence
of God inevitably implies that "anything is permitted," the
assumption is true only if no moral need of any kind exists to
shape the inward individual. The Superman of Nietzsche, who
theoretically allows himself anything, is not to be taken as merely
promiscuous or undiscriminating: a blank which the use of a
theory will make a successful Prometheus. Raskolnikoff's sincerity lies in the *failure* of his programmatic crime regardless of
whether it should have led to repentance. If this hero of Dostoievsky is a philosopher of crime who exposes himself as a failure,
Gide's Lafcadio is a dilettante of crime who exposes himself as
a success. The judgment of the professional criminal, Protos, is
perfectly apt: as yet, Lafcadio is a brilliant dilettante; he has only
the taste, not the technique, for crime. One feels that no matter
what will happen to Lafcadio after the novel's final page, his
purity, if nothing else, will go down the drain.

The Roman Pope, of course, is a phantasmal surrogate for the
imperious parent. How plainly we see through Henry IV's playacting that it revives in allegory the disobedient son suing for
forgiveness of the male parent, represented by Gregory VII, and
procuring the intercession of the female parent, represented by
the Countess Adelaide, for whom there is also (logically through
guilty desire) an ambivalent feeling. Henry, like Hamlet with his
mother, has to endure the sight of the incest surrogate with her
paramour. At least, his retirement to insanity has previously
given him the privilege of continuing his insolence toward the
father surrogate and the disguised motivation of his suit to the
mother surrogate to intervene in his favor. When this mode of
repetition-life is rudely spoiled, the catastrophe takes place.

The Pope has a curiously light-shedding role in Gide's *Les
Caves du Vatican,* translated as *Lafcadio's Adventures.* The

book's motivated criminal idea is a scheme by a gang of clever swindlers to bleed wealthy Catholics. Posing as secret agents from Rome, they allege that members of a Freemason plot have kidnaped the Pope and daringly placed an impostor in the Holy See; to restore His Holiness requires, naturally, large sums of money. It is possible to see a faint but firm line of connection between Lafcadio's parody patricide on the train ("motiveless" and fatal aggression against an old man) and the melodramatic farce of the supposed Papal imposture. Here the circumstances of Lafcadio's birth have a bearing. He is the illegitimate son of Count Henri-Juste de Baraglioul and has lately become privy to the fact through the Count's own initiative. Lafcadio will receive a patrimony in money but not family recognition, not the title of which he has not delayed to dream. Thus he has cause for aggression against his natural father, whose immorality has deprived him of legal rights and privileges.

The tendency of his psychological displacement in the railway coach becomes evident. Secretly he would have liked to clout the dignified old nobleman before whose bed he has actually knelt and shed tears during his first sight of his father. This same man, his father, has even sneered at his pretensions to being a Count de Baraglioul. Lafcadio is humiliatingly convicted of an imposture, since he has had his calling cards already printed, but at heart he believes that the imposture is not his but that of his father against himself and his mother, whom he enjoyed and on whom he begat illegally.

The "need" for Lafcadio's *acte gratuit* is now exposed as a normal demand for a parental oracle and a childish, irresponsible reaction at lacking one. He is far too shallow, too little of a genius, to exalt the consequences of this basically emotional need. On the contrary, one feels that, in the therapeutic sense, a libidinal purge has been achieved. As with the youths whose perverse crimes get into the newspapers, the indecent murderer has gotten the aggression against his father out of his system by choosing a scapegoat, and now, logically, is just another lamb for the hangman's noose. It is simply that a technical error has been made. Lafcadio's real character is that of a fugitive from psychoanalysis. His pale though pious contrition for his crime is possibly Gide's naïve contribution to a portrait intended to be delicately sinister.

It seems only symmetrical with this portrait that the sublimated and general father surrogate for Catholics, the Pope, in whom God and the natural father meet in symbol, should be treated by Gide as a mere counter in an imaginary criminal plot; indeed, as a supposed object of prestidigitation. The spirit of prestidigitation is exactly what governs the displacement in Lafcadio's psychology and what brands his crime. Momentarily the old man in the train becomes a blind surrogate for the natural father as easily and irresponsibly as the myth of the false Pope in Rome appeals to the imagination of hysterical Catholics, whose sense of guilt is directly attacked by the swindlers. This light spirit of the symbol, this gay sort of theatrics and alleged stage-business, is a far remove from all those of true importance which have been discussed here. With Lafcadio, it is as Hollywood itself might have said: He had no father to guide him.

Myshkin: Angel without oracle

The only hero-star whose rays do battle with Hamlet's in the heaven of gratuitous action is Myshkin, who is the opposite of Stavrogin. Stavrogin is gifted with the insight of crime, but no crime that he can commit will satisfy him; therefore, having abandoned the "crime" of revolution, he does not concentrate on big crimes. Oedipus, Hamlet, Stavrogin are demonic, but the only medium which the Devil has found in Dostoievsky's angelic prince is epilepsy. The rest of him is goodness, an instinctive Christianity that is pure grace, so pure that its juncture with the world is often awkward; it is a goodness abiding in the within, where there is no ferment of the passions and where the will cannot reach. The gratuitous heroes discard everything but the monolith of the will before which they prostrate their spirits. Albert Camus has portrayed the doctrinal demon of gratuity in the hero for whom his play *Caligula* is named.

Cadenza: *Caligula, Julius Caesar*

Caligula's will is rooted in his frustrated passion for his sister, who is dead. Life becomes for him a huge appetite, a drunkenness of the Superman empowered to do anything—and with the Hamletian wit to do it; anything but what would cure him. The contrast between the Hamletian Caligula, for whom all programs are parodies of art, and art a parody of life, and the poet Scipio, who must hate Caligula for his absolute tyranny while loving him for his conscious incarnation of the tragic, makes beautifully clear the relation of the Hamlet-being to his poetic self, which will never find its freedom except in death. "I don't need to make a work of art," says Caligula, "I live it." This is the awful hermeticism, the "fierce, joyless pleasure" in which the Hamlet hero ascends and falls as though in one uninterrupted arc. Shakespeare's Julius Caesar sentimentally believes that Brutus will be loyal to him, and his pathetic surprise that he isn't occasions one of the most familiar moments of the play. Caesar's phrase, in which he names his friend, is an elegy for human brotherhood. No such worldly sentiment appears in the character of the philosopher of cruelty, Caligula, whose "Brutus," Cherea, is a politician alienated from him throughout the play. Caesar is not Caligula because he believes he can carry along his personal faction in a moderated tyranny; Caligula makes no such concession by individualism. He is an emperor who faces the world, fundamentally, only in his private breast, and who, because his mistress does not embody the impossible, strangles her before accepting death at the hands of the conspirators. Not much of a politician, Shakespeare's Coriolanus has only a Hercules-delusion and suffers his end as the Promethean punishment. But nothing could be more gratuitous, from Caligula's viewpoint, than his own assassination. This is expressed superbly at the moment of the knives' work when, from the dreadful knot of human confusion, he suddenly breaks clear, his face bloody, and (laughing and sobbing) cries with the final irony: "I am still alive!"

No knowledge darkens Myshkin's soul. This condition too is an absolute, but achieved by means opposite to the absolute of Hamlet or Stavrogin. And in the same sense as is Hamlet, Stavrogin and Caligula are charged with nothing but the past, so that their very existence—as Igitur understood the most consciously —is, as a continuity, a contradiction in terms. Hamlet and Stavrogin exist and act because, however great the will with its insight into truth, the libido which supplies all energy works with an irresistible skill in the courses of the world where the outward individual tends to entangle it.

It is the life in their bodies, their strength as men like other men, that electrifies Hamlet and Stavrogin with the irony by which they transform the world (whose objective existence itself seems gratuitous) into utter triviality. Hamlet, especially, lives in a horror of self-loathing that he lacks the simple consent to die physically as he has willed to die metaphysically; instead, he is tempted to fight, to leap into graves, to obey the parental oracle. Myshkin is tempted to do nothing but give, but what he can never really give in any moral sense is the individual self. He has neither the power nor the right to really give himself, and precisely not in marriage, because he is not properly speaking an individual; he would like to be two selves and marry both Aglaya and Nastasya. When he acts on an impulse of pure charity and offers Nastasya his hand and his fortune to save her from selling herself to Rogojin, not only does Nastasya divine the fundamental spirit of the offer, but she realizes that Rogojin's money is sound after all because it is desire's own vehicle; genuine love, to possess, will buy. She even mocks Myshkin for offering to be her nurse: "Why, he needs a nurse himself!" In other words, Myshkin has not reached even the age of proposal.

Christ had anger. Thus, Christ was more of an individual than Myshkin, who had none. Myshkin's only true anger is quasi-mimetic and involuntary: the fit. But as we learn from the episode of Rogojin's insidious pursuit of him in the streets, even the fit is a defensive agitation, a kind of terror whose magic suspends the pursuer's intent. Is epilepsy Myshkin's only form of demonic knowledge? Is it the vestige of the personal will and intellect, the state to which the libidinal appetite has been reduced?—but by what? If we accept Myshkin's own conclusion following the dramatic incident of Hippolyte's near suicide, after the consumptive youth has boasted so elaborately of his design, nature itself is too much for Myshkin. Even before the beauty of the sky and the earth, we suddenly learn, he has felt outside, useless. What can the personal biological past mean if the root of the individual is not covered by the miraculous flesh of the ground? This tragic confrontation of the natural scene, after which the prince has his fear-dream of "the strange woman," is oddly reminiscent of the ritual of Igitur and the schism from nature which that hero invents. But before one can leave nature by an act of will, one must have had it. Before Stavrogin dispossessed himself of love and revolution, he had to dispossess himself of the old naïve magic of nature, the very animism which would have given Myshkin the eyes to see the meaning of the dawn and his part in it. The theory that Myshkin was intended by Dostoievsky to be a version of the legendary "fool of nature," who is so wise after all, seems hardly tenable. The people whom Myshkin affects do not profit by the "lesson" of his wisdom, it only confuses them to the last.

Myshkin not only enchants but also puzzles and disturbs, because he lacks the one trait which human beings usually value most in others, moral positivism. It is not that anyone thinks of him as a cad and an adventurer, but virtually as of an orchard which bears its fruit to rot upon the ground, be caught as it falls, or stolen, but never picked by anyone who permanently or individually has been given the right to harvest. Myshkin cannot be possessed because he has not the power to give himself any more than he has the power to leave Mme. Epanchin's expensive vase in its place. And the sorrow of it is that he wishes with all his soul to preserve the vase, as he wishes for Aglaya's happiness and for Nastasya's redemption from guilt. The power to give the self resides entirely in the individual will, and such heroes as Stavrogin, Hamlet, Des Esseintes, and Axel wear that power in every line of them, but especially on the bare brow where it is written largest. Verhovensky can see it there when he looks at Stavrogin, and so is rendered foolishly incredulous through wishing on what seems impossible. These heroes of gratuity invoke the glory of the possible in others' imagination and then crush all hope, aroused thereby, with the *gratuitous act*.

Without arousing anything but the despair of this hope, Myshkin's social fate is in the crash of the vase when his aimless elbow displaces it. What can be *morally* expected of him or Stavrogin, once they are understood? Of Stavrogin, nothing; of Myshkin, nothing but a truly humanitarian, perfectly genuine and spontaneous, compassion. That this aptitude (and not epilepsy) is the very sign of his mental enfeeblement is demonstrated in the very last scene when, sitting by the raving Rogojin, who has murdered Nastasya lying outstretched beside them, he strokes and comforts him. "If Schneider himself," writes Dostoievsky, "had arrived then and seen his former pupil and patient, remembering the prince's condition during the first year in Switzerland, he would have flung up his hands despairingly and cried, as he did then: 'An idiot!' "

It is hard for Myshkin to understand the moral nature—no, even the logical nature—of events as they take place before him, as he fails to comprehend the social commotion occasioned by Hippolyte's staging of his suicide attempt. And during the incredibly hysterical scene when Nastasya provokes Gania to draw the burning money from the grate, the prince is said to watch the whole scene "silent and dejected." Later, he knows very well that the two maddened women, who confront each other for his sake, want him to choose between them, but even when Aglaya shrieks that he has to do so instantly or else she will give him up forever, *choose* is exactly what he cannot do; instead, he apologizes to Aglaya for not doing what apparently he wants to do: choose *her*. Pointing to Nastasya he murmurs: "How can you? . . . She is *so* unhappy!" The only human signs he really understands or can respond to are the phenomena of the human responses themselves: the grief or the gladness of others. He is empathetic toward human emotions but he feels powerless to prevent, control, or induce them, or to shape them coherently to each other. In this manner is reproduced the anarchy of *the fit*.

Myshkin's idiocy is the sub-intellectual form of Igitur's *folie*. Its absolute alienation from an objective dynamics of life has the same personal movement of destiny. The blind automatism of Myshkin's responses disqualify them as specific and relevant: they revolve in a subjective vacuum. Igitur's destiny is achieved through will, Myshkin's through a basic defect, or at least distortion, of nature. The case of Henry IV is problematical according to this pattern. An accident—something close to what the Surrealists have termed "objective hazard"—intervenes in his case and brings, as it were, disease to the aid of temperament and will. However, we cannot depend too strictly on so fantastic an art as Pirandello's. Henry's fall off the horse may have been chosen as symbolically apt, or merely plausible as realism, for the philosophic conflict with the world which was portrayed, and perhaps does not rightly belong within the structure of that conflict.

The freedom of idiocy has been admired by men apparently because it is without responsibility or fate. Certainly the incidence of "going mad" is at least partly a liberation from suffering or responsibility, or from both. Catatonia is a wholly passive retirement from sanity and the world. But even in the case of catatonics, it seems permissible to speculate that some emotion of horror coincided with the main stress of their passage into a different world of spirit—that is, a positive feeling helped this passage. All this, surely, is the fruit of Hamlet's own knowledge. To know what he knows is maddening because he has recognized the horrible and also is part of its constitution. Hamlet is saying: "I know enough to drive me mad. Yet I am not mad." No, the great in will are not driven mad by horror, which on the contrary is utilized as the final food of their decision. Myshkin has a *mimetic* nature; Hamlet has a *creative* nature. Myshkin knows some old horror and through forgetting it has become its obedient child.

Hamlet knows a new horror and through remembering it has become its disobedient child because it is primarily his own guilt —as Myshkin's conceivably was his guilt. It is selfhood which Myshkin does not perceive in the spectacle of calm, beautiful nature, because the childhood and youth of his horror have been spent in epilepsy, a violence of nature. Epilepsy is the concrete form of his great disremembering and his invisible future alike, for it is the remedy of the horror no less than its enigma and its net.

But religion delivers men from horror, at least when there is nothing else to effect the delivery. The horror of the First World War did much to throw Rilke into his great Orphic poetry and the profound, nameless religion of the *Elegies*. The dwindling of mundane program before the prospect of immortality and a hastened way toward bliss and the evolution of the soul has been a moral problem for man throughout the ages of the earth. In terms of culture, only the individual can deny the potency of the great religious mirage of a world beyond this one. Des Esseintes delivered himself to a ritual of the senses which failed. But this is no indication that he rescinded the validity of his individualism thereby unless we take him as a mask for Huysmans, and then he is seen to be a primitive sketch for the early Durtal; however, Huysmans was careful to conceive Durtal as an aristocrat, and as such, Durtal makes religion, as a poet would,

a quite personal and even critical foray into Catholic orthodoxy.
The potent charm of Proust resides in his implicit, artless belief in the sensibility, a thing quite unlike Des Esseintes' intellectual, methodical, and doctrinal assumption of the supremacy of
the senses. Proust was born into sensibility as certain saints were
into innocence. Des Esseintes regarded sensibility as though it
were only the duty of a gentleman to acquire it at more than its
best. When I thought of Myshkin in this context, I immediately
thought of Proust too; that is, in the name of a personal quality
rather than a nature of man. A kind of innocence is common to
them, but whereas Proust is positive toward nature, Myshkin is
negative. Myshkin is an exile from nature inside and outside
time's continuum. All that binds him to the world is the image
of suffering or the gesture of human gladness that spells release
from suffering—unless, of course, it is the untouched happiness
of the child itself.

But proust's tentacular sympathy makes him a zoöphyte, a
"collective individual," who absorbs as much as possible of the
world that comes his way, not to devour it but to consolidate with
it. Proust is a natural believer in the religion that is sensibility.
The existence of his disease is a gauge perpetually warning him
of overindulgence with life, as comes out so clearly in the devious project of his first going to see Berma on the stage. But the
anticipation of pain through pleasure links Proust's disease in-
versely with Myshkin's, which held in its cataclysmic heart all
the mythical plains of peace. It was a cultivation of psychological
mechanism which enabled Proust to arrive at his formula that
he made the basis of his great work. Such a cultivation is utterly
lacking in Myshkin, for whom the intellect is a more or less useless machine. The intellect for Proust was only a huge toy which
performed a super-Kierkegaardian repetition of sensible experience. But nothing in Myshkin's life was repeated except by permission of the fit.

Proust and Myshkin come closest of all to each other in ordinary social relations. They are naturally drawn to people and

people are naturally drawn to them. What ruined Myshkin was the social agendum of marriage; no such moral obligation bothered the individual in Proust's milieu, so he was freer than Myshkin to devote himself to all kinds of sympathies. Proust had an almost idiotic admiration for exclusive aristocratic society, an admiration which authenticated itself through sensibility rather than sense. Marcel's reverence for the Guermantes family borders on awe. His social orthodoxy was recognizable at once, translated as it was into the most flattering manners. Thus, in one aspect, that of etiquette, Proust's susceptibility to the world had a social status opposite to that of Myshkin: it was the acme of reliability, the unquestionable, enduring, pre-eminent article. What shone out from Myshkin regardless of form was the golden substance; what shone out of Proust was a golden form whose substance was valued at gold by a vain aristocracy. The subjective identification of the untitled Proust with titled society seems naïve because of its purity, so that by one hand at least, the left, his susceptibility to the interests of others is joined to the titled, but less socially qualified, Myshkin's.

Despite Proust's respectful portrait of his father, his muse was entirely maternal. Myshkin's parentage is invisible, but notably he is a prince on the female side of the family and it is this phase of his blood which brings him to the Epanchins, Mme. Epanchin being his mother's relative. To women especially, Myshkin is an angel, and assuredly Proust was no less to several women, including first his mother. But with our heroes who may be termed demonic, the mother symbolizes that from which one revolts in favor of the father or the ego. With Igitur, Rimbaud, and Stavrogin, it is the ego. With Axel, Kierkegaard, and Hamlet, it is the father. Of course, in such cases, as that of Henry IV too, there is an implicit ambivalence toward the mother to be correlated with a more or less speculative ambivalence toward the "virtuous" father.

In general, however, the demonic is associated with the impulse of the pure ego to release itself from the conflict of parent authority and set up its own oracular mechanism. The oracle cannot exist without the will. It is the will to fate which animates all oracles. Proust's problem of will was immensely simplified because the oracle, established once and for all in his life, was merely his mother's kiss. Myshkin had no problem of will; all pride and all grace, things he possessed without will, were cast automatically, if in fear and trembling, at the feet of epilepsy.

Rimbaud has been portrayed by biographers as an angel gone astray; certainly he had the will to the demonic if at first also the outward aspect of a seraph. His filial disobedience is part of his legend. The filial obedience of Hamlet and Kierkegaard, as has been seen, is ambivalent at its roots. Myshkin's relations with God are implicitly conventional—very much doubtless, like his relations with the Czar, remote and inconsequential. He did not have Rimbaud's genius, yet he too might be called a wandering angel, an angel who has forgotten his original home so that his hesitation before nature, that wistful confession of non-kinship, may mean that essentially he is *beyond* nature, beyond the libido which harnesses the will and despoils the self and others in the terrible pride of knowledge; "despoils" in order to reach the final initiation of the Cell: consciousness of the world and fate *in* self. Because the fit is so terrible, knowledge is redundant to Myshkin; so is the past and the future, and program itself, for the fit is all program. The fit is the natural "abyss" which prevents Myshkin's being claimed without reservation for the Christ of theology; for if Christ was really an epileptic, he ordered his destiny to avoid the disease's significance. It is otherwise with Myshkin. The fit has the dark voicelessness of the silver trumpet of fate. It is the flood and fuming of the dark force which his golden head would outride.

At least, Dostoievsky has given us in this hero a profound enigma of goodness, a portrait of Christlike compassion. To the Christian, as to Christ first, the world is desiderated because the human fate is God's judgment, its supreme hope an eternal place in Heaven. In this case, human program has no self-contained fatality: it has meaning only to the world of transcendent value which it indicates and which is God's property and responsibility. Under Christianity, occidental drama for society at large would mean, properly, only the drama of belief and unbelief; man had been deprived of the tragedy of death and personal failure. Caligula is inconceivable under Christianity. To Igitur, Christianity or any religion was irrelevant; to Rimbaud, as to Baudelaire, it was a dialectic of good and evil which offered rich esthetic possibilities. If this dialectic is to lead to repentance, as it did at the end of Rimbaud's life, then Christians may consider it worthwhile for the demonic to have a large share in the personalities of artists.

But the main thing is that, whatever its Christian status, the demonic is uncontrollable and often of a surprising independence, especially among artists. Hamlet is not defined by a Christian sentiment and if we examine the play it is possible to see that the assumption of a Christian milieu is not necessary to its validity. King Hamlet's Ghost, in being tribal, a scion of the Furies, is pre-Athenian, thus outside both Christian and the highest pagan justice. Specifically, Hamlet's drama invokes the primordial incest crime as having precedence over any conception of the social vendetta or of "divine" justice. Considering that it was only *through* the vendetta idea that Elizabethan tragedy could exfoliate under Christianity, Hamlet's situation is of the greatest psychological and moral interest, not in the ordinary relation to what Gide, deriving from Blake, has called the Devil's Party (to which willy-nilly the artist always "belongs") but rather in relation to the Cell's magic, which is demonic only as the pure ego is demonic: as a conscious or unconscious renunciation of both Christian salvation and pagan drama.

Myshkin is a nonparticipant in the fate processes of salvation and drama simply because he is without ego. Rogojin is the *participating* hero of Dostoievsky's novel. Myshkin is without even the oracle of the Socratic *daimon,* the inner whisperer. He is simply without oracle. This automatism represents a twist in the genealogy of Hamlet's strain, a twist which deprives of drama because it deprives of motivational drive. Hamlet's motivational drive wished to frustrate the dramatic program. For Hamlet's intense personalism, Myshkin substitutes intense impersonalism. Hamlet, though compelled to take his father's part, is really willing to take nobody's part but his own. Myshkin is willing to take anybody's part but his own. And it is merely his objective existence which decrees this perfect empathy. He is wholly "available" . . . Myshkin's chief descendant in the mutation of the genealogy I have set out to trace here is Melville's Billy Budd. Of him, and of Milly Theale, more is to be said in these pages.

7
JOSEPHINE'S SITDOWN STRIKE

According to a legend, Aesop was sent on a mission to the Delphians, and inadvertently arousing their hostility, was condemned to death by the Delphic Oracle. In his defense, like Socrates, Aesop had recourse to his peculiar instrument of power, inventive discourse, and told the fable of "The Eagle and the Beetle," whose moral was that the oppressed shall inevitably avenge themselves on the oppressors, no matter how high they are. Aesop, a slave, was consistent in taking the attitude of all the typically victimized, weaker animals of his own fables. In this sense, any individual before the majesty of the people's law feels weak, and has recourse to his personal instrument of power.

In "Josephine the Singer, or the Mouse Folk," * Franz Kafka makes his clearest statement on the position of the artist in society, and for the first and only time, completely generalized and objectified that candidate for achievement who is so often the protagonist in his stories. An important, if somewhat neglected, aspect of Kafka is his attitude toward himself as an artist. He regarded being one as an integral part of human unhappiness and did not place in art the confidence which so many great men have manifested in it as a self-aggrandizing, even though treacherous, weapon. This could not have been so because Kafka underestimated his intellect or his ability to create. Still, if we glance at many of his contemporaries, such as Gide, Proust, Pirandello, Joyce and Mann, we see that each has shown a profound faculty for utilizing the tradition of individualism as well as the special sensitivity of the imaginative man. Joyce's *Portrait of the Artist as a Young Man,* Gide's *Counterfeiters* and other novels, Pirandello's plays involving interchange of identity between author and character—all these works have the narcissistic quality of making a generally plausible structure out of speculative private problems; the artist has objectively dramatized his role in the midst of society.

In "Investigations of a Dog," Kafka includes the "flying dogs," evidently the artists, but these remain humanly vague in comparison with the specific, individualized portrait of Josephine the mouse, a supreme artist. Gregor Samsa of "Metamorphosis," K. of *The Castle* and *The Trial,* are bureaucrats or humble professionals—thus "common" men. They are unsuccessful in that, lacking jobs, they remain unemployed, or having jobs, they become unhappy and guilty of "dangerous thoughts"—an intolerable kind of moral hypochondria. The hero of *The Trial,* indeed, has a good job in a bank and to all appearances is an average, law-abiding citizen. Why is he arraigned, without notice, before an existent if never quite materialized court of civil justice? Why

* Translated by Willa and Edwin Muir, in *The Penal Colony,* Schocken Books, New York, 1948.

is he plucked from his position and finally put to death for a crime whose nature he is unable to discover? In answering these questions anew, a critic who failed to relate them to the pivotal case of Josephine the mouse singer would be at a disadvantage in arriving at a decisive estimate of Kafka's meanings. Duly, in this story, Kafka wrote a fable formally narrowing down and personalizing his own art and yet according it a new, definitive horizon.

Kafka's philosophy of practical frustration, signified by the inability of his heroes to advance beyond a certain point in their careers or fatally to backslide, is much investigated ground; this stasis, this appalling sense of disorientation from movement, is properly regarded as the basis of Kafka's metaphysics. Yet on this basis he has built considerable ramifications and the story I am considering fixes on his own powers as an artist—insofar, that is, as he may be identified with any of his protagonists. His view of himself as an artist, a professional being, is the underlying cause of the very shape taken by his special art: the fable. For, being a form whose division from real conditions is implicit, and thus in a way irremediable, the fable automatically satisfies Kafka's impulse to slice reality in the middle, to show its conclusive split.

As a tacit opponent of bourgeois and scientific materialism, Kafka does not, like the artists whom I mentioned above, take a self-conscious attitude of defense when writing specifically of the artist's professional urge. Stephen Dedalus is virtually a classical monster of wit, capable of shaming all philistine opponents, a champion whom Joyce covered with all the glory and humiliation of the artist at this stage of human history; at bottom, Stephen is not fabulous but realistic. While Joyce produced in his hero the extreme of social arrogance, Kafka (though his own stature is unquestionable) calls on all his resources to reveal the fatal lot of the victimized and weak, the outcast and miserable, hero who lacks any trace of what could be called narcissistic grandeur—the personal pride true of a "professional."

The outstanding characteristic of the Kafkan hero, therefore, is the opposite of individualistic heroism with culture as its weapon. The bank clerk in *The Trial*, eventually taken out secretly and knifed by official executioners, has nothing to say in his defense at the crucial moments, nothing at least but inner outcries; no eloquence for eloquence's sake forces its way to his lips. From the beginning he had not tried to escape, but rather, like an ordinary, literal-minded citizen, has sought to have the mysterious charge cleared up, disproven. Unlike the traditional protestant or romantic hero, he has not tried to anticipate and outwit the mechanism of destiny, voluntarily becoming an outlaw from society. He has waited patiently in the charmed circle of the law-abiding until he is trapped beyond rescue.

How plausible it is, and how characteristic of Kafka, that when turning upon the artist and society his fabulous lens, he is not confined to the artist's subjective view of himself (though he discloses this view systematically) but rather extends the artist's self-view by uniquely qualifying its well-known narcissism. Josephine, the great songstress of the Mouse Folk, is shown conducting a lifelong, unsuccessful struggle to be exempted from the work which is obligatory—apparently by rigid statute—to every individual of her race. The Mouse Folk, superficially implying a socialist economy where an equitable division of labor prevails, is actually, of course, a figurative image of present-day bourgeois capitalism, where, in the United States, poets such as William Carlos Williams and Wallace Stevens, in order to support themselves, had also to be a doctor or business official.

For his Aesopian nation, Kafka took care to choose a mammal species in which every individual—whatever the hierarchy of the strong and the weak—has the necessity of shifting for himself as a grown animal. One could have speculated that in a Kafkan fable the artist would be projected through some extravagant biological metaphor, by a creature fabulously rich in lassitude, such as the Queen Bee, who is equipped for isolated "great deeds" only. But what would have provided Voltaire or a mere social caricaturist, would not do for Kafka, who as a modern could realize how thoroughly discredited is the bourgeois fable of the artist as a lazy man or do-nothing. On the other hand, the unquestioned social datum of the artist as one who experiences a temperamental revulsion from "ordinary" work served not only Kafka's purpose in "Josephine the Singer" but is the pre-eminent theme of all his work. If he did not choose for this story an insect kind having aristocrats and nonworkers, such as termites and bees, it was generally because he wanted the Mouse Folk to have a plausible parallel with humanity; he wanted Josephine's race to be in the same bio-evolutionary category with man, the highest mammal.

The weight of Kafka's reason here was an urgency that affected the whole range of his art. Physiological analogy with mental sickness in modern novels, that character aberration which took the form of "psychosomatic fiction" when Proust, Mann and Joyce treated of artists, was subtly but positively in *dis*harmony with Kafka's desire to grasp everything at its deepest moral center—a desire which caused him to dispense with all the natural and social paraphernalia in which individuals are usually shown in fiction. This economy was part of the fable's simplifying function, for which Kafka, in spite of his complexity, had the strongest feeling. But aside from this point, his simplicity in creating Josephine, the mouse artist, flowed from his refusal to consider the artist as in any sense a biological *freak*.

This attitude is consistent with his procedure in "Metamorphosis," where the hero, Gregor Samsa, does not *begin* by being an insect but *becomes* one. The moral dislocation—the meaning of the "metamorphosis"—is not precipitated by an aberration within the norm of the animal species, but issues from a violent displacement of the animal kind itself: *man* becomes *insect*. Moreover, Gregor becomes an insect peculiarly repugnant to man: a cockroach, a domestic scavenger. The horror of his consequent position in his family, with whom he lives, is made all too plain: if conceived as a bedbug rather than a cockroach (the insect is never named), he has the function of the nonhuman in its most repulsive intimacy with the human. In cross-reference to Josephine, Kafka fertilized his metaphor of cockroach or bedbug with a remote application to the theme of the artist. Not only is the artist traditionally accused of parasitism, but a part of the modern artist's legend is his role as scavenger: the role half seriously, half humorously bestowed on him by the Dadaists and Surrealists. It is one which artists such as Kurt Schwitters have seriously and continuously exploited, usually in the medium of collage, often salvaging waste materials, fragments and disused things to make aesthetic patterns and objects.

However oblique or fragile, the bridge in *Metamorphosis* between the artist as scavenger and the ordinary man as scavenger (that is, "tramp"), is not only evident, but very real. The story of Gregor Samsa remains the most tragic and uncompromising of Kafka's fabulized metaphors of man. The metamorphosed clerk is an analogy, so to speak, not *to be crushed* but *to crush*. Within his fabled environment, Gregor is an outcast individual just as the roach, insidiously present as it is, is an outcast among men. The person of Gregor is an analogy which becomes a metaphor. The tendency of the fable's figure of speech, *animal as man,* is to change into a moral biomorphism: the hidden animal part is behaving in a speculative universe. Kafka emphasized this natural faculty of a form. His animals are concepts of the subhuman aspiring to be human—human, we might say, *because of their aspiration,* just as man "is" divine because of his aspiration to be godlike.

Kafka's mole, dog and ape are more "Aesopian" than Josephine or Gregor. But inveterately Kafka transcends the simple dramatic irony of Aesop's method, which is schematic rather than speculative. Aesop's fables are prototypes of the medieval bestiaries, where the respective characteristics of animal kinds correspond to moral traits in humanity. Mankind as it is, both in virtue and fault, remains the master metaphor of the bestiaries, making the analogy between man and animal fixed and schematic. For Kafka, every species (including man himself) is an anarchic or "open" figure of Man the concept; biologically, man is not the highest mammal in his fables but shares with all planetary kinds the awful predicament of a present dominated by an unknown, usually threatening future.

For Kafka, the master metaphor of race is the abstraction of a monolithic social hierarchy, and within this hierarchy—whose framework becomes clearest in "Josephine the Singer"—he manipulates at will the lower and higher animal impulses that appear fluidly human or animal, insect or mammal. The fabulous horror in Kafka is that *nothing* is fixed. By bringing man as a dramatic actor within the total planetary scheme of unceasing competition and persecution, Kafka both reduces the human stature and aggrandizes it: a paradox which he pinpoints above all in his heroine, Josephine, whose successful profession and pride of caste as artist do not prevent her feeling socially oppressed.

The framework of oppression and persecution, the master-slave and tyrant-victim relationships, is as implicit in Kafka as in Aesop. Yet it remained for the former, as exemplar of the modern spirit, to interpret the entire range of this framework in terms pointing to the broadest tradition of the master-state as opposed to the slave-artist. This happens in "Josephine the Singer" where, as a matter of fact, Kafka uses the fable to compass the legend of Aesop's own trial at Delphi as well as the sum of his (Kafka's) story as an artist. The story of Josephine is basically the story of Man as the Socratic Animal: the supreme philosopher or artist as persecuted by his political peers.

Supremely equipped by his genius, the artist still remains vulnerable to reproaches that may lead to fatal predicaments. Kafka understood it as part of the inalienable duty of an animal-fabulist to depict this sort of preying, too. How vast are the phenomena of the planet's endless, mutual persecution! Not only is there the persecution of the subhuman natural world among its own members, but also the persecution of man by this world—especially by pests and germs of all sorts—this world (for example, insecticides) by man, and man by man. For his part, Aesop took for granted all this preying as a given and inevitable, even unchangeable, condition; preying was preying as man was man. Thus, Aesop's moral universe was an egg whose shell enclosed certain laws of struggle governing the interior but incapable of breaking the egg. In a somewhat different sense, the scientific fabulists, Fabre and Maeterlinck, make the same assumption of a closed human world, employing the same implicit analogy between man and the rest of the animal world as corresponding and parallel, but closed, systems.

Fabre's account of the prodigious erotic effluence of the female Emperor moth, tending toward the esthetic effect of a metaphor, is as lush as certain French narratives of human sexuality.* Kafka aims, with "Josephine," far beyond such a conventional technique of fable, whether involved with science or fantasy. He is monolithic, therefore, not on the level of biological analogy, but on that of metaphysical essence. It is not that a mouse may be "Josephine" or "Mickey," or that a man may "be" a mouse, but that all biological levels as such are artificial: *seeming* rather than *being*. Biology, like morality, is metaphysically homogeneous. So Kafka's fabulous world is not an egg but a broken shell, and observing it in action, we have to ask: *What emerges?*

His metaphoric animals, with one foot in nature and one in metaphysics, keep the door of natural possibility perpetually open. Gregor Samsa's step from the human to the subhuman is really an access to moral anarchy which only a philosophic fabulist such as Plato, whose fabulous "animal" was Socrates, would have understood in ancient times. Ultimately, Kafka's animal heroes are to be seen as evolutionary symbols of human society in the highest philosophic sense. They project a dynamic philosophy of social vision in which the actors wear masks of metaphysical despair over variable animal countenances. All of

* Proust was familiar with it.

them, including the ape, are ironic declassifications of the Superman, the human ideal.

Heroes of Joyce and Mann sporadically don similar masks: one thinks of Bloom rampant in Nighttown. And yet, at their most involving, masks of animal lust or suffering really flatter, with their starkness, devious human motives; so is Stephen Dedalus oddly flattered by the orgy to which he ironically abandons himself as Leopold Bloom's companion. But Dedalus is an artist; Bloom is not. Dedalus, that is to say, is a man of plural masks: to be donned at whim or will. If both men are "sick," they are not so in the same way. Dedalus' reunion with Bloom as his lost father is a dramatized personal motif (i.e., dramatized by Dedalus as well as by Joyce) which a competent artist can control and therefore deprive of its disturbing quality: its role in psychic illness. The morbid grandeur squeezed by Dedalus out of his experience in Nighttown has long been recognized as a normal product of art. Nowadays such exploits, if nicely conducted, tend to be regarded as society's self-therapy, its "catharsis," with the artist directing his own surrogate as the scapegoat.

If not only Dedalus, but also Aschenbach and the Magician shot by Mario, be examples of the artist as scapegoat or sickman, the fact would plausibly follow that Joyce and Mann, by analysing and rationalizing their personal demons in fictitious flesh, successfully exorcised them. Hence, modern clinical theory may argue that artists restore themselves to secular health by confessing the peculiar sickness of their profession. Perhaps the best term for this "sickness" is chameleonism. It is the trait which so much preoccupied Pirandello as the whole world's moral disease: instability. Pirandello was right. It *is* the whole world's disease because the world aspires to a systematic, foolproof rationalism which basically is disowned by the artist. What is a malaise in common humanity therefore becomes the artist's characteristic virtue. Even Joyce, who was decidedly less friendly than Mann to the bourgeois order, capitalized on his "sickness" in the way that satirists have always capitalized on the generic weaknesses of a given society. The artist, governed by his moods, changes the cap of castigation for the sackcloth of sympathy, his own exaltation for his own depression, and ascribes it to "characters." Above all types, and whether feeling "good" or "bad," the artist is the chameleon of human animals.

Presumably a *needed* social critic, the artist or philosopher is such in a special sense and degree when he turns to *himself* as a social type. The trial of Socrates, furthermore, made it evident that this self-criticism, if tragic in outcome, may have a deep social irony. The artist's humiliation may be more than a routine therapy of self-and-society. It may be a divine sacrifice in a supreme ordeal where all participate. As this sacrifice, it becomes a mythic paradigm: the Fable of the Artist-Philosopher. Aesop as well as Socrates is supposed to have lived it literally. As the fable of fabulists, it is the unified framework of all Kafka's fiction. Its moral structure is that of the Trial, the applied power of the law recognized by Socrates and placed by him, in effect, above even that of philosophic inquiry insomuch as the freedom of this inquiry is subject to the law's verdict which, by decree of death, may eliminate the philosopher himself. Kafka's Josephine does not bring on her head the ultimate lethal verdict—but she fails in her struggle and eventually retires from both it and her profession. "She hides herself," says Kafka's narrator, "and does not sing."

From Socrates' times till now, every artist, every public performer, submits himself to the people's "verdict" in the most elementary sense. Josephine, apparently providing "what the public wants" in her artistic capacity, receives a negative verdict on her economic demand of the state. Is she, losing this fight for a revolutionary regard, to be considered another "rejected artist"? Well-known statistics tell us of the rejected artist's compensative mechanisms; in cases of avant-garde artists, pitted against overwhelming tradition, the personal stories are sad enough. But whatever triumphs such artists have won, they inevitably have tended to be based on pride of caste, on conscious community with the limited élite and disdain of the rabble. If the artist also has deep private problems of moral or philosophic sort, it is reasonable for him to suppose that by the same valid token that he is "different" he is also an "artist." Is this not true, in fact, when his differences are defined as *quantitative* rather than *qualitative*?

It is the *sum* of his differences, the cycle of his masks, that makes an artist: he can be a mouse as easily as a man; he can likewise be an angel or an ivory trader. For him, the door of the future is always ajar. . . . Necessarily, the artist's program, like all human programs, has its own hazards. During our time of much criticism of man by man (psychoanalysis being its most widely accepted form), both personal and professional happiness is subject to self-accusation—the more so as the artist exercising the accusation may have compromised to gain popularity, may have degraded his art to advance himself; in brief, his impulse to "change masks" may have sloughed off taste and even intelligence. Then the "purity" of professional pride would be corrupted, the distinction between sickness-as-an-artist and sickness-as-a-human-being would be fatally blurred. Suppose an artist were nominally a "deviate" of some sort, and in the Deweyan sense of instrumentalism, attempted to cure himself of alienation from society's mass by union with it through art? He is in danger of catching in the mirror his own face in the mask which is perhaps the worst of human ills: self-deception. A modern playwright, involved with his own psychic therapy, finds himself in the paradoxical position of being called vulgar because he allows his works to be vulgarly inflected on the stage; hence, at least ostensibly, he has "vulgarized" himself as an artist in order to be "healthier" as an ordinary human being.

In "Josephine the Singer," Kafka makes a supremely decisive comment on the situation of the artist in regard to such controversial values. With masterly simplification, he isolates in the character of his mouse artist that grandeur of professional health which convinces the artist that nothing is wrong with his art, and so nothing wrong, tacitly, with himself: *the wrong lies wholly with the social-economic system.* Josephine does not dream of vulgarizing herself: she directly accuses society of ignorant injustice. Is *this* the worst sin of pride of which the artist may be capable—or is it, as I think Kafka means, a kind of Socratic mask in which the chameleonism of the artist becomes a noble and single obsession—an *aggressive monolithism* of the exempted artistic character?

Kafka's singing mouse is the profoundly inspired animal of art. The law implicitly proposed by her heroism is that the artist be exempted from any contribution to the social good except the pleasure transmitted by his art. This remains the slogan on the figurative picket sign at last discarded by the despondent songstress. For her, the only "sickness" of an artist is the burden of ordinary labor to which he must submit. In effect, then, Josephine turns inside out the supposed correspondence among the *extraordinary,* the *artistic,* and the *sick:* for *her,* the "ordinary," in relation to the artist, *is* the "sick." We may be reminded that Freud's term for our great social sicknesses was "civilization's discontents." The artist's discontent is simply specialized, rarer than another's. The question, of course, remains: *how rare* is his discontent?

That the preciseness of this degree must not be ignored is Josephine's unique inspiration as a character. Fortunately, too, it is part of Kafka's inspiration to have used such rich and ingenious touches to show us Josephine that she suggests a measure of the artist in reality. Such an artist, significantly a masculine sort of woman, was Gertrude Stein, who in her time represented the artist as the acme of individualistic petulance, cabalistic airs and specious imitation of humility. Without either self-accusation or accusation by the state, Miss Stein embodied some of the traits of which Socrates' enemies, though he did not possess those traits, accused him. Some critics accused Miss Stein of unrestrained mystification. What is certain is that her esoteric mysteries, like those of Socrates, were morally in earnest and that, like Socrates himself, she exerted a fascination on the young, apparently to their advantage. Sherwood Anderson's style, and that of Hemingway, would not be the same without her influence, while a composer, Virgil Thomson, understood the "music" of her ideas well enough to turn them into brilliant operas.

Gertrude Stein, most of her life an eidolon of High Bohemia, became popular as an interesting sort of freak. Quite conscious of the kind of theater she created, she wrote a very sensible biography to help along her legend. Although sibylline charm and an expansive warmth of personal presence took the bite out of her unfailing self-assurance, the bulk of her later literary work remains strange and peripheral: an eddying pool beside the mainstream of literature. Both her personality and her art are closer to Josephine's than might seem true at first glance. The fabulizing Kafka makes Josephine's singing stand for the Orphic supremacy of all art as a human medium. If Gertrude Stein's substantial value as a literary artist is not in itself major, I think the propaganda of her style in a time of artistic crisis was of major political importance. She was a partisan of the "common sense" inherent in the art mystery, and if only as an abstract example of the irrational in art, was a considerable force in the twentieth century struggle of the arts against the rationalist attitude.

Still more than symbol and legend connect Gertrude Stein with Josephine; temperament also does. "We are quite unmusical;", says the mouse narrator of Kafka's fable. "how is it that we understand Josephine's singing or, since Josephine denies that, at least think we can understand it." Still more significantly, Josephine "wants not only to be admired, but to be admired in exactly the way she decides. Admiration alone is of no importance to her. And when you sit in front of her, you realize that what she squeaks is not ordinary squeaking." Alter the "squeaking" here to "speaking," and it might well be Alice B. Toklas explaining Gertrude Stein's effect on an audience when she read her work aloud. The paradox was that Miss Stein felt she was so extraordinary because she was more ordinary than the ordinary; she felt, that is to say, that the apparent ambiguity of her speech was the underlying truth of the ordinary.

Josephine becomes as one with Gertrude Stein in believing that, no matter how strange the mystery of an art, it becomes ordinary in giving pleasure—and what is *more ordinary* than giving pleasure? Why did Josephine claim that the Mouse Folk did not "understand" her? Only because it did not agree with her that art was ordinary labor. *This* is the embarrassing ambiguity shed over her success in practicing her art: its doubtful equivalence in material remuneration. In all truth, Kafka does not reveal whether Josephine must contribute ordinary work because artists are poorly remunerated among the Mouse Folk or, while needless economically, ordinary work is forced on her to remind her that after all she is not "divine" but, like all mice, "mousish." The public-minded Josephine is really most Gertrude-Steinish when she transforms the difficult mystery of being an artist (ultimately a *musical* quantity) into the moral position of Socrates at his trial.

The ambiguity of Socrates' situation was that he insisted on the "musical" mysteriousness of all thought, which he usually called the quest for knowledge, but which also and necessarily, as the impartial pursuit of the power to create beautiful things, is art itself. The society that put Socrates before a tribunal resented his philosophic abstraction of mind as the pursuit of a mysterious, elusive knowledge; above all, it resented and feared the proud independence of this position as exempt from political criticism; it abhorred the "divine" pride of the artist-philosopher in his *exclusivenss* as such. No state—to generalize the matter—can ever recognize the Incomprehensible as a value in itself. Since, with the advance of science, human society has increasingly rationalized itself, "incomprehensibility" as lodged alike in art and religion cannot be creative and open in action without exciting, in extreme cases, a fatal suspicion in the public.

We have good reason to believe Socrates was involved with an esoteric sect and thus was committed to unofficial as well as official mysteries of divine belief. In later centuries in the West, art's peculiar nexus with science as well as religion has been its recognition of secret, underground forces. The term "underground" has developed a curious semantic ambivalence, being applicable to all kinds of secret societies, to ancient chthonic forces and to modern political resistance, to natural germination and to the Id of psychoanalysis. The possible maturation and explication of all such forces might be a new god or a new state, a new art or a new science. Thus the Incomprehensible as a principle, as the pursuit of still hidden, still elusive things, must always be contrary to the Law as a fixed and cautiously closed rationalism that must apply to all citizens of the state. Although emergent changes in social structure enforce what are known as economic and political reforms, no less than religious and artistic reforms, the tension between the Comprehensible and the Incomprehensible, the Known and the Unknown, as separate standards of value, can never be relaxed, can never be eliminated from political consciousness. Josephine wanted ordinary bank credit on an exclusive mystery: *that* was what made her uniquely "extraordinary."

Aesop, wielding his professional skill, prophesied that as a slave-artist, he would one day be revenged on the tyrant-state, Delphi, whose oracle condemned him to death. In the person of the humble Beetle, he would be revenged on the majestic Eagle. It is an all too familiar political fable. What was alarming about it at the moment that Aesop told it? It pretended that the power of an eagle might exist behind the mask of a beetle. It implied not only that appearances might be deceptive but also that they might conceal the possibility of a complete "reversal of form": the "strong" might become the "weak" even while still wearing the mask of the strong. . . . If the artist is a seer, he is a seer above all in understanding the nature of the forces of change. His uniqueness is that he understands and strives to understand them, not on the level of the politician, whose interest is in governing material reality, but on his own level, where his interest is in governing symbolic reality. The reason that the artist's intuitions have commonalty with those of the political and economic underdog is that, for both, the future is a realm of aspiration, a realm where possibility is what one seer has called "the truth of masks."

Morally, however, the revenge of the Aesopian Beetles on the Delphian Eagles was a vain boast on the lips of an artist who was less philosophic than Socrates. Neither Josephine nor Socrates prophesy the downfall of their oppressors. It would be a profanation of art or philosophy to make a *political* prediction as such. This humility that is also a great pride has, for Kafka, the quality of insoluble paradox. As the fabulist of Josephine, his subject is the drama of the chameleon artist whose "trial" is endless. If, in her final retirement, Josephine suffers a symbolic death, the inconclusiveness of her story may well throw decisive light on the inconclusiveness of Kafka's novels, *The Castle* and *The Trial*. The truth of masks is itself endless. If the artist may be an ordinary man, the ordinary man may be a public monument.

In Josephine's story, Kafka adds a vast ironic dimension to his testimony on the human condition. Here is the final sentence: "She hides herself and does not sing, but our people, quietly, without visible disappointment, a self-confident mass in perfect equilibrium, so constituted, even though appearances are misleading, that they can only bestow gifts and not receive them, even from Josephine, our people continue on their way." An individual artist dies sooner or later, even the tradition of his art may die; society goes on. At least, society wears the mask of permanence, and *this* Kafka seems to take for final. But Josephine, in a way, remains the animal mask that *does* exclude his other animal masks: the masks of the underdog that are sucked under by the massive sea of ordinariness. Josephine and Socrates are "different" from Gregor Samsa and K.—*they* can understand what happens to them in terms of social logic. It is only that

Socrates and Josephine hold a view of social justice different from the state's. The logic of Socrates' justice, as of Josephine's, is that *the state should transcend itself*. For only by an act of the Mouse Folk as a political body will Josephine the singer ever be truly united with her race. She knows that she can only appeal and rhetoricalize till the moment when Monumental Mousishness, transcending itself, takes her to its living bosom— till, in substance, it recognizes *her* mask too as "ordinary."

III
MARTYRDOM BY INSTINCT

8

THE SACRED FOUNT

When a friend, some years ago, read aloud to me *The Sacred Fount* (my first experience of it), I found it, in R. P. Blackmur's happily Jamesian phrase, "in the degree of its fascination quite ineluctable." But I think Blackmur was signally wrong to term it "the nightmare nexus in James's literary life, between the struggle to portray the integrity of the artist and the struggle to portray, to discover, the integrity of the self." This "nexus" is quite un-Jamesian. James never left a struggle, in his fiction, in the balance, as Blackmur's wording indicates; never established the conditions of a struggle without deciding their issue. This is true, I think, even of *The Sacred Fount*.

When I heard the work read years ago, I thought I was ingenious to interpret its "secret" as a unique sort of flirtation, that between Mrs. Brissenden and the Narrator. They had found, it seemed, a very strange way of making love to each other by speculating on certain strange effects of love on the two partners. Their flirtation ends in harsh disillusion, but so any flirtation might end. I think my solution was superficial: too *simply* ingenious. The truth of *The Sacred Fount* is much deeper and broader in meaning. When I read it recently, the truth as well as the fascination of the work came to me naked and "ineluctable."

The Narrator (who sometimes shall be called, here, HJ) *is* having a flirtation with Mrs. Brissenden (who shall hereafter be called Mrs. Briss even as James calls her). But their flirtation is of a kind never portrayed before James portrayed it. Who is Mrs. Briss? She is no other than James's symbol of his own readers, a reader perhaps of all his previous books, as may literally be the case, who has caught some of their fascination, and takes spark as we see her doing; doing so fiercely, indeed, that she seems to contribute to the "idea" which HJ has started to develop on the train to Newmarch, their mutual destination where a weekend party is being held. I think James's own personal tone never sounded so purely and genuinely through a fictional "I" as in the Narrator of this story. His "idea" is that when two people fall in love and have an affair, they wage (so he tells Mrs. Briss the first day) a kind of battle in which one grows weary, old and witless, the other strong and youthful, acquiring a charm and wit he—or she—never before possessed.

This idea, by all means, is explicit in the novel's own terms. The problem is whether it is true or not, true to the bottom; whether it applies in more than one case (there are two hypothetic cases at Newmarch), and whether even one case can indubitably confirm it. During the weekend, we observe another person, a male "reader," reacting to HJ's idea: the painter, Obert. He too seems to sanction it, appreciate it—his is the esthetic reaction of one *visually* sensitive and perceptive. He underwrites the idea provisionally to the end, though without being thoroughly convinced; it is as though his particular sort of interest exhausts itself before the story is over.

James has provided elsewhere, in his prefaces as well as his stories, much evidence of the "struggle" between ideas of truth as possessed by inspired writers and the capacity of readers to understand such ideas and to be persuaded by them. *The Figure in the Carpet* is based directly on this struggle. One may recall that, in prefatory remarks made about that story, James wrote that the "Neil Faradays . . . Ralph Limberts . . . Hugh Verekers and other such supersubtle fry" did not exist. "But," he proceeded to add, "this is exactly what we mean by the operative irony. It implies and protects the possible other case, the case rich and edifying where the actuality is pretentious and vain." James cannot be competently understood on any score, I think, unless a certain saturative irony is assumed of whatever he wrote, whether creative or critical. In the preface just quoted, he stated the matter urbanely, with a certain detachment. But the Narrator of *The Sacred Fount* is much closer to the heart of the same alternative cases. At his most perilous moment, he informs the reader: "I was there to save my priceless pearl of an inquiry and to harden, to that end, my heart." The point is that "the case rich and edifying" is being directly attacked by "the actuality pretentious and vain"; that is, in Mrs. Briss's mouth, the former is being turned into the latter.

On the last night of the weekend, the Narrator and his female confidante have turned up, after everybody else has retired, to have it out as to whether his "idea" is true. After seeming to go along with it, after in fact helping to advance it, she claims to have made the dramatic discovery that it is all a myth. Gilbert Long, whose new personality seems to have proclaimed him the profiting partner of a loving pair whose female element is speculative, is (Mrs. Briss says) the fool he always was. Therefore, as the amatory "case rich and edifying" he is unmasked as one "pretentious and vain." Whatever the fictionizing Narrator has seen in the social life at Newmarch he has "read into it." For if Long is still a fool, at bottom, the fact demolishes the Narrator's whole theory of his love affair with May Server, the lady first suggested by Mrs. Briss as the sacrificing and bereft partner. Meanwhile, the Narrator seems to have confirmed this identification by observing and conversing with Mrs. Server.

The rudimentary aspect of James's own creative method is no mystery. He himself said that he was always on the alert for interesting motifs, shreds of anecdote which caught his mental ear, things dropped at the dinner table or anywhere else. Out of such a rumored "actuality" he might well weave one of his cases "rich and edifying." But here, inevitably evoked, is a world-wide problem among James's readers: Is anyone in the human race quite so subtle and intelligent as Henry James, in famous instances, makes out his characters to be? Does he not, in general, exaggerate about his *dramatis personae*? Does he not contend that lovers experience nuances of consciousness, about choice and scruple, such as it seems most unlikely that real people ever experience? James, beyond doubt, was so demonic a connoisseur of human relations that, in most readers of his work, a fear is raised, however hypnotic his effects, that he is flattering the race's intelligence. His works, therefore, lack a core of truth—that core of truth, at least, associated with the idea of the novel as a representation of actual society.

For his part, evidently, James always tried to believe in that "possible other case" that would look neither pretentious nor vain. His achievement ought to be defined, I think, as a very special reconstitution of the literary romance. The Romance had come down to his time as a transparent fiction written, acted or sung as entertainment (Mozart's operas are first-rate examples), and it was supposed to portray certain extreme emotions and situations that had existed in the past, but not the present, or existed in the present only as "motifs"; that is, they might be conceived, these emotions and situations, as "carrying one away" but only to a land of dream, of aesthetic illusion, not to real places or to the people who lived in them.

The chief content of the traditional Romance is the effects of emotion raised to the level of passion. Its function was therefore simple: its material being emotion and its method a stimulation of emotion to the point of madness, it used the crude calendar emotions of the race for theatrical indulgence, massive extracurricular "purges." But this situation, during the nineteenth century, was changed by a series of innovative intellectuals in all countries of the West: the Age of Reason had earned its fictional heirs, and Balzac's and Dickens' romantic caricatures of society were changed into studies of human psychology and close observation of manners and situations.

Two women novelists of England who attracted James's own qualified admiration, Jane Austen and George Eliot, had established a "tone" as realists and explorers of the moral situation. Henry James could understand them better than he did the Naturalist school of France, where he found great clusters of physical facts substituted for the mental operation he so much admired—and of which *he* became the greatest explorer. But James decided that the nineteenth-century novel, even as he endorsed it, was far too modest before the self-evident possibilities of the creative medium of fiction. He replaced the moral situation of the calendar emotions—love, hate, jealousy, envy, pride, whatever you like—with the moral situation of the creative intelligence as a free agent; this is one reason that his *dramatis personae* are so often artists themselves: those with professional creative responsibilities.

I believe it was André Gide who reproached James with this: replacing the emotions with the intelligence. But here Gide's own creative intelligence failed him. As a new romancer, James specifically replaced the *passion* of the *emotions* with the *passion* of the *intelligence*. This, however, was not a schism in human situations, but a reorganization. It was fully as *logical* a thing to do as to replace the *romantic* situation of the emotions with the *moral* situation of the emotions. James's replacement may be less "realistic," but for that reason it is not necessarily the less truthful; in fact, it consciously aimed at a truth greater than realism. His moral premise, infallibly, was that intelligence is, or at least can be, compact with all that is passionate; that is, the intelligence may be a passion in its own right, and thus a creative qualifier of all other passions; primarily, in James's work, the passion of love. Why should the intelligence, as a free and creative agent, be confined to the professional interpreters of life—the "Hugh Verekers"? It is James's tribute to the faculty of the human intelligence that he shows it revitalizing existence, giving human passion a rebirth on a higher level.

It is his special strategy that he associates youth with the "rebirth" of intellectual vitality. All of his heroines whom he sets on pedestals are young; even their deaths—like those of Daisy Miller and Milly Theale—are early so that the magic of rebirth can be worked on others (if simply on the reader). Daisy is a sketch for Milly: the missed biological chance turned into the succinct biological triumph; Milly dies to save both Densher and his confederate, Kate Croy, who are in love but have misused their intelligence. Ideally, to James, the passion of love stimulates the intelligence rather than drugs or perverts it. Milly is a symbol of the dawning *passion* of the intelligence that transmutes, at the very end, Kate's and Densher's love.

The "idea" of the Narrator of *The Sacred Fount* therefore relates closely to other works of James: the passion of love is capable of a supreme, even impersonal, sacrifice by one partner for the other's benefit, whether or not it be established that the sacrifice or its acceptance be conscious: its *product,* however, is always present by signs, and the signs are the charms of intelligence and youth, which HJ (the Narrator) thinks of as going hand in hand. Gilbert Long *looks better* because, according to the Narrator's "idea," he has absorbed all the intelligence of an unidentified partner who is to be sought among the guests at Newmarch. Mrs. Briss herself has acquired youthful charm and vitality because she has drained her husband, Guy, of his—and Guy's own looks and manner support the assumption. Long's new wit, new personality, also support the assumption until Mrs. Briss believes she discovers, in a short tête-à-tête with him, that he is really the dull, vacuous person he always was.

Perhaps we should pause to ask if HJ's idea is not, really, a far-fetched one: a romantic misapplication of Faustian rebirth to actual life. Mrs. Briss's final judgment, in fact, seems to represent this viewpoint. But to believe in the transmuting nature of a passion is to believe in a kind of magic. That James played with the idea of the existence of supernatural forces as such is attested by many of his stories and much of his language. Is it so far-fetched to believe that love exalts and even *converts*? James wanted, as *The Sacred Fount* above all his works is evident, that it convert to intelligence. In Faust as a hero, there is a rebirth of all the faculties, even if the sexual passion is his prime motivation. To attain this rebirth, he had to call up the aid of the Devil. But the Devil is simply a figure of romantic mythology. James's stories entertain devils of his own invention—if they are not always so sinister or conspicuously a "devil" as the ghost at Bly.

In the main, James was not a romantic mythologist, however, but a student of life as it was lived; or more accurately, perhaps, as it should be lived. For this purpose, the intelligence of his *personae* was a "devil" of passion. In the intelligence, James discerned no creative limits; thus, in his works, it tends to have a limitlessness that makes it a romantic passion on the grand scale. *The Sacred Fount's* Narrator is simply another professional incarnation of this "devil," but one to whom, for reasons of his own, James decided not to give an unambiguous triumph; anyway, not without first taking it out of his hide. Mrs. Briss is the whip. The whole structure of his theory, the idea which he himself calls his "palace of thought," depends on the identification of Gilbert Long's partner: one of the female guests (of whom two are candidates) who will fit the pattern. But on Mrs. Briss's fatal discovery that Long is the same dreary fool, the ground is yanked from under the feet of the theory.

As Mrs. Briss (even in the Narrator's eyes) is superbly sure of herself, we could conclude from the end of the story that the theory has been a snare and a delusion. But this would be to take James "straight" in a way that he never meant to be taken straight. The final long scene between HJ and Mrs. Briss is obviously a miracle of virtuosity. Between the simplest, most direct conversational sentences imaginable, James interlards (in the form of an accompanying narrative of HJ's thoughts) the most extravagantly nuanced prose. Something far more important than the destruction of his theory is taking place, and this is nothing but, as I suggested at the beginning, that strange perennial duel James had with his readers (so significantly his *female* readers!) here fictitiously transposed into its social setting.

As James was so immensely scrupulous in conversation, and often fenced with distinguished men and women admirers far more qualified on their own grounds than Mrs. Briss, the issue of the crucial "case rich and edifying" against that "actuality pretentious and vain" could never be brought into final dramatic focus. But in *The Sacred Fount,* James very precisely and deliberately (and, I think, movingly) did bring it into focus, and so the irony, as usual, is far closer to the surface than his self-bewildered readers would imagine.

Naturally, few unconvinced "readers" had had the courage—even if they had had the impulse—to be so direct, so bluntly pitiless, to James's face as Mrs. Briss is to the Narrator's face. Yet we know, if only from incidents related by others, that James must have suffered much from "Brissian" wounds dealt far more tactfully. Mrs. Briss displays an unsheathed sword and deploys it like a veteran; finally, when meeting stiff resistance, she tells him that he is "crazy." James is surely relating in this scene the sense of his emotional violation from a vast accumulation of smaller but very real wounds from many a Mrs. Humphry Ward and Edith Wharton, who were never sufficiently incensed to risk calling him "crazy." This scene in *The Sacred Fount* is a Laokoön of the drawing room taken from many models of which he himself was the suffering hero.*

I find the scene, therefore, full of an exquisitely affecting and expressive pathos, and all the more so because it is an anticlimax for the growth of that fond intimacy between himself and Mrs. Briss which I have called a "flirtation." Indeed, it may be the very model of James's actual "literary flirtations" with his distinguished women readers. How romantic and how extravagant, then, is Mrs. Briss's savage "intelligence." Each new blow becomes harder; one feels them in poor HJ's midriff. The Mrs. Briss of fiction, if not the Mrs. Briss of life, is trying for a knockout. Technically too she may achieve one. But the Narrator, as James's *persona,* does not take it, I think, lying down. After all, James was an indefatigable recoverer of his own dignity and his magical salve was always the ultimate refinements of irony. These are the Narrator's closing sentences and the story's end (he refers, of course, to Mrs. Briss, who has left him, at last, like an army under banners): "I should certainly never again, on the spot, quite hang together, even though it wasn't really that I hadn't three times her method. What I too fatally lacked was her tone." The "three times her method" is typically decisive Jamesian plain speaking. And as for that "on the spot," its irony is charged with a magnificence. This is why I think that *The Sacred Fount* is Henry James's deep, personal *gloire,* not his "nightmare nexus," as a writer.

I think that James was never unsure of his private integrity as a self, or of its relation to his integrity as an artist. The scene of the struggle was always the objective relation of his art, and thus himself as an artist, to society, to his readers. It is well known that he yearned to be a "popular author," to have a large public. But, I think, this was partly due to the fact that he never quite converted even his élite readers, his fellow professionals, and

* See Ford Madox Ford's very funny "pastoral" anecdote confirming this —Simon Nowell-Smith, ed., *The Legend of the Master,* (London: Constable, 1947), pp. 43–44.

thus forlornly wished for quantity as a partial substitute for quality. He was always becoming entwined in drawing-room Laokoöns; ostensibly, many literate observers, who have recorded their impressions, took it that James was entwining himself with his own conversational prose; however charmed, these observers found it, at times, difficult to follow and listened, amazed, before the spectacle of the "struggle." What few or none realized was that *they* were part of the struggle, James was only its hero.

And what was it that James, the prose-entwined, was struggling *against*? What, indeed, but Mrs. Briss's *tone*—which was actually, in the society through which he moved, as much the vibrating, stubborn silence of his listeners as anything they said? However, at least once, James actually met with a "savage" much more dangerous than Mrs. Briss. The incident was related by Percy Lubbock and concerned a salon personality named Rhoda Broughton, who, says Lubbock, was "liked" by James "for being what she was, so authentic a block of character, a type so unqualified; and again he recoiled, he held up his hands in a horror of her barbarism—her slapdash cut-and-thrust at the questions and the issues that require so many a discrimination for any fitting exploration of whatever may be discernible as their last significance of implication. Rhoda came slashing into the argument as though it could be hacked in two, right and left, and a straight way laid open down the middle." Lubbock is describing a particular case from the chance, spontaneous warfare of the drawing room, and his rather self-conscious effort to justify James's elaboration by casually parodying it is, in fact, an image, if a crude one, of the way James, in *The Sacred Fount,* counterposes his elaborately shaded analysis with the extreme simplicity of the Narrator's and Mrs. Briss's conversational give-and-take. But James's aim at ultra-simplicity in dialogue (its syntax being quite unparalleled in articulate fiction) has consistently been scouted by critics for the sake of his complex sentences of analysis. The last scene in *The Sacred Fount* is a perfect example of his inveterate aim: to charge the simplest words in the language, and the shortest sentences, with the whole world of meaning. His idea was that men and women, in ordinary conversation, might accomplish the elegance of an extremely simple "style." This bond is one which his characters tend to establish with each other and it is the bond which HJ holds with Mrs. Briss.

But it is not the one Henry James held with Miss Broughton. The specific exchange described by Percy Lubbock takes place when James begins a typically sinuous observation on Shakespeare, eventually coming to the epithet, "a lout from Stratford." * According to Lubbock, he hardly gets another word out before Miss Broughton exclaims, "A lout!—me divine William a lout?" Expostulating, but polite, James starts back, again and again, at the "lout," but Miss Broughton's cries interrupt him. She will not permit "me beloved Jamie" to call "Shakespeare a lout!" In brief, apparently, she never permits James to finish his thought. At last, it seems, he dropped the matter. But one can imagine what, at the moment anyway, James thought of *her* tone!

I fancy that James never quite recovered from what he may well have regarded as the root of the matter, of which Broughtonism was only the most violent, most shamelessly crude and open form. Simply by equating a Rhoda Broughton with a Mrs. Humphry Ward, he would logically have arrived at a Mrs. Briss. I see no reason to believe that this is not what exactly he did do. There would have been no point, or fun, to have drawn the portrait of a Rhoda Broughton as his arch opponent. To make it all real, to make it significant and interesting, he had to have a true collaborator, someone on his own level of literacy, who could make the game worth playing; someone who did not hate "talk" so much as to destroy it; in other words, he had to have someone who took literature with something like his own seriousness. Hence: Mrs. Briss. She had to have enough charm, enough presence and "authority," to overcome the deep irritations he had

---

* Nowell-Smith, pp. 40–41.

suffered in society. To actually prove that the game was worth playing, however, he had to make the Narrator as vulnerable, in his "palace of thought," as Henry James was in his intellectual amour-propre. It is a sublimely comic tolerance that HJ has for the aggressive Mrs. Briss and a sublimely comic pity that he has for the Narrator. But I do not think that this prevents our perceiving the exact nature of Mrs. Briss's position, as the lady herself is allowed to define and isolate it. It is simply that vulgar positivism which consistently set its face against all the finest-spun revelations of James's fiction. A consideration of the nature of the *Narrator's* position should show what the quarrel is really about.

The Narrator's position *is* "the sacred fount." And it was the new Romanticism of James: the premise, I think, on which the verisimilitude of his stories was always based. The Narrator's position is that his "idea" is not necessarily true in this or that case, discoverable at some house party, but that it is possible to the human imagination, and that being so, its realization in some actual love affair is also possible. I have already referred to the idea of magic involved with this conception of what may be called an "operative irony" in cases of love. If the exchange of vital energy that is visualized between partners of a love affair by the Narrator of *The Sacred Fount* is, indeed, possible, I don't think it takes only a naïve credulousness to ratify it. Of course, Mrs. Briss, finally, shakes off her naïve credulousness, and as it were "comes to her senses"; so she thinks, and asseverates. This was James's type-experience with élite readers who seemed about to go the whole distance with him, and then turned on him with a challenge—based, often, on a common sense criticism of his extravagance.

James saw this challenge—and I think he was right—as the failure of belief in the unlimited powers of the intelligence as a passion. One feature of the great romantic passions of love is death. This romantic "feature" appears in the Narrator's idea as, not the sacrifice of life itself, in either partner, but the sacrifice of one partner's vital energy to the other. The one word to cover this sort of energy properly, in terms of the human personality, is that "intelligence" which illuminates the subject and dazzles others. It is, as it were, a pure gift, and is an intellectually dynamic conception of the act of physical conjugation. In the eyes of HJ as the Narrator, it forms an energy as comprehensive and basic as Faust's magically recovered youth, Freud's libido and Don Juan's unstintingly dispensed sex. This is perfectly coherent. It is "the sacred fount."

The Narrator, with a sort of passion, wishes to communicate this same subtle gift, this "sex" which operates through the intelligence, to Mrs. Briss. At first she seems to accept it, and eagerly, but then she refuses it; moreover, she denounces its intention. HJ, therefore, is a sort of rejected lover, but as such, he is still, leaving Newmarch in an odor of defeat, intact. This story curve, to be gathered from the present work abstractly, is, actually, explicitly the situation in *The Figure in the Carpet,* where a lady makes a certain literary critic's solution of the great novelist Hugh Vereker's creative "secret" the price of her consent to marriage; on the wedding night, the secret supposedly is communicated by the critic to his bride, who herself is a novelist. Then the bridegroom dies (symbolically?) in an accident.

The Sacred Fount might well be a parable of Henry James's own erotic experience: a mighty speculation-in-little about the terms on which he has escaped giving himself in love, which might be the same as those on which he has been able to retain his belief in the unlimited powers of love *as intelligence.* Is there not a curious sense of identification between the Narrator and May Server in his moving portrait of her during their evening colloquy, when everything points to her identity as Gilbert Long's lover who has made him the supreme gift of her vitality? James might say: "There, but for the grace of literature, go I."

Many fictional motifs of James attest the dangers of so potent a literary imagination as his, especially as it touches upon supernatural powers. James repeatedly shows us persons possessed by supernatural visions. It is with the ultimate of gentle tact, and tactic, that he declines, too, ever to admit that these persons are hallucinated. The great case in point, of course, is that of the governess in *The Turn of the Screw*. Seemingly, and ultimately, James wished to leave the "reality" of the ghosts at Bly a problem. But it is noticeable that, all in all, the "evil" there is itself an unsolved problem. This was because evil, to James, was never, in a final sense, *the* problem. The struggle at Bly, like the struggle at Newmarch, is not one between good and evil. Gilbert Long would not be evil to accept May Server's supreme gift any more than she would have been evil to make it. It would simply occur, this exchange, as the result of a great natural dialectic. Like tragedy itself, this dialectic would absorb good and evil into the immense turn of its fatal wheel. But Mrs. Briss is no longer in the groove of her opponent's "idea." This is plain when, pushed beyond her endurance by the Narrator's plaintive protests, she strikes out with: "Don't you sometimes see horrors?"

Here is the "turn of the screw" in *The Sacred Fount*. It— "horrors"—is what the governess in the other story thinks her little charges, Miles and Flora, have seen and learned. The Narrator, who has been doing his best to get Mrs. Briss in deeper, counters:

> "People catch me in the act?"
> "They certainly think you critical."
> "And is criticism the vision of horrors?"
> She couldn't quite be sure where I was taking her. "It isn't, perhaps, so much that you see them—"
> I started. "As that I perpetrate them?"
> She was sure now, however, and wouldn't have it, for she was serious. "Dear no—you don't perpetrate anything. Perhaps it would be better if you did!" she tossed off with an odd laugh. "But —always by people's idea—you like them."
> I followed. "Horrors?"
> "Well, you don't—"
> "Yes—?"

But she couldn't be hurried now. "You take them too much for what they are. You don't seem to want—"

"To come down on them strong? Oh, but I often do!"

"So much the better then."

"Though I do like—whether for that or not," I hastened to confess, "to look them first well in the face."

Our eyes met, with this, for a minute, but she made nothing of that. "When they *have* no face, then, you can't do it." *

This slice of the agonic dialogue contains—besides erotic innuendoes of the flirtation going on—a gloss to the psychology of things at Bly. It is a veritable nest of Jamesian ambiguity and serves as another token of the author's claim of an "in-law" relation among his works. Two stories are locked together by the testimonies of witnesses with similarly prejudiced psychology. We have only the governess's word that Miles dies from the sight of his former tutor's ghost. He could have died from being scared to death by *her*. His very death, I have always felt, has a curious air of being nonessential—nonessential, I mean, to the basic idea James had there. Miles's death is required by the overt melodramatic structure. But this, like all "overt" structures in James, is merely one element of the total irony.

Mrs. Briss's triumph and the Narrator's humiliation are just as "technical" as the governess's victory over Miles. The effect of the imaginative energy in the one case is simply reversed in the other. Instead of being converted by it, Mrs. Briss (unlike Miles) comes out and wipes up the floor with it. But we know, as James wants us to know, that somehow the "face," the vital energy, the towering and even torrential *intelligence,* is there. Does it kill or does it resuscitate? Or does it merely anger and alienate? It may die in its own, beneficent blood. But it can come out—at Newmarch, at Bly, amid the manners of France, with clairvoyant intentness, in Maisie Farange—full blast. This, I think, is the unavoidable lesson of the master: the "sacred fount" is that bap-

* *The Sacred Fount* (New York: Grove Press, 1953), pp. 298–299.

tismal source that converts "the actuality pretentious and vain" into "the case rich and edifying." We can take it that James regarded his artist-heroes as surrogates for himself and that he consistently, and conspicuously, inquired into the true nature of their ordeals. The artist is one who sacrifices his life to the idea of being utterly good; that is, *utterly comprehensive.* If he does not succeed he is still a fountain and still sacred.

9

THE FIGURE IN THE CARPET

The ambiguous relation between lie and truth, fiction and reality, is one which has fascinated modern writers, notably Gide and Mann, and has a very vital, very prominent place in the novels and stories of Henry James, who was a forerunner in this type of ambiguity. Inevitably, as James was perhaps the first novelist to reveal, the distinction between, and identification of, fiction and reality must extend to a judgment of the artist's quality as inventor rather than reporter. According to Coleridge, who distinguished between fancy and imagination in trying to formulate the "truth" of artistic invention, *fancy* was transparent fiction and *imagination* a higher sort of truth. Yet the rise of scientific inquiry and modes of thought in the nineteenth century (reflected

by the growth of psychology as a separate science) tended steadily
to bring into focus a contradiction between "fact" and "fiction";
and so, in the twentieth century, Mann's "Mario and the Magician" finally passed a social judgment on the artist as a kind of
charlatan, a creator of illusions without substance. Henry James
would have found such a social judgment vulgar and incomprehensible. For everything in his writings points to his belief in the
ethically ideal role of the artist as inventor. James's deep sense of
reality was devoted to showing how human beings, such as they
are, can morally perfect themselves by guiding and disciplining
their passions with the intelligence. Even if we could not infer
this much from his fictional treatment of human beings in general, we have conclusive testimony from his fictional portraits of
artists and writers themselves.

If James's works are ambiguous, if they are full of subtle
irony, it is not because their author was confused, superficially
ornate, or quibbling—that is the false tradition of James's ambiguity. He knew how hard really valuable knowledge, really
competent morality was to come by, and how heavily the social
dice are loaded against human virtue. Hence the struggle for virtue, for the "moral sense," is full of traps, temptations and dis-
guises; above all, the trap of *cheap* virtue and a *facile* moral
sense. Yet James complimented the race by assuming that its
highest types were people naturally endowed with and committed
to a "moral sense." Artists he visualized as higher beings, who
saw this effort to attain truth and reality as an unrelenting moral
struggle between the individual and the world, and whose deepest
impulse was to devote themselves monastically to revealing the
principles and conditions of the unceasing struggle. His very
early story, "The Madonna of the Future," about a painter who
idealized the Madonna so much that he could never get around
to finishing his painting of Her, warns against too much esthetic
metaphysics, but in contrast, the same story's portrait of the vulgar statuette maker, whose simian imitations of men and women
are made overnight and earn him instant fame and money, leaves

no doubt as to which path of "truth" James considered the more honorable. Moreover, though he himself learned to practice his art copiously, he never changed his mind about inventing as against reporting or "imitating." For in his preface to the volume of his collected works containing "The Figure in the Carpet," he admits that his esthetic heroes, the "Neil Faradays . . . Ralph Limberts . . . Hugh Verekers and other such supersubtle fry" do not exist. "But," he adds, "this is exactly what we mean by operative irony. It implies and projects the possible other case, the case rich and edifying where the actuality is pretentious and vain."

One is tempted to think that James had reached the point where the neglect of the large reading public pushed him to the extreme of bitterness, and that when he said a Hugh Vereker did not really exist he was exercising, and with a special irony, a speaker's sovereign privilege to except himself from his explicit judgments of the general. Long before, James had dedicated his literary life to being "supersubtle," and as for "the figure in the carpet," there is ample reason to suppose that (as we constantly find from his pained reaction in documented conversations) what he thought he had made beautifully visible on the surface of his fiction lay concealed from the general gaze as a "figure in the carpet." It was something to be divined magically as the critic, George Corvick, divines the hidden organic pattern of all Hugh Vereker's novels. Considering everything, it would not be in the least surprising if "The Figure in the Carpet" did not contain a kind of wish fulfillment in James, who was fancifully imagining the method by which some future critic, merely by understanding the basically "ideal" nature of his fiction, would be discovering what has traditionally become James's "figure in the carpet" —his famous ambiguity.

In arriving at the conclusions set forth in this essay, I was struck by the degree to which, taking the whole view of James's fictional canon, his stories of artists and writers are involved with the same theme, the morality of love, courtship, and marriage, as

are most of his other works. In offering the concept of the child
as "the figure" of James's carpet, I refer to that symbolic off-
spring of the artist, his fictive progeny, as much as to the actual
children who appear in his stories. My direct authority for this is
in the Prefaces, where James not only mentions an "in-law" relation among his works but also, in his preface to the volume containing *The Aspern Papers* and *The Turn of the Screw,* speaks of
"fitting . . . all my small children of fancy with their progeni-
tors, and all my reproductive unions with their inevitable fruit."
James was not a casual stylist, and it is needless to insist that in
visualizing his works as a race of beings, with an intrinsic genealogy, he was expressing the nature of his feelings about them as
products of his marriage with the Muse. The special aspect of
these feelings which must concern us, in the light of the "figure"
which is my subject, is James's actual and personal view of marriage for an artist, for just preceding "The Figure in the Carpet"
in the same volume of the collected works, is "The Lesson of
the Master," and here James makes his clearest fictional statement about the undesirability of the artist's having any but the
Muse for wife or any but the work of art for child. James's own
biological metaphor is our authority for assuming that an important family relationship exists between these two stories placed
next to one another. We must never fail to consider James's
prodigious urbanity and the extreme shyness with which he made
personal statements. Part of the "operative irony," inevitably,
was the freedom of speaking through the first person of his many
narrators, Regarding what he terms "the all-ingenious 'Figure in
the Carpet,' " he also writes in the preface: "All I can at this
point say is that if ever I was aware of ground and matter for a
significant fable, I was aware of them in that connection." So
much for those who would claim that James's somewhat "horsy"
humor in this story indicates that it is a bagatelle.

"The Lesson of the Master" is a typical exercise in the author's
ambiguity and irony. The novelist, St. George, is a master past
his prime and worshiped by a young apprentice, Paul Overt,

who in the story's course becomes enamored of a Miss Fancourt. Overt hopes to wear the mantle discarded by St. George and is rudely surprised when St. George, whose first wife has died, precipitately marries Miss Fancourt. The master then points to his lesson: the artist should never marry and he has elected this way to demonstrate it to his protegé. Part of the irony is that Overt has been robbed of marital happiness for the mere prospect of success as an artist. But this is a sign of James's own idealistic faith. Here we must participate with him in the fervor of artistic idealism as a faith rather than as a demonstrated fact, just as we have to take the grand existence of Vereker's "figure" on faith since it is never explained to the story's narrator and thus he never tells it to us. However, the point of the story *is* its grand existence and the equally grand effect its discovery by the critic has on his own sexual destiny.

Name symbolism is one clue to the nature of Vereker's "figure," however, and James seems to have paved the way for using it by name symbols in "The Lesson of the Master." St. George is also the name of a legendary knight who slew a dragon. Therefore the novelist St. George slays the dragon of marriage standing between Paul Overt and fame—standing, as it were, between Overt and his *overt* fame, since at this point the younger writer's fame is merely potential. The irony is ambiguous because St. George has actually prized his dead wife, who, he claims, was "everything in life to him." Yet, since paradoxically the marital happiness she gave him worked the opposite way for his art, he has concluded that such happiness should be sacrificed for the flowering of genius, which tacitly represents a higher happiness than love or marriage. So he expressly tells Overt.

That Overt might *not* have the caliber of a genius (that he might not be the novelist's "*St.* Paul" and triumph with the master's gospel), that St. George himself might *not* be sincere but simply desirous of Miss Fancourt as his next wife—these are things James leaves cavalierly, rather than ambiguously, to the everyday world of reality. The subtlety is: we must have knightly faith in virtue and ideals and tacit faith in St. George's devotion and judgment inspired by artistic mastery. Moreover, St. George *is* doing something concrete in his ironic lesson: he is at least showing Overt that Miss Fancourt is more attracted to past-mastery (St. George's) than to speculative mastery (Overt's), a fact placing in question her own faith in love itself as an ideal.

James's fusion of humor and satiric irony with idealism and the deepest moral seriousness is a unique characteristic, yet one which is relatively difficult and has often, perhaps, thrown his readers off the track of the hard irreducible meaning, the indissoluble *truth,* of his fictions. James made his meanings "hard" because to that end he believed he was being lifelike, more so than a thousand "imitators" of life. Life itself, James is always saying implicitly, is not easy, and above all not easy to serious and intelligent beings; to pretend that it *is* is simply the biggest lie anyone could possibly invent. But that his work constantly strove toward truth and communication, that he always consciously put his fictional message *on the surface,* seems plain from the words in the next story, "The Figure in the Carpet," placed in the mouth of another ambitious writer's fiancée. This lady was won by a feat which we are enjoined by a dozen allusions to take as one of knightly prowess: the feat of valor by which gentlemen in the Tournament of Love and medieval romances proved crucially worthy of their chosen ladies. James sounds a note of high culture when Gwendolyn Erme says of her fiancé Corvick's final victory in solving the "figure" in Vereker's "carpet": "Now that it was there it seemed to grow and grow before him. . . . When it came out it came out, was there with a splendor that made you ashamed; and there hadn't been, save in the bottomless vulgarity of the age, with everyone tasteless and tainted, the smallest reason why it should have been overlooked." Miss Erme had made Corvick's success the price of her hand.

One of the easiest accusations against James is lured into the focus here: the charge that, in all his characters' moralizing and hesitation, and the idealistic cast their sexuality often takes, he failed to appreciate the sexual passion for what it is worth, and that his personal poverty of sexual experience (to all appearances) is to be held responsible. The just answer must be that sexual passion has no true human existence until it is given a *definite* worth, and that the omission to assess it truly, to give it shape and proportion in relation to the conduct of life as a whole, is perhaps the most fatal error an individual can make. James, it seems to me, held this belief as securely—if with a very divergent temperamental emphasis—as Freud did. Sexual attraction is his constant theme, and if he very seldom wrote of it sensually or sensuously, he always wrote of it poetically, intelligently, and concretely. Sex is as much a moral passion in his writings as anything else is; in fact, it is the chief moral passion there. Primary evidence of this is available from "The Beast in the Jungle," where a love affair comes to nothing and a woman's attraction for a man remains meaningless as he cannot experience the spring of "the beast in the jungle" which is passion, though at last he senses its presence and imagines its spring. Part of all knowledge is intuitive and James knew the sexual passion by consummate intuition. Perhaps his own personal detachment from it enabled him to observe it so minutely in the manners of others. In *What Maisie Knew,* for example, we never doubt the lower kind of "beastliness" in the passion of most of the frivolous adults, any more than we doubt, in *The Tragic Muse,* the erotic drive of the actress-heroine as being of the higher kind. James's craftsmanlike concern for symmetry and his deeply situated consistency caused him to repeat certain key images. One of these repetitions occurs in "The Figure" when Miss Erme, carried away by Corvick's spectacular means of winning her, communicates it thus to the story's narrator: ". . . it's the thing itself, let severely alone for six months, that has sprung on him like a tigress out of the jungle." The cross reference to the other story tells us something of the nature of the "figure" Corvick has divined as well as his own authentic relation to it: his passion for Gwendolyn has lifted his intuition to the heights.

Necessarily suggestive, too, is the relation between a tigress, a "beast in the jungle," and a dragon, the beast which, legend says, a true and loving knight had to slay to win the hand of his lady or to protect her virtue. Does not St. George slay Paul Overt's dragon for him and win a lady in marriage because her marriage to Overt, he thinks, would end in disaster to Overt's genius?— and does the same act not insure the virtue of Overt's Muse? James's irony has great elegance, for in the subsequent story the lady elects the "dragon" her suitor is to "slay." It is nothing but Hugh Vereker's literary "figure," a secret which has eluded all the novelist's reviewers and commentators till Corvick comes along. The truth is that Gwendolyn Erme, the courted lady, is herself a novelist, and her excitement may be due in part to her anticipation that so profound a secret of creative literature might improve her own fiction—though nothing so bald is ever said by her or anyone else in the story. Let us call it part of the "operative irony." James's high tone about the matter, despite his satiric quips in passing, is sustained. In the end, the secret won by Corvick's intellectual sweat is presumably communicated to his wife on their wedding night, though sadly an accident immediately puts an end to the bridegroom's life. However, the "figure's" sacrosanct value is preserved by token of the Widow Corvick's habit of referring to it as her own transcendent "life." This is the more significant in respect to the present purpose because she cannot bear Corvick a child, though later she marries another critic, to whom she bears two children. Obviously the "life" given her by Corvick's critical genius was not physical progeny but intellectual or spiritual progeny, that of literary creation. In this light, a clue transmitted by Vereker to Corvick is highly tendentious: "What I contend that no one has ever mentioned in my work is the organ of life." More name symbolism becomes persuasive here. While Gwendolyn Erme's first book is called *Deep Down* and reviewed in a magazine called *The Middle,* the book she writes following her marriage to Corvick is called *Overmastered.* She too has received "the lesson of the master."

If I have enumerated the essentials of a clear pattern, as I think I have, it remains to be noticed why James wrote the story in the way he did, through a narrator whose main virtue is curiosity and a restrained envy of his betters (the persons of the story), and why there should be all the *mystery* . . . why a "concealed" pattern of fiction should be so important and why in this case, even as elucidated here, it should remain an abstract idea or "ideal." At the end, the narrator feels out Drayton Deane, Gwendolyn's second critic-husband, to whom the whole existence of the secret, and its function in the life of his predecessor, comes as an embarrassing surprise: Gwendolyn has kept it to herself! James's high comedy flowers perfectly when the narrator anticlimactically observes of Deane: "The poor man's state is almost my consolation; there are really moments when I feel it to be quite my revenge." Deane, narrator, reader—all are "technically" frustrated.

The comedy has been one of stupidity as well as wit. Yet even the narrator's naïveté has gotten onto the ritual nature of the proceedings by noticing just what *we* might notice: part of Corvick's gifted wit consists in talent for puns. That James, for his part, should let us have the heart of the story (i.e., the "figure") through punning, among other devices, shows the debonair quality of his urbanity as an intellectual artist: "Vera incessu patuit dea!" writes Corvick to his Gwendolyn while engaged on the great mission away from home, and the narrator, noting the sentence (he is in Gwendolyn's confidence at this stage), deliberately puns on the "dea" as "dear" in addressing her; in other words: dear Gwendolyn, dear truth, dear goddess. Both truth and love are dear because dearly bought by wisdom. Vereker's own name looks like a combination of *veritas* (truth) and *eureka,* and thus means "found truth." The point seems clinched in Corvick's victory telegram to Gwendolyn: "Eureka. Immense." Love, truth, virtue are all identified in this way as integral with the "figure." There are other signs too that Gwendolyn is not wrong in her faith in the high spiritual nature of Vereker's "figure." The narrator, on hearing that Corvick has been in India while letting the problem incubate in him, imagines the critic surprising "the goddess in the temple of Vishnu" and repeatedly refers to the "figure" as "the idol." We already know from hints benignly thrown out by Vereker, as though leading Corvick on a treasure hunt, that the nature of the "figure" is integral with Corvick's very situation of winning a wife. Vereker says that "the 'figure' would fit into a letter" and that it is something "a lover would have told the girl he loved."

Squeamishness should not prevent our grasping, furthermore, James's waggish and discreetly blasphemous play on the metaphor of the Immaculate Conception. Corvick's adjective for the "figure" in the telegram is "immense." This intimates pregnancy, which is also implied in two quotations of Gwendolyn's words given above, where Corvick's intuition is said to have been "let severely alone for six months" and to have "grown and grown." When Gwendolyn replies to Corvick's telegram, "Angel, write," the Annunciation seems daringly hinted. That Corvick declines to put the secret in a letter, however, presumably saving it for his marriage night, further implicates the ritual nature of the whole affair. James has found a way of insisting indirectly on the sexual passion as a ritual mystery (that is, more commonly speaking, as a sacred moral responsibility), and that this, in substance, is Vereker's "figure" as well as James's is what the present essay has sought to establish. Since ineffable, it can exist only in symbol.

The name symbolism is so conspicuous that none should be omitted. If we transpose the syllables of Corvick (vick-cor) we have a rhyme for victor, which is what Corvick—and every "true knight"—is. Moreover, the syllable "cor" is a pun for both *core,* the heart of the matter, and *corps,* the body, possibly as a notation for the "beast in the jungle." But Corvick's total name (including that of his patron saint, George) establishes that he is a victor *over* the body, so that the exact nature of the Vereker figure may well be what the whole canon of James's work attests as James's own "figure" and which I have already defined—the secret of converting the sexual passion as such into the civilized status of *moral* passion. We need not accumulate the great body of evidence for this contained (not too ambiguously) in James's creative literature. Moreover, we have his word as quoted above for the family relationship among his stories, and so are free to seek the pattern of this relationship anywhere among them.

I think that James has told the story of "the figure in the carpet" many times in many forms. I think it is in the closely inter-related "The Author of Beltraffio" and *The Turn of the Screw,* each of which contains the death of a little boy indirectly brought about by a woman's mistaken impression that she is saving his "innocence." James had a most sophisticated view of innocence in children; for him, such innocence was compatible with intuitive knowledge of the most comprehensive kind, as proven by *What Maisie Knew,* which immediately preceded *The Turn of the Screw.* The little girl Maisie matures in virtue and achieves a "moral sense" by learning practically everything about adult sexual relations the nineteenth century considered it wrong for a little girl to know. In *The Turn of the Screw* the governess forces Miles to look at the ghost, which he denies he sees, but whose existence, by suggestion, he intuits from the governess and therefore dies not from knowledge of Peter Quint—which he already has—but from contagious fear of his ghost. In "The Author of Beltraffio," Mark Ambient's wife is so puritanically opposed to her novelist-husband's licentious esthetic (he is a sort of pre-Raphaelite) that she lets their little son, Dolcino, die of a fever rather than permit a doctor to save him to grow up under the influence of his father's literature. James does not leave any doubt that he is on the child's and the father's side. As a writer visiting another writer, the story's narrator gives us a vivid incidental insight into James's conception of fiction as the ultimate authority for reality: "It was not the picture, the poem, the fictive page, that seemed to me a copy; these things were the originals, and the life of happy and distinguished people was fashioned in their image." Mark Ambient is shown us as "happy and distinguished" while his wife falls short in such qualities. Into the above quotation, I think, can be read the symbolic reality held in minor form by letters and other verbal documents having such apocryphal significance in James's fiction and almost invariably involving love or marriage or a cognate aspect of these.*

In *The Turn of the Screw,* it is the letter from Miles' school explaining his offense (so we hear vaguely by report of its contents) as the utterance of certain taboo phrases, which are to be inferred from the text as sexual or "obscene." James does not question the good intentions of either Dolcino's mother or the governess in *The Turn of the Screw;* he simply feels that their morality is inferior. James is very "modern" about the education of children. It is moral character which determines sexual virtue, he demonstrates, and the sooner children learn the "awful truth" about the sexual passion, the better, but they can never really learn it from lies about sex or from having sexual knowledge held up to them as unmitigated evil. Certainly, Miles and Flora have been in danger at Bly, but the climax of their danger is the hopelessly neurotic governess, a vehicle of misdirected "goodness." Sex *is* a "beast in the jungle" to James; a prime danger for children, a possible boon to them and to adults. But to James this beast was, in its larger and final aspect, a mythological dragon to be allegorically slain, something whose spring was to be mastered and moralized; in short, resurrected in a *higher form.* As "the figure in the carpet," this pattern of resurrection, this "child" of the wisdom of life, can be traced over and over in James's works. His fabulously triumphant Masie is like the virgin who tamed the Unicorn, the incorrigible wild beast, and so is his heroine whose first name rhymes with hers, Daisy Miller. James's innocent and

---

* There are the author's posthumous papers in *The Aspern Papers,* the unopened letter from Gray Fielder's father reposing in a secret drawer in *The Ivory Tower,* Millie's bequest to the Denshers in *The Wings of the Dove,* and the dead man's love letters in *The Abasement of the Northmores.*

triumphant girls and young women are bound together, indeed, by the names of four of the most important. All these establish their "innocence" as a virtue maintained *despite* knowledge or *through* its intuitive mastery: Daisy Miller, Maisie Farange, Milly Theale, and Maggie Verver. But actually James thought the lack of genuine appreciation in his readers a scandal of a thousand facets. His fabulously well-mannered irony forbade him to do anything about it in print but expose its shocking conditions and indicate its causes. He never named it. His silence was one long process of fastidious yet positive enough examples and allegories. The fate of his artists—more a matter of suffering than he usually lets on—says everything but refrains from crying it from the housetops. This, as the crowning irony, was his own, personal artistic progeny.

10
MILLY AND BILLY AS PROTO-FINNEGANS

What is the keynote of the Hamlet-being? It is the instinctive withholding of the mind and/or person, under the sovereignty of the ego, from the dialectic of society, the drama of "real experience." The greater and more conscious the withholding, the greater the chasm between self and world, personal entity and the objective cosmos. The lyric afflatus of identification with nature which we find in different forms in Wordsworth and Valéry, and still differently in Blake's *Songs of Innocence* and the primitive ballad, *Tom o' Bedlam,* is echoed in *The Drunken Boat* of Rimbaud as the Odyssean (or anti-Hamletian) phase of the individual: the journey represented with a symbolic elision of time and space.

This occupation means a more or less sincere challenge to fate through experience; a challenge which Rimbaud carried eventually into real action. On the other hand, the emblem of the Cell of Pure Contemplation, with its Hamlet enigma, is the capture of fate without the chronological future, simply by means of a reading in the mirror of the past. As a result, all real action becomes more or less gratuitous; there is never a full commitment of the moral will to the dialectic test. There is only an instinct, as with Kierkegaard, *to repeat;* and to achieve *novelty* only in this philosophical sense, *comprehensiveness* only in this sense.

Basically Hamletian, both Fabrizio and Julien Sorel are heroes of what may be termed the romantic excursion, which in the related incest context, would signify search for the mother surrogate and dalliance with Ophelia; the role of the actress has been mentioned in respect to this search. Such heroes are intellectually naïve in comparison with Hamlet and Stavrogin, if culturally more valid than Melville's Pierre, whereas Axel, Des Esseintes and Igitur, scions of a proud aristocratic tradition, have respective ways of isolating themselves (as was noted in previous pages) from the vulgarities of the world, chief of which is the stupid illusion that immersion in material experience and chronological time will bear worthwhile fruit; will influence fate or help in attaining perfection.

Des Esseintes' way is that of the pure sensualist, Axel's that of princely haughtiness, Igitur's that of the most refined and absolute intellect. The most objective of the signs by which, aside from the work of art, such heroes are known, is the rejection of marriage. Although Mallarmé himself was married, his hero is essentially wifeless and loverless, though not motherless. To Stavrogin, as we have noted, marriage was a mockery, and to Hamlet himself, Axel, Des Esseintes, Henry IV, Kierkegaard, Myshkin, Caligula, and Pierre, real marriage or a permanent love affair took various shapes of the impossible.

It must be noticed that whereas Myshkin and Billy Budd are angelic, the artist-as-Hamlet is far from having the traditional role of priest which, in one perspective, he may be said to inherit by way of the Renaissance from ancient times: the expounder of magic and religious learning. The priest, whatever his historic cultishness, ultimately belongs to the people; the pure Hamlet-being never belongs to anyone but himself. And yet, as incarnated by Myshkin, there is a type of Hamlet-being naturally chaste (that is, nonsensual), significant exactly through being without ego or will, held together only by some miraculous integrity not of his own making, and yet who has neither the power nor the impulse to withhold himself from temporal experience, from nominally participating in human situations if it be only to excite in others large hopes and incoherent passions which are never satisfied.

Has Henry IV's accident perhaps an obscurely symbolic meaning?—is it to be aligned with Myshkin's epilepsy as something that nature rather than the will may impose on the individual to achieve the leisure and advantage of the Cell? Such a thought suggests the observation by Richard Chase in his book on Melville that the creator of Pierre included in the poem, *After the Pleasure Party,* "a denunciation of whatever meddling god it was who separated the original hermaphrodite human being—that old Adam of the occult myths—into two beings of opposite sex." We may speculate of the Hamlet-being and of his angelic conversion in Myshkin that the whole character of his impulse is the determined survival of a transcendent protest from the Old Adam himself against the blow which severed him.

Thus the presence of the incest motivation would be accounted for, within the conventions of the Cell, by assuming that it represents a suprasexual desire for a past state that is an original unity; that is to say, on the philosophic level of the Cell's existence, *coition* is really *consubstantiality.* In terms of Renaissance idealism, this concept is stated in the esoteric love dream of Francesco Colonna, the *Hypnerotomachia,* when the dreamer Poliphilo, at a crisis in his progress, chooses of three portals the one marked "Mater Amoris." Igitur's "Héros = Hymn" equation is also evidence: his lyric soliloquy, through death thoughts, reunites his being with the immortal maternal.

It is suggestive that Melville's Amor-possessed heroine of *After the Pleasure Party* should recall her former monastic self as "In cell an idiot crowned with straw." This is the same idiocy which serves in the sight of the world as Myshkin's token of separation from the sensual pleasures of Eros. But epilepsy is a natural parody of rage, the malign term of the angelic innocence, so that detectable in its nervous eruption is the complex image of a protest such as Urania's against the "human integral clove asunder" as well as a quasi imitation—transmitted perhaps through unfathomable race memory—of those personal dismemberments of the male undergone, according to myth, by Osiris, Dionysos, and Orpheus. It should be noted that however fictitious are the literary forms of myths, they are based upon actual religious sacrifices of human beings, a fact consistent with this most "positive" instinct of Myshkin's: self-sacrifice. The fit remains the only passage which "Amor incensed" can make through Myshkin's body, charmed as it is normally through the spell of its own innocence.

If Myshkin is an angelic wanderer destined to do no one any final good except as an otherworldly symbol, like an ikon, Billy Budd is conceived as a body of innocence destined to be sacrificed without mistake, as in the Eucharist ritual itself, to satisfy the spiritual appetites of man. The rage of the Bassarids in dismembering Orpheus, who shunned the Dionysian revels in honor of his dead wife, may be considered a destructive rage: the fury of the love goddess that was manifested in another form against Hippolytus, mangled on the seashore by his own horses.

As to this hero, his fate in the tragedy by Euripides may be only a secular variation on the historic sacrifice of virility to such pagan deities as Cybele, where the general mutilation was self-imposed through ecstasy (and here, once more, Myshkin's complex image in the fit is called up as a facet of involuntary self-abuse, a transcendent onanism, or more precisely perhaps, a symbol of the *inhibition* of the self-directed impulse). Virtue, we must note, is synonymous in the fertility sacrifice with virility and virginity; the pure seed, sanctified by an untouched integrity, must be spilled to the goddess—at least, this was the best, the most effective.

In this sense, Billy Budd and Myshkin are alike virgins, and their "destruction" logically has a benign and creative side. This side is so muted and fragmentary in Myshkin's case that it is hard to claim that it exists; nevertheless, its hypothesis is present. As Chase notes in his book, Billy Budd is only a variation of Melville's Handsome Sailor whose virility and beauty are implicitly negotiated qualities, things eminently used for the secular world of the senses. This empirical version of the projected "ideal sailor" is by no means, of course, essentially Billy, who is the ideal incarnated without reference to reality. Melville's own ideal, evidently, is that of virility's transcendent sacrifice, not its natural consummation.

Thus, like such disparate Hamlet-beings as Igitur and Des Esseintes, Billy, no less than Myshkin, is alienated from nature— if only, in Billy's case, to rejoin it in a quasi-supernatural sense. In being a sort of allegory—as critics, chief among them Chase, have exhaustively demonstrated—the story of Billy places its hero among the semifabulous company of the gods. But we can perceive, as I have been trying to show, that the efforts of such as the Mallarméan hero, and to lesser extents, Axel and Des Esseintes, have a Promethean metaphysics: an interior logic of the Superman arriving at his consciousness of fate without the assistance of time and the world. Perhaps, indeed, it is precise to define the Hamlet-being as one who steals fire not from Heaven, to which he aspires as the mirage of his own personality, but from Hell, whose Luciferan demon he wishes to re-exalt on a height which has no naïve directional gauge such as that availed in the *Divine Comedy: above* and *below.* The Cell and Igitur's dynastic moment are outside even an allegorical time and space, for they are not allegories, but emblems, and as emblems are personal, not tribal or social. They are *symbols* in the Jungian sense: unique, indecipherable, omnipotent, and final enigmas.

The instinct of the Hamlet-being is not to be sacrificed unto the world, either as a ritual object, such as the sacred kings or the scapegoats who were killed, or as a counter such as Oedipus in some divine plot, but to achieve autonomy in defiance of all natural and supernatural oracles, and to reside there in security.

Hamlet was sacrificed unto the convention of the revenge melodrama, which became for Shakespeare (in all probability) some such personal compensation as Stephen Dedalus more than playfully propounds in *Ulysses*. In this light, Shakespeare can be considered to have used Hamlet, in his high mightiness, as a scapegoat in the solution of a private theme altogether hidden from the public. This hypothesis, in fact, would hold good for all the relations implicit between the various Hamlet-beings and their creators. The projection of the ego into the person of the fictitious hero is a form of self-punishment, a Promethean punishment such as is meted to Pierre; only, if Pierre be compared with Des Esseintes, we see that the important thing was successfully to visualize, as Huysmans brilliantly did, *the true terms of the project and its practical metaphysical strength,* its authentic glory, a thing which Melville failed to intuit, or at least to find relevant for his purpose.

Pierre is a sacrifice to human personal pride, Billy is a sacrifice *by* human personal pride *to* the world. Billy's own personal pride is akin to Myshkin's in being unusually passive and submerged. He is a human catalytic agent which by itself is at peace, but which stirs up the sleeping or subsurface passions of others, as he arouses the avidity of the sinister Claggart but enlists other sailors spontaneously in his cause. There is no difficulty in identifying Captain Vere, whose duty compels him to bring Billy to trial and condemn him to hang, as the benign father surrogate, and Claggart as the malign father surrogate. This dual nature of the father is perceptible in Kierkegaard's view of his father through the prism of the son-sacrificing Abraham. Claggart, being unjust, is the real executioner for he falsely accuses Billy's innocence, thereby earning the violent denial of Billy's blow that kills him.

The psychology of guilt in Billy as a symbolic projection of Melville's guilt is not so important here as Billy's inheritance from Myshkin as a conversion of the Hamlet-being. His youthful inarticulacy (he stammers when excited), his infantile innocence emphasized by his very name (Budd), his awkwardness (as when he spills the soup at mess), echo Myshkin's traits and the knocking over of the vase. These two are personalities not quite of this world, both because they are somehow unequal to it and they somehow transcend it; their ineligibility is measured by their final disaster, and yet through this very disaster they attain their otherworldly apotheosis.

Chase's book provides an elaborate analysis of Billy as consciously intended by Melville as a symbol of the Eucharist ritual and the sacrifice that is "the Lamb of God." That Melville is allegorical in treating his hero, whereas Dostoievsky is not, is a trait of their differing cultures, yet Melville's method is a reversion to the emblematic and tropological esthetics of Huysmans and Mallarmé in that Billy represents Des Esseintes' and Igitur's didactic sort of morality, which is less easily transmitted from author to hero in Melville's case precisely because *intellect* is *not* the star in Billy's emblem.

One cannot be *consciously* innocent in Billy's way any more than Myshkin could have *chosen* epilepsy as an expression of his personality. And yet the mutual secret of their personalities is a *being* which does not perpetuate itself in will or device, or even in automatic commitment, but which remains master of their fates despite anything that may happen to them. Thus they are of the spiritual brotherhood fathered by Hamlet except that, for the demonic-ego, with its conscious absolute, Myshkin and Billy substitute innocent-being, with its unconscious absolute. Nothing to change his substance *can* happen to Billy; nothing to change his substance *shall* happen to Hamlet.

The original Hamlet-being dies primarily through self-will; the derived Hamlet-being dies primarily through lack of it (i.e., Myshkin's final idiocy is a way of dying to the world). Billy's blow to Claggart's jaw is the stupidest denial he could have made to the sailor's charge, the most catastrophic response; it is even more witless, conventionally and logically considered, than certain spontaneous actions by Myshkin. But it is the turning point of his story and the crux of his personality. It may even be accepted as a dumb, subverbal, quasi-natural, rather than verbal and sophisticated, form of religious positivism; for Billy's fist is directed at Claggart's *jaw,* which is too heavy for his other features and therefore probably represents speech, verbal articulacy, as much as it does the mechanics of eating that Chase analyzes. True purity and belief in virtue do not need the rationale of words. Billy is thus the subverbal, subintellectual, subadult Hamlet-being for whom the Cell is an unknown abstraction, for Billy is, above all, noncontemplative.

Before being hanged, he is tied up for the night and described as though he were inanimate nature; he dies in complete beatitude and his last words are "God bless Captain Vere." Thus he blesses the father surrogate as Hamlet with his dying breath might also have blessed his father had he accomplished all he did differently, for his father had ordered him to indemnify a crime committed in deepest thought by the son himself. That Billy, though technically guiltless of the charge brought against him, uses physical aggression against his accuser suggests that a modicum of guilt inheres all too humanly in him, too, if it be only the guilt of brute force, the flaw of the material body. It is the only sign of the demonic in Billy, as the fit is the only sign of it in Myshkin. But Melville had determined that Billy in death should be the very image of the angelic, hence his corpse fails to show the normal physical phenomena of a hanged man, those "spasmodic movements" of nature of which the priapic sign is the raising of the Devil's standard in the flesh. I have already referred to Myshkin's fit as the possible emblem of a sexual inhibition: a "concession to nature" which, provided such a weight is acceptable, Dostoievsky doubtless meant intuitively. Yet there may be in Myshkin's disease, truly, the antique reverberation to be found in the legend of Pan's pipes that their sound could produce epilepsy. And what could a Myshkin of this world hear of such things but the "unheard"?

Billy Budd seems not nearly so humanly intact or believable as Myshkin, and yet Billy is not compensated with that electric touch which is the token of the intellectual triumph of their authors that we find in Hamlet, Des Esseintes, Axel, Igitur, and indeed all the heroes I have discussed, as artificial in human personality as some of them are. Billy remains the contrivance of a religious allegorism the purity of whose form has been achieved best in *The Scarlet Letter*. But that he has a near relative in Henry James' Milly Theale is important to his genealogy as I have traced it here.

The religious symbolism of *The Wings of the Dove* has been concretely explored by Quentin Anderson. The symbolism is concentrated, of course, in the illumination of the title, which identifies the heroine Milly Theale with peace, Christ, and holy marriage. Complaint has been made by critics that Milly is too abstract a creation, that she is hardly even a character, that she does not act through will. Precisely, she is passive. Like Billy, she *is* rather than *does;* and if she meditates, the event has a religious secrecy. In view of James' treatment, and her place in the hierarchy of his American heroines, Milly emerges as the extremest idealization of the type of young woman in the aura of a moral mission to Europe. The great majority of James' critics, however apperceptive and sensitive to the James charm, have often failed to detect James' irony where it is not obviously to be looked for. Anderson's case for the religious allegorism of *The Ambassadors, The Wings of the Dove,* and *The Golden Bowl,* seems irrefutable. But this, though tantamount, is not the heart of the present matter. Moreover, Anderson's account of James' method leaves too much room for such adverse judgments as the one by Marius

Bewley that James does not "have hold of" Milly as he does all his other major heroines; the grand-scale metaphors that work with the others, Bewley alleges, do not work with Milly.

It seems to me that this point is not so much a question of literary *skill* as of literary, or fundamentally creative, *intention*. One may have a taste of heroines more of a wit, lustier, less weighted with high omen, and perhaps less "smug" than Milly Theale, but the art of James in creating the ambiance of Milly's personality in the reactions of the people about her, constitutes not merely a legitimate poetic device (I avoid the "problem of the novel" deliberately) but a clear philosophic statement. Milly, in brief, contains the immanent in the inexpressible sense; she is an immediacy as a physical presence and yet by the same token a transcendent, exactly as Billy and Myshkin. As I have said, Billy is not to be compared as a human presence with Myshkin, nor is Milly. James, however, makes his intention explicit by remarking of his heroine in the novel: "She worked—and seemingly quite without design—upon the sympathy, the curiosity, the fancy of her associates, and we shall really ourselves scarce otherwise come closer to her than by feeling their impression, and sharing if need be, their confusion." James, by stating his desire to create a magic in Milly, is thoroughly aware of the problem and its technical irony. Myshkin, Billy, Milly, all three, "seemingly quite without design," tend to "confuse" as well as charm; their power is equally *mysterious*. Milly's magic is to arrive, as it were, second hand. The art of the novelist, stumped by the phenomenon of the female-inexpressible, can only devote itself humbly to exposing Milly's effect on others as tender for showing her directly to the reader. In this project, James certainly succeeds. One feels overwhelmingly throughout the prose the emotions of an indirect spectator.

Making Milly so hermetically an object, and constantly implying the preciousness and purity of that object, James also is carrying to an extreme Melville's method in characterizing Billy Budd. The only logical test for the validity of this method of communication is reference to the empirical. Did *you*, the reader, ever sense in a young man or a young woman that indefinable presence as of hidden gold and greatness which does not reside in esthetic or intellectual gift or any overt, concrete term of the social dynamic, but that seems, even so, unquestionable, intrinsic? Of course, on the realistic level, this is essentially a religious feeling the same as the belief that the Host is the blood and the body of Christ. Judged *formally,* Milly may seem a hollow heroine; judged not metaphysically but religiously, she is full of dynamic being. As a female image, she is the beloved, a value consistent with the corollary fact that James supposedly is giving in Milly a portrait of his early sweetheart, Minnie Temple. Just as one can only *assume* rather than *observe* the qualities in a man or woman that causes someone other than oneself to love them supremely, one assumes rather than observes Milly's charm in the articulate responses of her admirers. It is exactly by the *abstractness* of his esthetic method that James has accomplished this effect.

On the other hand, it is concrete enough that Billy and Milly have kinds of physical beauty. Though beauty, even in the written word, is not to be taken too conventionally, the fact remains that a certain physical charm, in Myshkin's case as well as Billy's and Milly's, is the keystone of the reader's participation in their meaning as objects. This beauty, however, is but the secondary or outward show of the inner, which in Milly's case, ironically enough, has also an "inward" show: money. Milly's greatness is only nominally and quantitatively reflected by her monetary wealth, which is never made a show in the vulgar sense, but is only immanent as her virtue and desirability.

It is essential to the reality of Milly and Billy that they both arouse excessive appetite. They are, variously, riches, as all heroes are, and they "withhold" even as do the earlier Hamlet-beings, while this very denial provokes the greed of others. As Stavrogin's dormant personal gifts inflame Verhovensky's political imagination, Billy's inaccessible, enigmatic riches arouse

Claggart's greed, and Milly's material riches excite the covert avarice of Merton Densher and his fiancée, Kate Croy, who plot together rather like somnambulists to acquire it. We recall Axel's golden treasure which insolently he refuses to yield to the world. *His* treasure too is an *immanence* but an immanence of virtue through conscious ego and willed isolation, and thus the contrary of Milly's and Billy's kind of virtue.

Both Billy and Milly can yield this wealth, in any final sense, only through dying, for essentially Milly is a virgin—her sickness indicating this peculiar worldly handicap—and therefore is as unavailable to a sexual mate as Billy in his way and Myshkin in his. But in dying, Milly and Billy yield their bodies for the benefit of others precisely in the sense of the most ancient sacrifices: they are the earth's bride and bridegroom, and thus not one man's and woman's lover but all the world's. It is for this implicit reason that Merton Densher and Kate Croy reject the material coefficient of Milly's legacy, her money, and accept instead the tremendous sum of her spiritual image, which presumably is to guide the course of their marriage, place it consciously upon "the wings of the dove."

The design of the Ivory Tower, as a spiritual armature consanguine with Hamlet's Cell, has matured steadily in the complex movement of this investigation. The parallel between the untouched letter in Gray Fielder's ivory ornament, the taboo treasure in the depths of Axel's castle, and the unopened, burned bequest that has come from Milly's Venetian palace, is unmistakable. *Such riches are unavailable to ordinary human programs; they are unconvertible into the social dialectic, into drama or the holocaust of the passions, beside which promiscuous trouble and blaze they burn apart.* This hermetic stubbornness exists because they contain an impenetrable secret as the principle of their organisms, the same sort of secret that was projected by Igitur in terms of the absolute but which, by authors other than Mallarmé, has been conceived as residing in a blind product of nature—a disease or an accident—or as immanent in the universal virtue lying in the highest fusion of physical and spiritual beauty in man. The obvious nature of the secret in Hamlet's case has filled his cell with the noise of counterfeit fame though, in truth, his black walls are lined only with the gold of the ego.

The moral issue raised by these views of Hamlet as artist and individual would seem to be that centered in the most consciously and technically philosophical of the heroes that have been invoked: Kierkegaard. By lacking implicit faith in the goodness of all God's oracles, Kierkegaard became a Hamletian kind of Christian and specifically so through an ambiguous filial relationship. He, like our other heroes, had specific reason to refuse to help perpetuate the race. In this light, Abraham's sacrifice of Isaac, with which Kierkegaard was obsessed, is the symbol of death and rebirth that inheres in all fertility sacrifice; it is even a paradigm of Christ's crucifixion and resurrection. Kierkegaard could not consider such a thing was more than a parable of the spirit, could not believe it possible *as action* in the natural world. And if it was not possible as action in the natural world, its equivalent was impossible in the physical union of the sexes, in which analogously love would not survive, or at least was not even involved in, the mimic death of coitus; therefore sex is an animal appetite resurrectable only as such an appetite is resurrectable, by a recurrence of physical conditions, and is not a structural element of the ideal design of marriage. Yet logically Kierkegaard could perceive no other reason for marriage than the dialectic function with its inevitable property of sexual intercourse. Marriage could revive itself otherwise only through the child, the physical issue, but Kierkegaard's skeptical obsession with the mythical meaning of the son's sacrifice seems sufficient proof that he very much feared the terms of the child-father relation if only because of his own filial status. By conceiving love in terms of repetition, its metaphysical status, marriage as a social reality became redundant for the individual and the issue of marriage, progeny, just as redundant by another remove. Psy-

chologically, Kierkegaard's reasoning is very close, as we have
seen, to Axel's and not too far from Hamlet's. We are reminded
that, according to the Cell's morality, one gives birth not to
someone else but to *oneself*.

The moral of the genesis and spiritual-literary perpetuation
of the Hamlet-being is thus abdication, through the will, from
man's role in the dialectic of material nature, including procreation. If incest implicitly is the "natural" motivation of this abdication, as indeed it would seem from much of the evidence adduced here, it is a point to be argued with psychoanalysts and
perhaps others. My own concern is primarily the moral phenomenon of the intellectual and esthetic assertion which regards
fate in the Kierkegaardian sense of "the single individual," i.e.,
a childless man or woman, and essentially a parentless one.

If we glance at every outstanding image of a hero that has been
seen here, as though suddenly visible in one flash of light, what
single quality unites them as one body?—the impulse to negate
(in the most normal of human quests, that for the self) the usual
commitment to reality as a dialectic program of conversion,
change, and maturation, in which the individual consciousness
is to be achieved arm in arm, heart in heart, with other human
beings, and in which pride, a given integrity of the ego, and the
past are perpetually *risked*.

Billy *cannot* risk this integrity except in death; Hamlet *will not*
risk it except in death. The Hamlet-being constitutionally does
not admire a group salvation such as the Christian finds in
church, and he perceives—at least through Kierkegaard's eyes—
no prospect of personal salvation or rebirth in life into anything
but what he is: Kierkegaard's omnipresent repetition. It would
be useless to relate Kierkegaard's idea of fate to the more orthodox experiences of the Christian saint any more specifically than
they have been already. Valéry's *Cimetière Marin,* or the metaphoric reconstitution of the world in the individual consciousness,
is the orthodoxy of the Hamlet-being in regard to all rituals of
mystic union with the universe. Igitur's metaphysical reconstitu-

tion is the most *radical* version of this ritual in that the individual will annihilates the real universe symbolically by absorbing it into the exclusive consciousness of the ego . . . a *"bruit de folie"* perhaps, but the star song which dominated Mallarmé's most subtle rhythms and shaped his greatest emblem.

It is Myshkin who must be recognized as the prismatic lodestone of the Hamlet genealogy, the moral step which frees Hamlet himself from his mock drama, Igitur from the frozen aridity of his fathomless victory, Stavrogin from the terrible humiliation of his suicide, Axel from his castle, and Des Esseintes from his curse on the world. For Myshkin is the opposite of their stupendous adulthoods. He is the child, as Schneider says, with "the face, form and habits of an adult." Life that is wonderful is lived on the level of fused extremes. Stavrogin is all-idea; Myshkin is non-idea. Both are equally *ideal*. Each is absolute, too, because each—one consciously, the other unconsciously—identifies his being with a secret which enslaves the future. This viewpoint may seem to negate the element so dear to many, especially to the realists: experience. All this is idealism; and worse: *romantic idealism!*

This thought might be correct if one did not suppose, as I have supposed from the beginning, that Hamlet and Stavrogin, Myshkin and Billy, belong *to one family.* We may turn back to the pages on Julien Sorel and Fabrizio, or to those on Proust, to visualize how the blood of the Hamlet-being may be converted to the world's uses. In Fabrizio's life, the Cell of Pure Contemplation was merely an orientation to what was a life of great worldly experience. The Cell remains the steadfast symbol of the moral nature of all Hamlet-beings: the place of rest, the still star born from the heart of midnight.

Man the individual is torn between giver and taker, between the consciousness of the subject and the consciousness of the object. Of all the heroes I have mentioned, Proust doubtless achieved the most lyric equilibrium between subjectivity and objectivity. Think of the awful temptation of the Cell's occupant, when the door is barred, to burst through it and cast himself into the world as into a new womb! The single-individual-in-himself-a-fate? The Hamlet-being spends many hours staring at this paradox alone, and yearning for the experience of procreation. Every Dostoievskian character has the same natural impulse: the instinct to participate, to achieve friction and feel the outward stab of growth. In Myshkin it reaches a felicity of selflessness the more real because less consciously religious and moral than Zossima's or Alyosha Karamazov's. Billy Budd and Milly Theale might be thought of as slightly self-righteous, as all too piously aware, in obscure ways, that they are the lamb and the dove, the preordained victim, the "chosen one." This accounts for the irritation that Milly may awaken in certain readers, the sense of unreality that Billy may occasion in others. Nevertheless they are vessels for the blood of the Hamlet-being, though they spill it perhaps in vain in a world which at least Melville had in mind as the real world.

The secret of life in this hero-perpetuation is, in effect, that of inbreeding, for in the spiritual crucible of the Hamlet strain, the members of the family fecundate only each other. Billy's blood is shed for a Henry IV that he shall not go insane; Myshkin's epilepsy is spent for an Igitur that he shall not petrify in his pride. Milly's wings are spread not merely for the married Denshers, but to bear a Stavrogin that he shall not die alone and a Des Esseintes that he shall not think of woman only as a machine. Thus if Hamlet-beings shun the dialectic of society, they reach each other, and pollinate efficaciously, on the wings of time. Without the Hamletian Stephen of *Ulysses,* who set out to find his father with an Olympian arrogance (and mostly to please his creator), the hero of *Finnegans Wake* would not have been availed his colossal revelation, could not have achieved with mere commonness his death-dream transfiguration—an irrational more intellectually complex than any known rational.

Is this the meaning of the difference between the real and the fictive hero? Perhaps no man could ever possibly be as pure as

Axel, or Igitur, or Des Esseintes; no man at once as powerful and negative as Stavrogin, no "Oedipus" so knowing and so obedient as Hamlet. And to take it the other way, no epileptic perhaps so charming and princely, so *philosophically pure,* as Myshkin, no big blond beauty so magnetic and unconsciously effective as Billy Budd. Nor any young female millionaire, now or ever, so hugely pure and grand and magical as Milly Theale. To create heroes, I should say, is to live ideas. No writer who does not create a hero may quite live his idea to the full.

One of the most fastidious intellectuals of the modern world, Joyce, delivered himself unto the common man as hero in order to experience the most primitive and universal consciousness possible to his imagination. This was, yes, a form of egotism; possibly even an elaborate "wing" of the Ivory Tower; but it was also a socialization of the subjective personality; a casting away of personal identity to enter nude the metaphysical cosmos of man *in the reverse of* Igitur's gesture. Finnegan's night-mind, after all, is fed with the blood of Myshkin and Billy, may eat the body of sacrifice, may shatter the Tower in a twinkling, and resurrect Hamlet's Cell as the flaming seed of procreation.

Acknowledgments are made to the magazines in which some of the essays of this book have appeared, in different form and under different titles: *Kenyon Review*, *Accent*, *Modern Fiction Studies*, *View*, and *Chicago Review*.